Living the Shakespearean Life

Living the
Shakespearean Life:

TRUE STORIES

Edited with an Introduction by John Boe

[paperback]
ISBN 13: 978-1-58790-500-1
ISBN 10: 1-58790-500-0

[e-book]
ISBN 13: 978-1-58790-501-8
ISBN 10: 1-58790-501-9

Library of Congress Control Number: 2019932884

Published by Regent Street Press, Berkeley, California
www.regentpress.net

Cover and book design by Victor Ichioka

For Sam Wanamaker,
the onlie begetter.

CONTENTS

ILLUSTRATIONS

SOURCES:

*Sir John Gilbert's Shakespeare 1882

All others *Cassell's Illustrated Shakespeare 1875*

INTRODUCTION

You're living the Shakespearean life when, as Dame Judi Dench put it, Shakespeare is the man who pays the rent. While my Ph.D. dissertation was focused on Shakespeare, and while in my academic life I sometimes taught Shakespeare and wrote about him, I only began living a fully Shakespearean life in summer 2000 when I started teaching Shakespeare to American undergraduates in London. From then on, each summer was pretty much devoted exclusively to Shakespeare. I loved the experience and was changed by it. Much of my Shakespearean life centered at the Globe Theatre, the creation of the American actor Sam Wanamaker, who ended up in England because he had been blacklisted in the U.S. Thus the new Globe Theatre came about in part because of Joseph McCarthy.

Around 2010 I started wondering about how other people were changed by their Shakespearean lives and decided to do the interviews that led to this book. I first talked with Zoë Wanamaker, Sam Wanamaker's daughter as well as a notable actress. I knew I wanted to dedicate the book to her father, since the Globe had been so important to me, so I wanted to talk with her even if she wasn't primarily known for her work with Shakespeare. I met her in London, in her dressing room before she was going to act in *All My Sons* with David Suchet. She hand-rolled cigarettes as we talked and was as gracious and charming as I could have hoped. She told me stories of her father and of her own Shakespearean life. She introduced me to David Suchet, who burst into her dressing room saying, "I just had the most marvelous lunch. We spent the whole time talking about Shakespeare." "Then you have to talk with this man," she said, pointing at me, and he did.

So every summer in England and the rest of the year in the States, I interviewed workers in the Shakespeare industry: actors, directors, scholars, and voice coaches. I developed some general questions, which I hadn't had when I interviewed Zoë, but they functioned more as prompts than as a script. Here is a short version of my basic ten questions:

1. When did you first encounter Shakespeare?

2. When did you get a sense of how important Shakespeare was going to be in your life?

3. Were any people or experiences particularly important to helping you find your Shakespearean life?

4. Is there a particular Shakespeare play that you have found problematic?

5. What are your favorite Shakespeare plays?

6. Can you talk about favorite and/or problematic characters or characters you especially admire or even can identify with?

7. How has Shakespeare been useful in your life? Has Shakespeare taught you anything about living your life?

8. What is "Shakespearean," as opposed to Jonsonian, Stoppardian, or whatever?

9. Do you have any fantasies as to Shakespeare's personality?

10. Is there a quotation from Shakespeare that you particularly like or identify with?

I asked actors, directors, and scholars slightly different questions. When I edited the interviews, I eliminated my questions and comments, so the interviews appear as oral histories, as monologues. My goal was to get people to talk about what it had meant for them, professionally and personally, to have lived a Shakespearean life, to get them to talk about how Shakespeare had affected them.

The first questions brought forth memories of parents, grandparents, big illustrated editions of Shakespeare, specific productions and actors (often Peter Brook productions and Judi Dench), and teachers (often high school teachers). Interestingly, two renowned scholars (Stephen Greenblatt and James Shapiro) never studied Shakespeare in college.

Over time the discussion of favorite Shakespearean characters would sometimes take the form of what character would you like to have a drink with or hang out with. There were at least 17 different picks for favorite play, with *Hamlet* most often mentioned. The actress Robin Goodrin Nordli even suggested to me, "Maybe your question should be, 'What's your favorite play after *Hamlet*?'" After *Hamlet* the most mentioned plays were *The Winter's Tale* and, surprisingly, *Troilus and Cressida*. (Some of these latter votes may be suspect. As legendary RSC director John Barton told me, "If someone asks me what my favorite Shakespeare play I always say, 'The best play of Shakespeare is *Troilus and Cressida*.' That shuts them up. It's actually arguable.") I was surprised by how often *The Tempest* was seen as boring or at least problematic. Some of the plays labeled problematic of course included *The Taming of the Shrew* and *The Merchant of Venice*. *Timon of Athens* was most often mentioned as perhaps not a very good play. *Titus Andronicus* was the only play that scholar Tiffany Stern really didn't like, but scholar Farah-Karim Cooper (who has collaborated with Tiffany Stern) named it as her favorite play. Most people picked as least favorite or problematic plays ones they didn't like much, like *Timon, Titus, Taming of the Shrew,* and even in one case *As You Like It.* But a few people (including me) had problems with plays they nonetheless very much liked. Thus actor/director Nick Hutchison said he finds *"Pericles, Cymbeline,* and *The Winter's Tale* almost unbearable. We all know that the dead don't come back to life, but in *Pericles* for three hours we can see how great it would be if they did." And I find watching *Lear* or *Othello* almost too painful.

There was also a wide range of choices for favorite characters, with Rosalind the clear favorite among female characters, many of the usual suspects (Hamlet, Falstaff, Cleopatra) mentioned, and some unique choices among minor characters (like the scrivener in *Richard III*). Stephen Greenblatt memorably suggested that "there are lots of Shakespeare characters who have this weird effect that they seem to at least in one's imagination to exist outside the orbit of the play they are in."

When I finally sat down to answer my own questions, I realized that the hardest one was "How has Shakespeare been useful in your life." Scholar Steven Booth responded by saying, reasonably enough, "Shakespeare has taught me not one bloody thing." Others indulged me and tried to answer this impossible question. The director Michael Kahn said, "On good days I am more tolerant of people's ambiguity—well, contradictions—than I would have been if I hadn't done Shakespeare. And I am more aware and willing to live with ambiguity because that is the truth of Shakespeare." The actor Roger Allam said, "If you play one of those great roles, it expands your understanding of certain things about life." There was one thing that several people said they had learned from Shakespeare. Director/scholar Ralph Alan Cohen suggested that Shakespeare teaches you to "embrace what's in front of you." Similarly, Stephen Greenblatt suggested that a Shakespeare lesson is "Not to look away, to actually look at the people you encounter in the world, in a kind of unflinching way." Director Dominic Dromgoole talked about how the lesson of Shakespeare is "to try to enjoy everything." And in my own oral history, I tried to make a similar point in discussing Hamlet: he moves from the unsureness of "To be or not to be" to (in Act V) the accepting attitude of "Let be."

The voice coach Patsy Rodenberg perhaps best articulated an idea many others also suggested: "The Shakespearean life guides you, doesn't it? It guides you because the ethics are so clearly there. And in all the chaos of it, Shakespeare comes back to what it's like to be a human being. I always think he comes back to liking human beings in a way that Jonson might not. He believes in us. He is compassionate. He even likes his villains." Director Peter Lichtenfels summed up a typical director's attitude: "I don't really think in terms of favorite characters. As a director, you have to love them all."

Many people used the word "compassionate" in describing what Shakespeare was like. And often people pointed out how Shakespeare builds characters out of contradictions, giving them their "cracks," as actor David Suchet put it. Similarly, director Dominic Dromgoole (and others) pointed to how Shakespeare includes messiness (including mistakes and errors) in his plays and in his overall attitude. Scholar Jean Howard called Shakespeare "capacious and contrapuntal"; director Michael Kahn talked about his "building character out of contradictions"; director Adrian Noble emphasized Shakespeare's "non-judgmental view of humanity"; scholar Hugh Richmond talked about Shakespeare's "multitudiousness"; Stephen Greenblatt described Shakespeare with Yeats' phrase "the emotion of multitude."

A few people were unwilling to speculate on what Shakespeare was like, but most people played along. The most amusing response (but perhaps still accurate) was Stephen Booth's: "He was an insomniac who didn't like cats." Many people, especially those actively involved in Shakespearean theater, pointed out, as director Bill Rauch did, that "Shakespeare is the man of show business." And a number of people also suggested at Shakespeare's introverted nature. As actress Franchelle Dorn said, "It's hard to imagine that Shakespeare wasn't quiet, contemplative, and spending a lot of time alone." Director/Actor/Voice Coach Giles Block said that Shakespeare must have been a fantastic listener, that it was his ability to actually hear real speech that "probably made his first big shift from the Marlovian line." And scholar Andrew Gurr suggested something I had never heard before, that Shakespeare didn't value his plays nearly as much as we do, that "he didn't rate his plays as highly as he did the poems he might have written."

People told many personal stories out of their Shakespearean life. Scholar Fran Dolan told about her parents visiting a class she was teaching on *King Lear* where her almost blind father showed a remarkable understanding of the play. Scholar Velma Richmond talked about seeing *The Winter's Tale* with her then seven-year-old daughter, how when the statue of Hermione appeared, her daughter reached over and said, "Mommy, she's alive!" Director Rupert Goold said he never takes on Shakespeare plays casually: "I always feel like something's going to happen when I start one of them. I'll fall in love or have a breakdown—something will happen." And so he had a desperate horrible time doing *King Lear* "because it's a desperate, horrible play to go through."

I asked each person for a favorite quotation (more were from *King Lear* than any other play). I used these quotations as subtitles to the interviews. Some people offered more than one quotation, but they or I would usually pick just one for the title. I ended up using all four of Stephen Greenblatt's quotations as a subtitle, since they were all short and he quoted them so quickly and easily at the end of our conversation: "So I have heard and do in part believe it," "Simply the thing I am will make me live," "The worst returns to laughter," "The rest is silence." Director Barbara Gaines was insistent that she needed two quotations for her subtitle: "Lechery, lechery, still wars and lechery! Nothing else holds fashion" and "It is required you do awake your faith." As she explained, "That's the world. You can't let war and lechery keep you from awakening your faith." Director Jim Warren also chose "It is required you do awake your faith." He explained how the quotation suggests how most of us have faith in something and "it's required we shake it up and wake it up," but also that at his Blackfriars Theatre in Staunton Virginia (as at any theater, including the original Globe), the company tries "to awake the audience's faith." Another duplication was by scholars Barbara Mowat and Stanley Wells, who both chose *Lear*'s "Why should a dog, a horse, a rat, have life/ And thou no breath at all." Director Michael Kahn added an amusing qualifier to his choice of a favorite quotation, then kindly let me use it in the title: "It's too corny to say, 'The play's the thing.'" But I think my favorite choice was by director John Barton: "And that's true too." I must admit that I didn't immediately recognize it as from *King Lear*, but after talking to so many Shakespeareans, I more and more love this line and think it summarizes a characteristic Shakespearean attitude: Yes, that's true too.

Everyone I talked with seemed in their own way joyful, happy that they had a Shakespearean life. Director/scholar Ralph Alan Cohen said, "So there is something about a life in Shakespeare that really does mostly keep you happy." Scholar Russ McDonald said, "I came from a sort of Puritan background. My father was an electrical contractor who had no time for the theater or art or anything else, and so of course that's what I gravitated toward. For me the plays provide endless joy—intellectually, emotionally, musically, poetically— all different ways." Patsy Rodenberg said, "Shakespeare is so much fun. We are lucky, aren't we?" She also suggested that Shakespeare must be the human who has provided a living for the most people in the history of the planet. James Shapiro said, charmingly, "You're talking to one of the luckiest people in the world." As scholar Regina Buccola declared at the end of her oral history, "For me, the Shakespearean life is a good life."

I talked with more scholars than directors, more directors than actors. I talked with Americans and Brits, a Canadian, and a New Zealander. The Shakespeare industry being as large as it is, I could easily have talked with a hundred more people, and I would have enjoyed doing so. In the end, I think I ended up with a fascinating sample of people (35 in all) who have lived a Shakespearean life. Each person agreed to be interviewed specifically for publication in *Living the Shakespearean Life*, and each was given the opportunity to edit their oral history.

I enjoyed every one of these interviews, and there were some especially memorable moments: John Barton offering me a whisky when I came to his door soaking wet from a hard London rain, Hugh and Velma Richmond serving me a lovely traditional English tea after we had talked, David Bevington tearing up as he recited beautiful lines from *Twelfth Night*. Sometimes we talked a little after the formal interview was over. Thus before saying good-bye, I mentioned to David Suchet that I had just had a fight with my wife, and he offered me lovely advice: "Whenever something happens like that, never let the sun go down on it because it always gets worse. Ring her up and say, 'I love you.' I mean, to put a block between two people who love each other is just a waste of time. You may not have the time. Could be tomorrow. You don't want the sun to go down on that."

I talked with people in their homes and offices, in restaurants, coffee shops and pubs, in the Members' Room of the Tate Modern Museum, in dressing rooms, and in quiet spaces inside theaters. I thank everyone who talked with me. I am grateful for the few people who I talked to who didn't end up in this book, such as the couple who talked with me for almost three hours, leaving me with too much material to cut down to size, the scholar who talked so softly I simply couldn't transcribe what had been said, and a few others.

I have many people to thank. First, I thank all of the students who studied Shakespeare with me in London for almost two decades. Teaching them was the highlight of my academic life. For the opportunity to teach them Shakespeare in London each summer, I thank UC Davis's Summer Abroad and the UC Davis English Department. I also thank my last London class, a group of adults brought together by the generosity of Don and Dorothy Worth. I warmly thank Mary Hall, who started out as my London landlady and ended up my dear friend. I thank Janet Gift and Johanna Schmitz for transcribing some of these interviews, and I thank Johanna for good advice early on in this project. I thank Patrick Spottiswode, Director of Education at the Globe, for his generosity. I thank Pete Najarian for much needed literary encouragement. I thank Mark Weiman and Regent Press for publishing this book. I thank Paul Ruxin for putting me in contact with Chicago area Shakespeareans. I thank Victor Ichioka both for the design of this book and for almost 60 years of friendship. I thank Susan Palo for commenting on some of these interviews when they were in rough form. There were two people who read these interviews in their rough form, correcting typos and infelicities, suggesting improvements, queries, and cuts. First, I thank my dear friend Eric

Schroeder who despite the many demands on his time commented on early drafts of almost every interview. His favorite quotation is from *As You Like It,* "Men have died from time to time, and worms have eaten them, but not for love." And most of all I thank my wife Judy Boe, who is my first reader. I love her choice of a favorite quotation (also from *As You Like It):* "When I was at home, I was in a better place."

ROGER ALLAM

"THERE IS DIVINITY THAT HELPS SHAPE OUR ENDS,
ROUGH-HEW THEM HOW WE WILL."

*Roger Allam was born in East London and educated at Christ's Hospital and Manchester University. He joined the Royal Shakespeare Company in 1981 and has in his career played many of the major Shakespearean roles at various venues (including the National Theatre): Mercutio, Theseus-Oberon, Clarence, the Duke in **Measure for Measure,** Toby Belch, Brutus, Benedick, Macbeth, and Ulysses. In 2010, I saw him as Falstaff in **Henry IV Part 1** and **Henry IV Party 2** at the Globe, in a performance that deservedly won him an Olivier award for best actor (he has won three Oliviers in his career). Then in 2013 I saw him as Prospero (again at the Globe), in a rare (for me) production where I actually liked Prospero. He has of course gained renown for non-Shakespearean roles as well, including being the original Javert in **Les Misérables**. In addition to his widely praised stage work, he has appeared in many movies and television shows (for example, **Endeavour** and **Game of Thrones**). I talked with him near London's Globe Theatre in the Members' Room at the Tate Modern Museum, on August 3, 2015, just before he went to a rehearsal for that evening's wonderful performance at the Sam Wanamaker Theatre at the Globe of TS Eliot's **Four Quartets** (with Bach and Messiaen played by Angela Hewitt accompanying Allam's reading of the poems.)*

When I was a small child, I saw my sister in a girls' school production of *Twelfth Night*. I hadn't the faintest idea what was going on. When I was in secondary school, there were school productions of Shakespeare. I suppose that's really the first Shakespeare I saw. I was in a couple of them. But when I was a teenager, I was studying *King Lear* and couldn't make head nor tail of it. Then I heard a recording by Paul Scofield (I think the recording was made prior to him doing it on stage). Something about his extraordinary voice caught me and made the words alive, alive in a different way to simply their meaning and simply their sound. I suppose hearing that was my first really positive encounter with Shakespeare.

At school, I was Edgar in *King Lear* and Sir Toby Belch in *Twelfth Night*. Between those two times acting became something that I probably wanted to do. Then at the holidays I started going to the National Theatre when it was still at the Old Vic. You could get in very, very cheaply, so I could afford to go. If you queued on the day, it cost fifteen pence to sit on a bench in the gallery, and fifteen pence was the price of a tube from where I lived and also the price of a theater program. Today that would be about £3.50, £4, even cheaper than standing at the Globe. I saw Lawrence Olivier as Shylock there for fifteen pence.

I suppose when I first thought about acting I thought that what you do is be in Laurence Olivier's company. Then I started seeing stuff at the Royal Shakespeare Company. I was about seventeen when I saw Peter Brooks' *Midsummer Night's Dream*, which was the first time I'd seen the play. I'd never even read it. It was so intoxicating and exhilarating. It was so wonderful that a friend of mine and I ran the length of the Strand after seeing this matinee. It had extraordinary clarity and remains probably the best Shakespeare production I've ever seen. It was like having the play injected into your head. That's when I thought, "I want to be part of the National Theatre or the Royal Shakespeare Company." That's where I saw the life of an actor, I suppose, and after a while I did join the Royal Shakespeare Company. I stayed there ten or eleven years. The joint artistic directors were Terry Hands and Trevor Nunn, so it was old school.

Both of those roles at the Globe, Prospero and Falstaff, were difficult. I spent a lot of time thinking about Prospero and embracing the eccentricities of the play, which are many. I had a sense of wanting to go where the play goes, not trying to impose something on it. Sometimes Prospero's very funny, and sometimes he's furious and filled with rage and vengeance. And it's the only play of Shakespeare's that takes place within a brief allotted span of time; the play takes place in one day, between breakfast time and dinner-time. Prospero says so quite a lot. Also, from the first I thought about and found very, very difficult that long scene, Prospero's first scene. A number of people have spoken about how difficult it is. It's difficult to learn, it's very, very torturous, it's expositional, and you're talking about what happened twelve years previous. I found that very, very hard. I found it hard even to remember. But then I had the notion of it being something Prospero's never said before—because there hasn't been anyone else to say these words to. There's been Ariel, who isn't a human being, and Caliban (why would he say it to Caliban?) There's been no one to say it to, and so as the words are spoken, they're in a sense surprising and shocking to him. They reawaken the rage and the fury that he feels about what his brother did to him. The other thing that it made me think about was how difficult it must have been on the island when he was having to be father and mother (I know he had Caliban after a while). I started to think about how perhaps Prospero's magic hadn't been so powerful. If he was such a brilliant magician when he was in Milan, why couldn't he stop them taking him away and putting him in this horrible little boat with his young daughter. Why couldn't he have done something? In a sense, it's not until the island that he finds his Ariel. He has Ariel, of course, but he's also got his book, and so I imagine maybe it took quite a long time to free Ariel from the tree. Of course, what's most important to Prospero is his relationship with his child. That's his everything, that's his life, that's his future. So the father thing animated me first. That was the key experience that meshed the whole of the play for me.

Prospero was rather like another role I've played, the Duke in *Measure for Measure*. Prospero too is not in control. It's not necessarily some big plan that goes back five, ten years: "Ah, at this time they'll be on a boat and they'll be…." I suppose you could do it like that, but that's not the way I played it. It's that suddenly there's the ship and there they are, they're coming by: "I could do this now." And so it has to be thought of on the hoof, which is why he forgets that Caliban, Stefano and Trinculo have gotten together. There are so many things happening. It was important to me to try to keep everything very much in the present tense, so that it's not a story of "I'm going to avenge myself on my. . ." or "I'm going to forgive them" right from the beginning. It's not until they're there in front of you that you know. You don't know the end at the beginning of the day. Six, seven, eight hours before, you don't know what you're going to do if and when you get them all in front of you. And then at the moment in the present suddenly you do, and then you're leaving the island. I absolutely loved doing it and I'm very glad I did it.

I also found Falstaff very difficult. I thought I'd never, ever understood quite who Falstaff was. And then I started reading, dipping into it, because there's such a wealth of material written about Falstaff, a whole book written in the 18th century defending Falstaff from the accusation of cowardice. I read in Harold Bloom's book something about Richardson's performance, how he had the look of a tired old soldier. And I thought, "Oh, that's a way to go." And then I saw Mark Rylance in *Jerusalem*, and some of the critics referred to him as a kind of Falstaffian character, a kind of misrule character, so I thought, "Oh, that's a way to go." Then I started reading a book about how there are lots of characters like this in different cultures: a kind of tutor figure who educates the upcoming prince and who is killed or who is rejected and dies at the end. As in Mummer's plays, there's lots and lots of buried things in Falstaff about an older culture, an older England. There's one very, very good descrip-tion about how you meet at this kind of intersection time (which is what Eliot talks about) an intersection between modernity and medieval history plays with perfect knights; you see that all in these wonderful mummer's plays. And, of course, there's the whole thing about fathers and sons. I thought that there was room in these kinds of plays so that you don't necessarily impose a simple psychological reading on them. Rather you try and animate whenever you can of these different notes. John Barton used to talk about sounding all the notes: ring them like bells, when they're there to be rung.

One of the useful things about the Globe is that it makes you think of performance history. (I hadn't really been an admirer of the Globe before, having been so long at the RSC, and the success of the Globe having thrown the RSC into kind of a nervous breakdown.) There's a good deal of evidence that Will Kemp was the first player of Falstaff. Falstaff has a lot of speeches where he talks to the audience; he never stops talking to the audience. I became convinced that they were Shakespeare writing a version of Kemp's improvisatory style, so that the speeches remind me of certain comics I've seen, like Billy Connolly, long hair, beard, and stuff like that. And then you just snatch at things. Pete Postlethwaite was in a rather good television show called *Charm*, from 15 or 20 years ago. It was being revived, and I caught a bit of it. He plays a really awful, scurrilous, horrible character during the Napoleonic wars. Soldiers are attacking this town, and he hid under a dead body. I thought, "That's it, I'll have that, that's brilliant." So all these things—playing a role as rich as Falstaff brought in everything I'd ever done, everything I could possibly do—musicianship, singing stuff as well—and then it demanded more.

I felt that playing Mercutio, a long time ago, came easy for me. I had an idea about who he was, which I'm trying to remember now. It seemed to come easily I think partly because it was my first really good Shakespearean role at the RSC. It was at a stage of my career when I went, "Right! I'm going to do this." And it made sense to me, being in this group of young boys and feeling betrayed by Romeo, by Romeo being in love. There is some homoeroticism going on there, but I don't think it's necessarily conscious. It always seems to me a crucial thing to decide about when you're playing a character that something may be going on with you that you as a character don't know about. I think I felt that the whole Queen Mab speech was this huge critique of Romeo for falling in love with young women and therefore moving away from him and their group of young men, older boys. Mercutio's a wonderful part just as Romeo's a horrible part. I think Romeo's a really, really difficult part, but with Mercutio, everyone loves you and then you die and they miss you. Romeo gets behind the audience's knowledge of what's gone on in the play—he has to play catch up—and so there's a sense in which the people in the audience think, "Yes I know this, yes, yes, come on, Romeo." It's very hard. So Mercutio slipped on very easily. I was doing it in conjunction with Oberon and Theseus in *Midsummer Night's Dream*. That was 12 or 13 years after I'd seen the Brooks one but I could still hear in my head, Alan Howard and all of them. That was quite difficult but it was a joyous experience; it's a joyful play to do and audiences absolutely love it.

I'd love to have played Iago, but I think I'm too old now. Lear was the first role I ever wanted to play, and it sort of hovers there. But I don't know: whenever I see it I just think this is just the most difficult, impossible play to achieve. Lear is unlike Hamlet, which I never played and I never got until it was too late for me to play. Hamlet talks to the audience, so the audience experiences what Hamlet is going through; they experience the events of the play through Hamlet, while Lear barely talks to us at all. So Lear is a person that things happen to. It's just so difficult. I'd probably have to do it if I was offered it. It might be it's one of those things that's important to hover there in your own particular constellation because you find ways of thinking because of it; you refer to these things in your head. I was doing a scene in a television program I made called *Endeavor* with Anton Lesser, who is also an old RSC hound and a wonderful actor. In this particular scene, and you would never think this if you read it, we said the feeling of this has got to be like the feeling at the end of *King Lear.* We both knew exactly what we were talking about. You can think this is like *Lear*, but this isn't like *Lear*. So *Lear* becomes kind of a map.

Doing Shakespeare can make certain kinds of other acting very difficult because the wonderful thing about Shakespeare, especially if you're playing one of the great roles or even a good role, is that everything or at least 90% of the character is in what you say. It's spoken in the most wonderful, rich, varied, poetic language. Nothing in television is like that, so you really have to learn what else is going on under either the facts of the language or the facts of the rather poor expository nature of the language; you have to find something else to do. You have to find what you're not talking about, stuff like that. So in a sense Shakespeare taught me that, but that's strange, even if in a good way. Of course, Shakespeare does enliven you to the possibilities of expression.

All my education has been through the theater, and Shakespeare has been a large part of that experience. So you learn about fundamental things in life, like having a child as the character Prospero and also really having a child. Your life experiences feed back into the roles as well. If you play one of those great roles it expands your understanding of certain things about life, why someone might kill you, for example. When I played Macbeth for the RSC, there was a big shooting in Dunsinane. It's curious how when you're playing a character like that you pick up from the newspapers things that connect. This man killed a lot of children in a shooting in a primary school in Scotland (where Andy Murray the tennis player comes from). And so I thought about him quite a lot in relation to *Macbeth*, about how Macbeth in a sense wants to kill all the children so that there is no future; there's just this endless present. I think both feed off each other. If you read any great work it will hopefully rub off on you a bit. And if you act something, and especially if you repeat something, which we have the chance to do in the theater, you get to try it out quite a lot. You get quite good at it. And then you can lose it for a bit and then you can find it again. I find it endlessly interesting.

To find the Shakespearean is to find those images, those phrases, that break out of the scriptures of say Jonsonian verse or Marlovian verse, or break out of the superficial brilliance of say someone like Stoppard, something that can go deep: "There is a divinity that shapes our ends, / Rough-hew them how we will." There's a famous story at the RSC how Ian Richardson (I think it was) came into the Green Room, very, very excited and he said, "I've just heard it, I've heard the phrase." He was passing some workmen, some agricultural laborers in the Cotswolds and he said, "What are you doing?" And they said, "We're shaping our ends." Shakespeare had that ability to pick from everywhere. I really, really do believe he was the glover's son from Stratford. I don't hold with any of that other nonsense. I think at this fascinating, expansive, and difficult time in England's history, Shakespeare became one of those people who were educated enough but still connected enough with their roots to be able to draw these extraordinary poetic insights into what life is like and into who we are (such stuff as dreams are made of). Shakespeare is just packed with things like that.

I don't know whether Shakespeare was exciting to be with. He retired to Stratford and bought land; he didn't do anything tremendously revolutionary. But he was fortunate to live at a time when his great talent could become the most extraordinary skill in the world. If you think about the period of time—it's only like '40s Hollywood up to now. And as much as film has changed in that time, it hasn't changed as much as theater did in Shakespeare's time. I don't know what Shakespeare was like. I expect he was all that's best about the theater. One of the nice things about working in the theater is you're part of a tribe. Shakespeare was an actor as well as a writer, which I think is great, because he'd have understood the theatre from the feet up, from the ground up. If he was working at The Globe now, he'd be part of this team now, he'd be one of one's fellow actors, and then you'd think, "Wow, he's written this fantastic play, it's absolutely brilliant. And there's a good part in it for me."

I can't think of a favorite quotation at the moment, really. I think that one from *Hamlet*, although I've never been in *Hamlet*, is one of my favorites. It's the most beautiful use of a common, ordinary image—making a fence—and it speaks about destiny and free will in the most direct and brilliant and profound way. So I'll go with that.

JOHN BARTON

"And that's true too."

*John Barton, CBE, was born in London and educated at Eton College and King's College, Cambridge. He has been active director of the Royal Shakespeare Company for over forty years, where he directed or co-directed more than thirty plays. He is also well-known, indeed legendary, as an acting teacher and as a teacher of Shakespearean acting. In 1982, he made a series of videos with RSC company members, essential viewing (and reading, in book form as **Playing Shakespeare**) for any actor working with Shakespeare. He has also collaborated on adaptations of Homer, Euripides, Aeschylus, and Sophocles. He still conducts workshops and as well offers summer master classes for the British American Drama Academy in Oxford. In 2001, he won the Sam Wanamaker Prize for pioneering work in Shakespearean Theatre. He is currently an Advisory Director of the RSC. I talked with him in his London flat, during a summer downpour. Since I arrived soaking wet, he most graciously offered me a whisky. He was equally generous with his conversation.*

I can't remember exactly when I came across Shakespeare. It was at school, maybe when I was around sixteen or so. Shakespeare, yes, is my center, but it's not my only center because I'm also a writer, I adapt plays, and I teach acting Shakespeare. I've done a lot of things. I don't know if I've got a great deal to say about Shakespeare, but I do Shakespeare. I work on Shakespeare textually and I do workshops. I don't know if I have anything to say about Shakespeare other than that I'm keen on it.

I went to the RSC originally to work for Peter Hall, working with actors on text and language. Then we grew into other things. I don't know if I'm good talking about Shakespeare. Whenever I work with actors, I always make them do it. I say, "Do a bit," then I tell them how the text can help them do it better. That's where I come from most.

Peter Hall was important in my theatrical and Shakespearean life because he got me out of academic life and got me to go to the RSC, for which I'm deeply grateful. I'm also grateful to the actors, to lots of actors. I've worked with lots of actors from 1960 onwards, and working with them has taught me more about Shakespeare than I knew when I went there. Though I knew

Shakespeare, I'd never done it. I've learned more about Shakespeare from working with them. I'd read a lot and done a lot of plays at university before I'd come there. I'd sort of done Shakespeare, but I'd never worked with major actors until I got to RSC. So that's why I'm a bit hazy now—because I do it, but it just came my way. I didn't set out originally to go into theater. I wanted to do research. I got a fellowship and was involved with the college and did a lot there. Then I realized I shouldn't have done that, that it was a mistake. I was very glad to leave and go to Stratford. Peter asked me to go and help him because he hadn't done a lot of Shakespeare when he took it over. He wanted a colleague that he knew knew quite a bit about Shakespeare. When working with actors, I realized that it helped to talk to them about something important in the text that hadn't been raised for them before. This process still grows in a way, in my mind.

I don't have any favorite plays, but I've picked the best texts to use for workshop purposes. That's not to say that I would do them. I've found that the very best working texts, if you take the right ones, are the Sonnets. But I've never wanted to do the Sonnets publicly. You can get an actor to learn a short bit. If they're busy, you can't ask them to do a lot. You say, "Do one." Then you find out how the text works on it. So it's not a favorite text, but it's a favorite working text.

The choruses in *Henry V* are very good to work on. A lot of things that I'm actually more interested in I don't think are suitable for that kind of work. One doesn't often work on dialogue. But if somebody comes and says "Let's work on this," that's fine. I get them to pick what they've started and then I pick it up from there. I don't have a favorite one. I know certain bits of Shakespeare make bloody good workshops because you can bring out points about how Shakespeare works. There are a lot of wonderful, favorite bits of Shakespeare that I wouldn't dream of doing in a workshop because they're too difficult or you can't get there in half an hour or an hour. It's like two different things. But if somebody comes and talks to me and wants to work on some *Romeo and Juliet*, that's fine. I've worked on that several times, but I haven't used it as a working text for years. But I know it and I could pick it up.

If someone asks me what my favorite Shakespeare play I always say, "The best play of Shakespeare is *Troilus and Cressida*." That shuts them up. It's actually arguable. It's a pretty remarkable play. It's an extraordinary mixture of myth, politics, history, tragic, comedy, absurdism. It's got in it sections that do everything. But you can't do it. I was lucky when I did it because all the actors when I did it turned out to be major famous actors. You can't do it without a major cast. You can't do *Troilus and Cressida* without having at least the principal characters played by basically leading actors. I had to do it twice. I didn't want to do it the second time, and I didn't do it well. I had a pretty good cast, but it wasn't as good as the first one. It's surprising that *Troilus and Cressida* isn't done more often, but it's because it's hard to get a good enough cast. It's not that people are not interested in the play. They are.

To me doing a Shakespeare play is intimately related to casting. You can love a Shakespeare play, but there are one or two I've never done because I've never got good casts. I've never actually done *Antony and Cleopatra*, but I'm very keen on it. I was thinking of doing it when Greg Doran wanted to do it with me recently, with the two people I would have done it with, Patrick Stewart and Harriet Walter. But I was perfectly happy that he should do it and I didn't do that one. I've not done as many as Terry Hands or as Greg, but I've done about thirty. Nobody has done them all. Even Peter Hall never did all of them. There are some that people want to do, but they don't get to because somebody else does them first for different reasons.

I'm very keen on *Cymbeline*. I have done it and I didn't do it badly. It's frightfully difficult. The interesting thing about it was that an editor had just brought out a new edition of it. After watching rehearsals for three days, he said, "It's absolutely awful. I've realized I've edited it entirely wrong. I've punctuated it for the reader, but it's no help to the actors." He was probably right. But then the question of how you punctuate text is a choice that's made in rehearsals. In some plays, it matters a lot how you punctuate them and not so much with others. But he said: "I've over-punctuated wildly. I did it for the reader and I've done it wrong." That was really interesting. He spotted it immediately in rehearsals. That's why I don't like to talk much about punctuation. You have to make choices, and some places are easier than others. There's no general point one can make.

My main point always is that doing Shakespeare depends on casting. If you miscast, it's not going to work, even if you do it well. If you're blessed with a good cast, you'll do it well—I'm absolutely certain. I think the most difficult role to get a really good actress for is Rosalind. So I've never done *As You Like It*. There was never a Rosalind. There were ones that were around before I was doing them. I'm not saying they don't exist. Like Vanessa Redgrave is a famous one. But when I was thinking I'd like to do that next, there wasn't any girl that felt right for Rosalind. Today often you don't get the person you need or want, and you have to undercast it, and it doesn't work so well. I know this is true. This is the most important thing I know about Shakespeare. A lot of it is the luck of how you cast it. If you miscast or undercast it, it won't work. I'm absolutely certain of this.

This is all I have to say about Shakespeare. I'm talking about doing it. My prime thing is how would I, should I, could I put this on the stage. These are completely different questions than what I think about when I read it. I think the first play I ever read was *King Lear* and I've never wanted to do *King Lear*. I've co-directed it, but I've never wanted to do it because it's so extraordinary. I think it actually is one where the sort of Victorian idea that it's better to read it than do it is probably true. I've never liked it when I've seen it. I've never wanted to do it, because I thought that in this case the text itself demands more than you can achieve. It wasn't that I found it too painful. It was that I don't think one can really bring this off; it's so extraordinary. But I could be quite wrong on that.

I expect that working with Shakespeare has helped me direct other actors or other plays, but not in a very obvious way. I would stress the importance of simple things, such as the incredible importance of storytelling. It's led me to hate to use the word "character," because Shakespeare didn't have it or use it. It's not in the dictionary until the 18th century. He didn't use it, but he did it. He's the richest character writer there ever was. But actually I've found and tried that you can build a character by focusing on the text, without using the word "character." You can stimulate the building and interpretation of character without talking in the jargon of the 19th century. We use jargon that Shakespeare didn't use. I forbid people to say—I think they should be fined, if they say it— "iambic pentameter." What's wrong with "blank verse"? I suppose I'm talking about what I believe. I know what I react against, thinkers to be steered a bit clear of.

When an actor turned up and I thought, "I'd like to do *Hamlet* with him," I did it with him. He was a very good, well-known actor, Michael Pennington. I wanted to do it with him at that point because I was reacting against what I thought were perverse Hamlets. It goes wrong if you go with a hyper-psychological, hyper-poetical, hyper-magical. It keeps going wrong because each person who does it says, "I'll do it better that way." I tried to get away from the things that kept happening. I hate talking about what I believe about Shakespeare because I've learned a lot both in the study and by doing it. We'd talk about it more if we were actually working on a scene with someone. Absolutely. But if you ask me the general questions I'm not sure that I terribly need to talk about it now.

I hate any question about what Shakespeare was like because we don't know. We all have our own hypotheses. It's ridiculous. Hundreds of books are written each year and they all contradict each other. I think there should be a law written forbidding anybody to write a book about Shakespeare for ten years. That's why I never have. Well, I wouldn't do it even if there weren't a billion already. I do believe there are too many books on Shakespeare, even though some of them are very, very good books.

He obviously set out at first as a poet, not as a playwright. He became a playwright because he was knocking around in the building. The tradition of collaboration and commission writing does interest me. That was the norm to them. It's sort of extraordinary to people today, but that was what they did. He started a scene but then had to rewrite it because of a problem. That was the norm. It still happens on television and that sort of place. I dislike any question on what was he like. I always try to dodge that by saying he can't have liked anything very much because when everyone else was out at the Mermaid Tavern, they sent him off to finish the last scene of the play that he was writing. He used to work bloody hard, acting and touring. Certainly what is extraordinary about him is that he wrote so many plays in a short period of time. That is extraordinary. He also wrote very different styles and very different kinds of plays continually, from one to another.

The more I know, the less I know. The more I know the more hesitant I am to say that a play reveals the heart of Shakespeare. I'm being a bit reactive because I don't want to make speeches about it. I could do a workshop or something, and I have, but I don't particularly want to. I don't need to. Anybody who reads Shakespeare has their own view and they have a right to it. I don't feel like trying to unlock the mystery.

I know a lot of Shakespeare. I know it not by learning it, but if people start something, usually I can prompt them. I know what it is. When I'm asked my favorite quote, I don't particularly like that. But I can give you the answer: "And that's true too." That's a profound one. People like that one. Even if they know the play well, they don't know where it comes from. Nobody does. Directors who are doing the play don't know where it comes from. It's from *King Lear*. What does he reach at the end? If you ask Shakespeare what he thought, probably he'd end up saying something like that. The odd thing is this has happened to me a number of times (people not knowing where the quote is from). My wife is a Shakespeare scholar and she didn't know. She knows Shakespeare better than me. People tend to recognize it when they hear it, but they don't know where it comes from. I think that's a good quote.

In regard to changes in Shakespearean productions, I think the culture does shift. Nobody consciously does, but it happens. There are certain types and tendencies: romantic, anti-romantic, political, left-wing, right-wing. There are certain tendencies, but they're tendencies of the individual director. I don't think they're anything profound. And I don't think that things do change that much. As Peg Ashcroft used to say when asked about Peter's influence on the RSC and all that, "All this is highly overrated. We were doing it thirty years before you were born." She said when she was a girl, with Olivier and all these people, long before we were heard of, they were doing these things and working on them. That to me was one of the most interesting remarks an actress ever made. She knew what she was talking about.

I think that one change is that a lot of people who do Shakespeare now don't know Shakespeare and are frightened of it and therefore need to do display with it. I think the another really bad thing—perhaps this doesn't have to do with anything but directors—is a perversity of design and the fact that you almost have to do everything in modern dress. Of course you can do modern dress sometimes, but now directors think, "My version of this play is the important one because I am doing it set in South America." But they still have to do the play well. That's where it's gone bad. I don't think it's necessary. It's individual directors being perverse or humorous or not bold enough.

I don't think Shakespearean productions have changed, because they are about good acting. It was exactly the same at the RSC fifty years ago. I think it's hopeless having a set philosophy about what is Shakespeare. But sometimes Shakespearean productions go through silly periods, like when it's all got to be Brechtian or something. It doesn't prove anything. And they just don't do the play. With most actors, when you stop talking, you soon get through: they want to try things and open it up. I think acting Shakespeare has not changed hugely in the time I've been here. The most interesting paradox is that it's the exact same in America. I've done a lot of workshops in America. All the actors were very anti-method and wanted to get away from it. I wanted to get a method actor there, but I didn't get one. There isn't an English or American version. They're very very close.

I do a number of workshops. Groups come from America and I do them at the RSC. I've done them at Oxford, wherever they come. I like to do them. There's one major area that I'm most interested in, which we've not really mentioned: the history plays. I love the history plays. They do perform very well. They're not ever quite as fashionable. A lot of students don't want to do the history plays; they want to do comedy or tragedy. That's quite common.

I always wanted to do *Henry VI*, but I only got to do that one version of it. I've seen it five times. I know it very well and I'm very keen on it. *King John* I've done and am keen on. I think the history plays are terrific.

Of my favorite plays, I'd put *Henry IV* in the top three. They have a variety of worlds. They're very political, very human, and very not-political. It's all mixed up. But I'm not sure I've ever seen a Falstaff entirely work. I've seen two nearly work—Ralph Richardson and Robert Stephens did those. Mostly it doesn't work at all. And Hal is difficult to really bring off. If you have a major actor, he always seems a bit senior until the end. And you have to have a young actor.

DAVID BEVINGTON

"WELL, HERE IS MY LEG."

David Bevington is Phyllis Fay Horton Distinguished Service Professor Emeritus at the University of Chicago in the Departments of English and Comparative Literature, and he is Chair of Theater and Performance Studies. His extensive writing is used by students and scholars, including **From Mankind to Marlowe: Growth of Structure in the Popular Drama of Tudor England; Tudor Drama and Politics: A Critical Approach to Topical Meaning; Shakespeare; Action Is Eloquence: Shakespeare's Language of Gesture; Homo, Memento Finis: The Iconography of Just Judgment in Medieval Art and Drama; Shakespeare: The Seven Ages of Human Experience; Shakespeare: Script, Stage, Screen** *(with Annie Welsh and Michael Greenwald);* **How to Read a Shakespeare Play; This Wide and Universal Theater: Shakespeare in Performance, Then and Now; Shakespeare's Ideas: More Things in Heaven and Earth; Shakespeare and Biography; and Murder Most Foul: Hamlet Through the Ages.** *He is also prolific as an editor, having recently co-edited* **The Works of Ben Jonson,** *as well as previously the* **Longman Complete Works of Shakespeare** *(edited solely by Bevington), the* **Bantam Classic** *series,* **The Revels Plays and Student Editions, The Sourcebooks Shakespeare, The Norton Anthology of Renaissance Drama,** *numerous individual plays for the Oxford, Cambridge, and Arden editions, and much else. I talked with Professor Bevington in his office on the fifth floor of a striking old building on the University of Chicago campus. He was equally full of feeling and intellect, so I found it hard to stop asking him questions.*

I grew up in New York City in the Bronx during the Depression. We didn't have any money, so we didn't get out of the Bronx very often. But one time—I was seven or so— I was taken to see Helen Hayes in *Twelfth Night*. I mostly remember this secondhand, by my parents telling me about it, but certainly it was a wonderful event.

I didn't actually do much with Shakespeare in college. I didn't think it was terribly well taught at Harvard, to tell you the truth. I was interested in taking things I didn't know about, so I read widely in English and American literature. I majored in History and Literature, which I loved.

When I married Peggy in 1953, we were given a full recording of *Romeo and Juliet* on 33-1/3 rpm records with Claire Bloom as Juliet and Alan Badel as Romeo. It was so good that Peggy and I would put it on the way we might put on a Brahms symphony to sit around in the evening and just listen. And one time we were taking a car trip to see my family down in North Carolina, we realized that the two of us could recite the play (no doubt with some errors). We got through about Act 3. That was really quite lovely and ever since I've advised people to work on good productions as a way of really getting involved in a Shakespeare play. Claire Bloom is Juliet for me, always was and always will be.

When I came back to graduate school after being in the Navy for three years, I ran into Alfred Harbage, who had joined the Harvard faculty. He was a boon to me. I was thinking about going into the 19th century because I love Dickens. I actually wrote a Dickens paper that was published. But I worked so well with Harbage that I got into Renaissance drama and staging and went on from there.

Working with Alfred Harbage, I wrote my dissertation on pre-Shakespearean drama, which turned into my book called *From Mankind to Marlowe: Growth of Structure in the Popular Drama of Tudor England*. Then I taught at Harvard for a couple of years, mostly tutorials and composition courses, for which I was not especially qualified—but that's what they did with new instructors then.

Then I got a job at Virginia with Fredson Bowers. There was an older gentleman who was teaching the Shakespeare course, so I taught metaphysical poets, Spenser, and Renaissance prose and poetry, which I loved doing. I was interested in the drama, but I hadn't really zeroed in on Shakespeare. I took over this older gentleman's course when he was abroad for part of the year at the end of the spring semester. Then he died that summer in Europe, sad to tell but it was an opportunity for me. I got a cable from Fredson Bowers asking me if I would be willing to take over the Shakespeare course, which I was overwhelmed with pleasure at the thought of. So I worked that course up and it became very popular at Virginia. That's how I got started.

As far as problematic plays, I suppose everybody finds *Troilus and Cressida* problematic. I was invited at one time to edit it for the Arden Shakespeare. I was flattered to be asked, so I took it on and just fell in love with that play. So its problems to me are pure joy. *Troilus and Cressida* is extraordinary. I didn't know until I had a chance to work a couple years editing it for Arden just how extraordinary it is. There have been some bad productions of it, though, and I would love to see a good one. *Measure for Measure*, the same thing. I think problem plays are about as wonderful as they get. But there's some like *Timon of Athens* I can't say I really have ever succeeded in getting into. It's too austere, too bitter, but with wonderful poetry in it. I've never taught it as far as I recall.

I'm glad you asked in the plural about favorite plays because it's hard to pick one. I've been working a lot on *Hamlet*. I teach it a lot. At the moment, I'm editing it for a series called Internet Shakespeare Editions; this is very complicated. It'll be online and we'll have old spelling, we'll have the first quarto, the unauthorized quarto, of course a good part of the second quarto, and obviously the folio. I'm providing three complete texts with a set of notes for each. So I'm spending a lot of time working on *Hamlet* and it repays wonderfully.

I've just finished a book for Oxford called *Murder Most Foul: Hamlet through the Ages*, sort of the history of Hamlet. I had a lot of fun with that. But I've also really concentrated on teaching *Lear* and *Othello*, and among the comedies *As You Like It, Twelfth Night, Midsummer*, and *Much Ado*. It's hard to say anything unkind about any of those wonderful plays. Among the history plays, it's not surprising to say that *Henry IV part 1* is the best for me. I had a chance to edit that for the Oxford Shakespeare, and I've edited *As You Like It* for Internet Shakespeare Editions, and that's out and available online. And I was invited by Cambridge to do *Antony and Cleopatra*. Now there's a remarkable play. I mean, there are times when I think that's one of my two or three favorites. I don't know if I've ever really seen a good production, but I've heard good recordings. There's one with Peggy Ashcroft and Michael Redgrave that's everything one could hope for. I love listening to really good readings. You can get so much. There's one of *Coriolanus*, which is a difficult play in some ways to get into, but not if you listen to Richard Burton, who was born to play the part of Coriolanus, very steely and bitter and bright minded.

As far as characters, I feel very close to Antony and to Hamlet. I think about Antony in terms of the way most males are. I've never done any philandering, but I've dreamt about it: the imagination of the temptation and so on, the fascination with a remarkable woman, just in terms of erotic fantasy. And it's such gorgeous poetry.

Hamlet is something very different. I'm much persuaded that Hamlet is not a play about a man who couldn't make up his mind what to do. That's such an oversimplified psychological reading of Freud. Hamlet is a remarkable examination of how difficult it is to sort out when one should act and when one should not, an examination of the problematic nature of action itself. And Hamlet himself is so eloquent,

If we move over to the comedies, I can go with Jaques and Touchstone anytime. Or Corin also from *As You like It*, old Corin when he's telling Jaques that "the property of rain is to wet," and "I earn that I eat, get that I wear, owe no man hate, envy no man's happiness, glad of other men's good. . . ." He's a wonderful, simple man.

Richard III is utterly fascinating, wonderful, even if he's evil. And Macbeth certainly resonates with me. But some early plays of Shakespeare present few characters who are even occasionally like that. I would just as soon not ever bother to meet the Bishop of Winchester in *Henry VI Part 1*. Of course Shakespeare loves to see his villains in a more attractive light. Edmund in *King Lear* is fascinating. But I suppose Goneril is someone I would never want to meet. Or Regan in her own suave way is just as bad. Shakespeare doesn't often just portray certain naked, awful, corrupting villainy, but he does there. Cornwall is not much better, although Shakespeare is careful to make a case for him. But for Goneril and Regan, there's just sexual politics and power as far as I can tell.

Absolutely my Shakespearean life has changed me, but of course, one wants to steer away from the notion that these plays are offering nostrums about how to behave oneself. They're not sermons. Shakespeare is careful to avoid that. At the same time, they are at their best life-affirming in wonderful ways. Take *King Lear*. I think I find myself wanting to take seriously the idea that one should somehow learn not to covet things in this world; of course, that's not just *King Lear*, that goes back to the New Testament and is all over the place. But *Lear* makes me try to think seriously about how to avoid the corruptions of wealth and power, how to be charitable. I don't say that to those I'm teaching, but I am talking about the way I think. I want people to read Shakespeare because I hope it will make them better people.

It disturbs me that there's such a trend these days to regard Prospero in *The Tempest* as a dark character who's interested in power, is a bad parent, and all that. He may be all those things, but he is also a great theater person— a director. And he attempts to come to terms with the need to forgive and finally is able to do so as at the same time that he realizes that he must prepare for death. At this time in my life, that's something to think about.

Some years ago I was asked to give the Ryerson Lecture (a big annual lecture for a large crowd of faculty) here at the University of Chicago. I found myself wanting to title my talk "Shakespeare Faces Retirement." And people laughed, I think in part because I was not yet retired, but getting on towards that point. So with Prospero I could think about giving up one's daughter to another man, giving up one's art, giving up one's life, being ready to accept death and make the best you can of what little you've managed to do, and so on.

It worries me that too often people who teach in the humanities are not necessarily very humane. There are bitter fights, lack of charity, and so on. It shouldn't be like that. It's self-congratulatory even to suggest that literature can improve me even in a minor way. I don't suppose it really does, but it does at least sort of work in my aspirations, in my dreams to be who I would like to be. I try to be generous and charitable. One of the great books about Shakespeare from quite some time ago is *Shakespeare and the Comedy of Forgiveness*. That seems to me such a great argument. The importance of forgiveness runs throughout Shakespeare, and of course again it is at heart a Christian text. But I think and feel that Shakespeare's version of Christianity is very secular; it's very much divorced from service or indeed any sort of dogmatic statement of belief. It's more a deeply incorporated value system.

There's another way that I feel Shakespeare has helped me. I'm not church going—I used to be—and there are parts of church in terms of community that I cherished. But one has community at a place like University of Chicago. To see the world of art, teaching, poetry, and so on as a community is wonderful. Certainly Shakespeare and some other great poets can really help out in building such a community. It's very important to me in *King Lear* that Edgar, who in some ways is the most heroic figure in the play, is an agnostic. He's a skeptic, like his brother. But Shakespeare carefully posed them one against the other. Edmund takes the skeptical notion that you might as well rob and cheat because you'll get ahead of other people and you'll win all the marbles. Edgar sees all of that, but he sees there's nonetheless a reason for wishing to be good, to try to be good. And he does so without Christian example. He does so because it's a more universal, beautiful idea. And Shakespeare's very aware that you're never going to save this world, but one can try to do one's best to live that way. To me, Shakespeare is a deeply humane poet and dramatist.

He's extraordinary. To forgive the unforgiveable seems to me to be one of the great lessons in life. It's something that you see in Desdemona and Cordelia. When Cordelia's father says, in effect, "Your sisters were just awful, but you had some cause. You had some reason to hate me," she says, "No cause, no cause." It's like great music. Every once in a while, I just weep at something really beautiful. I was weeping this morning listening to a middle Beethoven quartet, the slow movement of the Opus 59 No. 2. I play viola in quartets and that helps. Music and Shakespeare come together for me in ways that are of course hard to describe. But Shakespeare has the cadences, the senses of beauty and sorrow, the harmony. It's clear that Shakespeare loved music. He writes about it in *Merchant of Venice* in the fifth act with the talk about the music of the spheres, which is, of course, commonplace. But he dresses it up in such beautiful, persuasive language about "choiring to the young-eyed cherubins." That kind of vision again! It is wonderful to be able to be in touch with that Renaissance sense of harmony. For him particularly the more dogmatic sides of Christian faith were, I take it, of less and less importance. And what remains is something described by Pythagoras, who of course was not a Christian but someone who loved music, harmony, and the beauty of construction.

I love science. I love astronomy. The propositions of geometry of Euclid or the study of the heavens are a part of that same utter beauty of everything. Shakespeare's good for making you want to be as much as possible a generalist in terms of humanities, to cross disciplines— music, philosophy, literature, history, and history particularly. It saddens me that so many people nowadays don't know much history. Shakespeare wrote a lot of history plays, partly for reasons about England's identity of course, but he goes back to the Romans and the Greeks as well. History is the great scheme of things. It's so useful to be able to identify movements in music, philosophy, history, and so on with different periods of cultural change: the phenomenon of the Renaissance, or the Middle ages, or Romantic period. It's beautiful to have a sense that when you read a George Eliot novel, say *Middlemarch*, of how exquisitely it belongs to that particular point in the 19th century and with the role of women and women authors then. It's lovely to see Shakespeare in that same framework, in the panorama of history.

It's easy to compare Shakespeare right away with Ben Jonson and the Jonsonian. Shakespeare certainly is not the strict neoclassicist Jonson tended to be. Middleton's a harder case. He's more in between, I suppose, although he did write mainly city comedies in his comic vein. But Shakespeare is just remarkable in his breadth of being able to appreciate the neoclassical world and to have learned tremendously from it in terms of structure and character types. But then he softens the edges and can be seen in terms of English traditions again in the more humane and generous side of things. Shakespeare has a wholeness, capturing that moment when the strength of the oral epic world of the middle ages is still there but is waning, so that the gods are not as present as they were, not as visibly present. But they're talked about constantly, worried about, interrogated, are there in *King Lear*, for example. Perhaps they are not quite there, but at least they're a presence so that we're acting out things here on this surface of the world but surrounded by above and below in the sense of the epic battle going on between good and evil in the universe itself.

That kind of grand scale you won't get in Ben Jonson or certainly not in Tom Stoppard either, whom I adore. Tony Kushner is somebody else I'm crazy about. I love modern drama. But you wouldn't go to it for this Shakespearean sweep of an affirmation. Even when they're affirming things, as Kushner certainly is, it would be hard to compete with Shakespeare in those terms.

A book published here at the University of Chicago, *Such is my Love: A Study of Shakespeare's Sonnets* by Joseph Pequigney, argues that the Sonnets commemorated an actual homosexual affair. Of course, the whole thesis as to whether the Sonnets are biographical is up for grabs, but he grabs the bull by the horns and says that it is indeed and that it commemorates not just a strong male friendship but a consummated homosexual relationship with the Earl of Southampton or somebody like him. Most people haven't agreed with that, but the notion that there's something bisexual there is an interesting argument. This is, of course, where anachronism becomes a serious problem. Today we're obviously getting much more accepting of homosexuality. I just ran across something where a critic was saying, "Of course, Antonio in *The Merchant of Venice* was a homosexual." The critic wasn't saying I think he is or there might have been or there's some tendencies on that part, but that he was a homosexual. Well, I'm glad he knows that for certain, because I certainly do not. It seems to me that it's much more arguable that he's presented as a gentleman of a certain sort who's not planning to marry but is perfectly happy to see his young man friend married. But the Sonnets do portray self-abasement, anxiety, a sense of betrayal. It's hard to believe that he didn't have experiences of that sort, and it's hard for me not to suppose that some of that rose out of a relationship, perhaps with the Earl of Southampton.

Did Shakespeare have affairs with women when he was in London? Yes, probably. (*Shakespeare in Love* of course experiments with that idea to a fare thee well quite wonderfully.) Was he guilty about it? Certainly. Did he have repressed unresolved feelings about heterosexual love? Yes. I'm on the whole inclined to believe that the marriage probably was difficult. It seems to me a little hard to explain why he would be away for so long when he could have moved his family to London. Then unquestionably he had strong feelings about his father and about the son who died, Hamnet. Did he have strong patriarchal feelings that his family ought to have a coat of arms? Yes. He went to a lot of trouble for that and when he died he was described in the burial record in Stratford as "William Shakespeare gent." So he made it! By that time he had bought a lot of real estate. His was clearly a first family of Stratford. And there they still are on the altar of the church for goodness' sake, he and his wife and some others. And there's the bust there too. He was a self-*made* gentleman, which was quite a thing to do in those days. That's where Greenblatt's book is persuasive. But I don't follow Stephen on the business with Shakespeare's Catholicism. He flirts with that rather fast and loose. But to see Shakespeare as a parvenu, someone with aspirations for being a gentleman, that is written loud and clear.

How kindly he was is perhaps the hardest question because there's the old tradition going back to Rowe and others about how generous he was. Henry Chettle back in the 1590s answered Robert Green's intemperate attacks by saying in effect that Shakespeare was really gentle. The word "gentle" has stuck with Shakespeare. That's of course the basis of Katherine Duncan-Jones's insisting that that's a mislabeled commonplace and needs to be interrogated. I appreciate her wanting to open that up for examination. Prospero's an interesting kind of portrait for Shakespeare: an overbearing father, grasping in his real estate dealings, something of a social snob, probably, albeit with a huge heart for ordinary people—and certainly not a democrat.

One thing that that portrait does— if there were ever any question— is to put to rest all the arguments about the Earl of Oxford. This portrait of Shakespeare as a parvenu from a provincial town who was in contact with local mores and local character types is plainly demonstrated in the things he wrote about. And Shakespeare was clearly a professional man of the theater, which was an awfully good place for him to be.

This portrait fits well with what we know about William Shakespeare and does not fit very well with what we know about the Earl of Oxford, who was a wretch, who abused his wife to the point of something close to the physical, and drove his poor father-in-law, Lord Burghley, near to his grave by being such a terrible husband. I once wrote a limerick on this subject:

> Will Shakespeare to Oxford once said,
> "My lord, you've an excellent head
> For a tragical line.
> King Lear is quite fine
> For a chap who for years has been dead."

There are of course so many quotations I could choose as favorites. An offbeat quotation with which one might introduce a lecture might be Prince Hal saying in *Henry IV Part 1* in Act 2, "Well, here is my leg," meaning, of course, I'm making my gracious bow, to which Falstaff replies, "And here is my speech." Then there's Viola who describes how she would simply not accept refusal when she's asked by the Countess Olivia what would she say if she was going to woo someone. "Why, what would you?" asks Olivia, and Viola says she would

> Make me a willow cabin at your gate
> And call upon my soul within the house,

Write loyal cantons of contemnéd love.
And sing them loud even in the dead of night;
Halloo your name to the reverberate hills,
And make the babbling gossip of the air
Cry out 'Olivia!'

I can't read that without breaking down.

Hearing Shakespeare out loud really does make it hit—as when you listen to Juliet saying, "What's Montague? It is nor hand nor foot,/ Nor arm, nor face, nor any other part/ Belonging to a man," or so many lines from that play. Thinking of *Romeo and Juliet* reminds me that one should have different favorites at different times of life. Shakespeare is awfully good in this way. I wrote a book called *Shakespeare: The Seven Ages of Human Experience*. It follows the seven ages through Shakespeare: for example to see the way he shows what falling in love can be in all its folly and beauty, then later on the struggle with something much like what we would call a midlife crisis in *Antony and Cleopatra*. My book goes through the seven ages pretty well, including of course at the end, "sans teeth, sans eyes, sans taste, sans everything." It's beautiful that Shakespeare was able to make that speech so beautiful and put it in the mouth of a skeptic, Jaques, who is offering it as his wry comment on the essentially meaningless pattern of existence.

Just before Jaques gives this speech, Orlando pleads for his old servant Adam, saying that until the old man is fed, he will not touch a bit. You were asking before about Jonson and Shakespeare, and I love that scene in *As You Like It* because it really sounds like a debate between Shakespeare and Jonson. Jaques is like a satirist who claims the authority to be able to call it like it is, to take the blinders off and let us see ourselves in our worst condition. And in Jaques' debate with Duke Senior, the Duke says, "Well, that's all very well this Horace stuff. I understand what you're saying, where it's coming from, but it seems to be that too many of you satirists are just using this as your excuse to get back at people you don't like." Of course, Shakespeare doesn't take sides on that particular argument. He's wonderful at being fair to both sides in a debate, isn't he? He allows you to sort the sides out yourself, although probably you and I seem to be agreeing that he lets the major chord come down at the end of the night for humor and forgiveness.

GILES BLOCK

"*MIGHT YOU NOT KNOW SHE WOULD DO AS SHE HAS DONE*"

Giles Block has been at the Globe Theatre since 1999. He has been called Master of Verse, Master of the Words, and (currently) Globe Associate in charge of text. His work, nonetheless, has stayed much the same: helping Globe actors with the delivery of Shakespeare's text and teaching for Globe Education. He began his career as an actor but in the seventies moved on to directing. He has directed **Antony and Cleopatra, Hamlet,** *and* **Troilus and Cressida** *at the Globe,* **The Tempest, Henry V,** *and* **The Comedy of Errors** *at the Blackfriars Theatre in Virginia, and numerous other plays in other venues. He has been Associate Director at Ipswich Theater, Staff Director and Director of Platforms at the National Theatre. He also directed two main house productions there in the early 80's. In 2000 The Association of Major Theatres of Japan recognized Giles for services to the Japanese Theatre. In 2011 he won the prestigious Sam Wanamaker Award. In 2013 he published* **Speaking the Speech: An Actor's Guide to Shakespeare***. This remarkable book is a practical guide for actors but is of equal use to any teacher or student of Shakespeare. We talked in summer of 2015, in the Member's Room of the Tate Modern in London.*

Second World War, both my grandmothers lived with us. And they brought to our family house these big three volume editions—I suppose they were Victorian editions, filled with pictures—of Shakespeare's comedies, tragedies, histories. I remember that pretty early on. For some reason, I'd decided even earlier that I wanted to be an actor. That seemed to amuse people, so I thought, "Maybe this might be a good thing to do." It was very difficult to get into plays until eventually I arrived at a school where we did a Shakespeare play every year. That was my first real introduction.

I played Prince Arthur in *King John* during my school days. Then I was lucky that in a neighboring school there was this brilliant man teaching English, Michael Croft, who founded something called the Youth Theater. Because I was so close, I auditioned, and got to be part of that. That was incredible. It's hard to believe it actually happened, but every summer we would play a West End theater. All the critics came and watched us. We were between about sixteen and twenty, that age group. We did a Shakespeare play every year and then we would tour our productions at Easter to places like Italy and Berlin. It was just an amazing way to grow up a little bit and also to get all this stuff in your head. I was an actor for several years, but not primarily Shakespeare. In those days it was a repertory system, so depending which repertory company you were in, you would always do at least one Shakespeare per year. And I had two wonderful years at Nottingham Playhouse where I think we did more, two or three a year. The first one I was in there was *Measure for Measure*, with Judi Dench playing Isabella. I was playing Barnadine. I was all of 22 or something. And then after a while I decided that I wanted to have more of a say than an actor sometimes gets. So I started directing. And I had a strange, wonderful period in my life for twenty years or so where most of my work was done in Japan. It was at the time our son had been born and was growing up. So I would go away from time to time and do shows over there. They were mostly Shakespeare; that's what they wanted me to do.

I suppose I realized two things from working in Japan. Because the plays were all in Japanese, I realized how you can never really get the feeling from Shakespeare in translation that you can when you hear it in your own language. But there was this wonderful translator who had translated all of Shakespeare's plays, Yushi Odashima. During this period of his life he apparently would go to a coffee shop every morning and slowly translate all the plays. I would meet him and get him to do two things for me: a back translation into English of what he'd written in Japanese, then a version of the Japanese written out in Roman letters so I could actually sound out the Japanese. Then in longhand I would write out these plays in English in Shakespeare's language, so I had these three texts to follow. Then my work became possible, because of the inestimable help I received from these wonderful— they were always women—interpreters. I spoke in rehearsals as I am speaking to you, and they would be translating into Japanese. I have a case somewhere of videos, but I don't know what state they would be in, probably decomposed by now.

In '77 I went to the National as a staff director, which is what they call their assistant directors. I could have been assigned to many different productions, but I was fortunate that I got to work two or three times on Peter Hall's plays; some of them took me to America. There was *Bedroom Farce*, the eight-person play that went to Broadway. So I went over there and helped put in the new cast when the English actors were replaced over a couple of months with the Americans who were taking over for them. And then later *Amadeus* happened and again I spent two or three years flying backwards and forwards as that continued on Broadway such a long time. I did most of the work of going over there and putting in new casts. After I left The National, Peter asked me to go over with him as his associate director when he was doing *The Merchant of Venice* with Dustin Hoffman. He wanted me to stay there, which I did. My wife, who is an actress, was free at the time and our son was 2 ½, so the three of us moved just off Times Square for three or four months while the play was running. I had worked with Peter already as a staff director on the *Othello* he did with Scofield, but he didn't really talk much about Shakespeare or about the texts. But there was this day in 1989—I do write about this in my book—when we first met the cast of *Merchant of Venice*. It had started in this country, but when we went to America for equity reasons we had to employ a lot of American actors to make the deal work. And he gave this talk to us all in the stalls where he talked about the importance of the line ending in Shakespeare. To be honest I'd never really thought much about the line ending. But the moment he said that, I just knew it was huge. And I remembered running home across Times Square to say to Penny, "It's about the line ending!"

And then I worked with him again. He got me to work alongside him at Stratford when he was doing *All's Well that Ends Well* because he was about to have a new child come into his life. He wanted someone to take over rehearsals when he had to be away. But I began to think that his way didn't quite satisfy me. I began to feel the wonderful language in which these plays are written. The mechanics of the rhythm and the play of line upon line are written in that way so as to release the text in the most luminous and clear way as possible. It should sound as natural as us speaking. Of course, the line ending is the most contentious area in this field, but if you think about how Shakespeare imagined these plays, you have to imagine he heard human voices expressing these thoughts. That idea really took me on a quest, trying to pin all this down. One of Peter's wonderful phrases was about the musicality of the line. Sometimes it is wonderful and musical, but a lot of lines are not musical. But there's always something about how the phrases within the line operate, difficult to get, difficult to achieve, but that's what I now realize is the key: we should be able to look at Shakespeare on the page and just begin to hear the voices coming off the page.

Shakespeare's writing develops over his life. He begins to feel that there has to be a different tone of voice when the characters are no longer really confident themselves, since most of the interesting characters are not always confident. Even Richard III has his disruptive night in the tent where suddenly the text is doing different things. I think *Macbeth* is a really hard play and I've never seen a production of it that gets close to what I feel should be there. I'm not saying it's easy to get there. It reads so well. When you're silently reading it to yourself, it blows you away. And usually when you see it, you think this is not what happens to me when I read it. Nevertheless, I'm sure it can be done. From moment to moment I've seen it, but I've never really quite seen it absolutely.

Leontes is a difficult character. But again, you start by giving yourself to his language or giving yourself to how the text is laid out on the page. There's a bit from Leontes I talk about in the book that I think is so extraordinary. It involves line endings: "Nor night nor day, no rest! It is but weakness/ To bear the matter thus, mere weakness. If/ The cause were not in being…." The "If" is at the end of the second line, so it's not "If the cause were not in being," it's "If… The cause were not in being." In thinking "the cause were not in being," Leontes' breath has been taken away by the enormity of his terrible thought. He has to breathe before he can express it. And it's such moments we probably notice when we listen to other people speaking. It's no different than the way we speak normally, where we breathe in most peculiar places. But it's in those moments that we alert the attention of the audience. Shakespeare doesn't write until he absolutely knows what these characters are doing to each other, what they are saying to each other. He gets to the point that he hears them breathing. And he knows when a thought is too complex to be said smoothly all in one breath.

It's hard for any actor to encompass a part in maybe five weeks because he's working out what he's going to wear, where he's going to come in from, and such. I need to get the time to share the possibilities of my approach, because you've got to do a double thing with Shakespeare. Of course, you've got to learn how all the words fit together, but then you've got to go back to the text and see where the breathing comes.

Shakespeare's characters do all seem to have an individuality. He writes a play and then he's done it and he hands it over to the actors, but then, my God, another one comes along which starts to obsess him. And sometimes the obsession with one play shows up in the course of the next or the previous one. So you get these little connections between plays written close to each other in time. For example, he writes *Julius Caesar* and then in *Hamlet* has Polonius talk about having acted Julius Caesar. And there are other such examples.

For me, doors opened and beckoned me in when I first came to The Globe when Mark Rylance was running it. There was a sort of double brief, which was come and direct some plays— well, a play to begin with, *Antony and Cleopatra*. And Mark also wanted me to be. . . what was I first called? "Master of Verse." I never liked that one, because I thought, "What about the prose?" So one drunken evening I said, "I want to change my title. I want to be called Master of the Words." So for a while I had that. Then all these titles went away when Dominic Dromgoole took over. Now I'm just called a Globe

Associate, and in brackets "Text." But I think the same things and just I try to do it better, I suppose. So I have this double thing: working with the actors on text generally and directing plays, which I did three times. I was doing both jobs and of course I learned pretty quickly that once you're also directing you don't get enough time to work on the text because you have to do all the basic stuff of deciding where people are going to come in from, what they're going to wear, what music to play when, and all that. And of course that was Mark's idea in having this Master of whatever. He felt it was like opera companies having someone doing mise en scène and someone conducting the music. Of course it's never quite worked perfectly. I always want more time.

It's a long time since I've done a non-Shakespearean work, to be honest, which really surprises me. But I suppose what working so much with Shakespeare has done is to make me more rigorous about what any author has written. I know with Shakespeare there is no limit to one's investigation into what he has written and how he's written it and the sounds that the words make and all that. So I think it probably has made me delighted in sharing with the people I'm working with how wonderful a phrase is. I pay more attention to the words. I now work alongside lots of directors, and I'm sort of surprised by how infrequently something about the text comes up in rehearsals. I do think I help.

It's really hard to do Shakespeare by half measures, you see. "How has having a Shakespearean life influenced you" is a hard question because it's a sort of question that affects me a bit with its implications. I think it's true that Shakespeare has taken over too much in my life. There is home life and working life. And I sometimes think that I've become too single minded—there's no end to it, you see. Just today, I've started reading *Cymbeline* again because I don't know it terribly well and we're about to do it in the Sam Wanamaker playhouse.

The "Shakespearean" is in the deftness of it. It is the simplicity of the plays, which yet seems original. It's the way Iago can say, "I am not what I am." It's how he works from the inside. I think what he does first is he gets fascinated by a story. Almost all the plays start with some story he's read. But stories frequently just deal in the action without any explanations of how the actions have come about. The story is intriguing and he doesn't doubt that the story has a truth to it, but he wants to make us see how the truth of that story has come about, and that means being the people in the story, not just observing them. So I think that's what he does. I feel it was probably a curse for him, really, that he had to do that, that he was drawn to do that.

He might have felt cursed in some ways. John Aubrey wrote that Shakespeare "wouldn't be debauched, and if invited to writ; he was in pain." It has been suggested that this might or might not be read as if Shakespeare was in pain when he wrote; punctuation is crucial here. And that he was in pain when he wrote is my reading of it. So that's why I feel perhaps it was a bit of a curse, that that's what he had to do, that's what he was drawn to do.

He must have been a fantastic listener. I'm sure he just listened to the way people talk and could recall the way people actually spoke. It was actually hearing real speech that probably made his first big shift from copying the Marlovian line. And he was probably intrigued by everything, all the travelers coming back from foreign countries. People must have liked him. He was a congenial spirit, part of a company. He must have been challenged by some of the actors: "What's happened to the text now?" And Shakespeare could have said, "Don't you hear? That's how you speak. I got that from you."

Some lines I know I can't do without. There's a line that tickles me because it puzzled me for a long time. It comes from *All's Well that Ends Well*: "Might you not know she would do as she has done." It's just eleven words and they're all monosyllabic: might-you-not-know-she-would-do-as-she-has-done. It's not obviously much fun as a line, but I wondered if it was verse or prose, and then suddenly I heard it: "Might you not know she would do as she has done." And it's verse! It turns out to be a verse line with a final (extra) unstressed syllable. It's the way you can just find music in it, and yet it's just so simple words. I also love, "O, she doth teach the torches to burn bright!" Shakespeare loves animating the inanimate.

STEPHEN BOOTH

Even as the sun with purple-colour'd face
had ta'en his last leave of the weeping morn,
rose-cheek'd Adonis hied him to the chase.
hunting he loved, but love he laugh'd to scorn.
sick-thoughted Venus makes amain to him,
and like a bold-faced suitor'gins to woo him.

*Stephen Booth is Emeritus Professor of English at U.C. Berkeley. He was educated at Harvard, then (as a Marshall Scholar) at Cambridge. He has been awarded NEH and Guggenheim Fellowships, UC Berkeley's Distinguished Teaching Award, an honorary degree from Georgetown University, and, in 1995, the OBE. He won the James Russell Lowell Prize from the Modern Language Association for his book **Shakespeare's Sonnets, Edited with Analytic Commentary**. His other books include **An Essay on Shakespeare's Sonnets; King Lear, Macbeth, Indefinition and Tragedy**; and **Precious Nonsense: The Gettysburg Address, Ben Jonson's Epitaphs on His Children, and Twelfth Night**. His work influences not only Shakespeareans, but also cognitive scientists, at least according to a recent article ("Shakespeare's Genius is Nonsense" in the journal **Nautilus**). We talked at a café in Berkeley.*

Aside from knowing what anybody in this country knows just growing up, like "parting is such sweet sorrow," I guess my first real encounter with Shakespeare was Laurence Olivier's *Henry V*, after which my mother made it very clear that she preferred Laurence Olivier to me. I don't know how far down her list of favorites Laurence Olivier was, but I came after him. I think that was 1945, and I was twelve.

One really early Christmas, 1942, I got a Christmas present, from what must have been a relative, called *The Pegs of History*. It was about twenty pages and it would have a picture and then it would explain that such and such was very important to history. (History of course did not spill over into Asia at any time.) The last peg of history was the meeting of Roosevelt and Churchill on a battleship or destroyer off Newfoundland. But in the middle of it was the Elizabethan period. The book said that ultimately Shakespeare probably mattered more to the world than Queen Elizabeth. I couldn't believe that. I ran downstairs, asked my mother, and she said, "Sure." I remain impressed.

I was always eager to see any Shakespeare play that I could. I liked them a lot. But it became clear that Shakespeare was going to be important to me professionally through an accident. Harvard used to turn out two distinctly different kinds of Renaissance doctorates, dramatic and nondramatic, and I was as purely nondramatic as they had ever had because I can't read plays successfully. I can read a play pretty well if I come back from seeing it, but in just reading it, I can't remember who's onstage, I get lost in footnotes, things like that. So I wrote my dissertation on Shakespeare's Sonnets. Berkeley used to pride itself— it probably still does— on seeing that its new instructors get to teach their specialty during their first year. So John George, the Vice Chairman for Courses—he was a hopeless romantic in everything but his private life—looked at what I did and he saw not the Sonnets but the Shakespeare and gave me a Shakespeare course in my first year. I didn't say anything. I was really happy. So I got to embark on about six to seven years of on the job paid training. And in my opinion, I had a big advantage because I didn't know all the stuff that got dished out in graduate school to people who were going to write and think about Shakespeare. For instance, I was thrown off that people spent so much time wondering where the damn doors in Shakespeare's theatre were. I didn't care where the damn doors were. And they were moralizing the plays, not openly, but closer to openly than people who moralize them all the time but pretend they don't.

At one time or another I have found all thirty-seven of the plays problematic. There's *Timon of Athens*, which is troubled by being no good. The first time I ever saw it was with Ralph Richardson, who was the best of the Timons. Laurence Olivier I think comes in third after Gielgud. But the greatest of them was Richardson, the least flashy, the ablest. He was so good as Timon that I thought for several years it was my imagination. But with Timon, a play I am unlikely ever to talk about either before or after this, it seems to me that with it maybe you get an idea about how Shakespeare worked. Essentially he wrote a flat-footed play like *Timon of Athens* and then went in and threw a monkey wrench into the show.

For the first six years of my career as a Shakespearean, the one I had the biggest trouble with was *Twelfth Night*. I would go into lectures and start to say the things that I knew from other people's lectures and books and I didn't do the students any good at all. I don't remember when the light struck, but I realized that *Twelfth Night* was the best play, and my favorite. I think that *Twelfth Night* exercises the listening mind more without letting the listening mind know that it's sweating. Even *The Winter's Tale*, which for me is number two, you might notice it sweating a lot of the time.

My big non-favorite character is Mercutio. The Queen Mab speech is unforgivable. You would think that Shakespeare's bottom drawer offered something richer than that. I think his bottom drawer also had the death of Ophelia speech. That feels bottom drawer, particularly when it's introduced by the queen, who says, "Your sister's drowned, Laertes." Then Laertes says, "Oh, where?" Which opens up the way for "There is a willow grows aslant a brook. . . ." But it is a great speech. The Queen Mab speech feeds into all the high school teachers and all the little old ladies who think the value of verse is the value that is in the Queen Mab speech, which sweats hugely and it leaves people the idea that what is described or talked about in a speech is what makes it great. And of course it's not.

Shakespeare has taught me not one bloody thing. Not one. God, no. I wrote a book some time ago—in fact, all the books I've written I wrote some time ago—in which I was talking about *King Lear* and *Macbeth*, and I said, "In the unlikely event that *King Lear* has anything to teach us," and the copy editor immediately changed it to "likely."

Shakespeare does have a way he moves in a speech and in a sentence. He flits into and out of topics, possibly metaphoric topics (one doesn't always know). But he's not the only person who does that. Coleridge does that. And Marlowe does it something fierce in Faustus. God, that's wonderful. From sentence to sentence and within a sentence he does something like theme and variation. Usually it is two or three themes, and you just never know what's coming next in terms of what the language is going to say.

I'm not sure writing came so easy to Shakespeare. Again, back to something I never talk about, *Timon of Athens*. If indeed he started by turning out a completely dead sturgeon and then putting in the caviar, it doesn't suggest the writing came so easy.

As to what Shakespeare was like, I'm not going to be very helpful. He was an insomniac who didn't like cats. For example, Bertram rejects Parolles in All's Well by saying "Now he's a cat to me." And I say insomniac because he's constantly talking about how nice sleep is. He keeps having characters who can't sleep. And in *The Tempest*, a big mistake on Shakespeare's part, that is, *The Tempest* as a play, his people are lying down sleeping all over the play. If you were in the pit you couldn't see most of the play what with all the people lying down. To me it's not so much the sleepiness of it— if the characters go to sleep then the audience is likely to— but that Prospero is such a bore. And he takes away the big musical numbers, just stops them. But I finally tumbled to what the main trouble was for me in *The Tempest*. It's a mean-spirited play.

Lately my favorite passage has been the first stanza of Venus and Adonis, which will make your head spin:

> Even as the sun with purple-colour'd face
> Had ta'en his last leave of the weeping morn,

Rose-cheek'd Adonis hied him to the chase.
Hunting he loved, but love he laugh'd to scorn.
Sick-thoughted Venus makes amain unto him,
And like a bold-faced suitor 'gins to woo him.

How come I'm noticing your head is spinning? It's an X-rated poem. And it's very funny without ever letting you know that it's being funny, because for a large fraction of the poem you've got this huge woman lying across this insufferable little boy.

There are a lot of Shakespearean plays that were stillborn and have stayed that way. The thing I'm most interested in in *As You Like It* is the curtain speech, which is beautiful and always makes me cry. Not much does. And I just like it, can see no reason for liking it.

You were asking about Shakespeare's personality. I am writing a paper for the Blackfriar's Conference that is just in the corner of that topic, "The Audience is Princess Anne." I unexpectedly came to the conclusion that Shakespeare felt the same kind of confident contempt for his audiences that Richard feels for Princess Anne and mistakenly feels for Queen Elizabeth. He doesn't like them, the whole audience. And the audience always likes to be spoken of contemptuously from the stage; I'm sure the groundlings all enjoyed Hamlet's view of them. For decades I've been tiptoeing up on the idea that Shakespeare doesn't like his audience. I finally realized going through play after play after play that it explains a whole lot. And also it might be that like Richard, Shakespeare sometimes overestimates his ability to make an audience follow him, as with *Two Gentlemen of Verona* and *Measure for Measure* and *All's Well that Ends Well*. There's not much sign that audiences ever were infatuated with those plays—now since it's even reached a point where productions turn the ending of *Measure for Measure* into "The Lady or the Tiger."

What I've found remarkable, the thing I'm working on now, are the things that Shakespeare does that he couldn't possibly do. For instance, when Mercutio does his "plague on both your houses" speech, he seems to be the victim, but he started the whole thing! What's remarkable is that one doesn't know this—just as one comes out of the play thinking that it's the play that the Chorus's first speech promised. But actually nobody takes the feud seriously except servants and Tybalt, and nobody takes him seriously until he's dead. And my current notion is that Shakespeare does such things because he likes manipulating those damn fools the audience. Any play or fiction thinks that to some degree. And while authors are writing, they're right—because the writer knows the butler did it and we don't.

So many of Shakespeare's sentences can be demonstrated not to mean anything at all. So it's sort of magic. You get the sense of what's going on from a sentence that actually says something else than you understand it to say or that actually says nothing at all. With "If music be the food of love, play on,/ Give me excess of it, that, surfeiting,/ The appetite may sicken and so die," everyone understands that it's the appetite for love. But if you look at the sentence it's the appetite for music, so the sentence is really about a jukebox junkie trying to kick the music habit. *Twelfth Night* is full of those things. There's the end of the letter that Malvolio gets stuck reading, "She that would alter services with thee, The Fortunate Unhappy." That doesn't make sense! One understands "exchange," but "alter" never means "exchange" anywhere else. Generally Shakespeare has a lot of sentences that don't mean anything or that can be demonstrated to say the opposite of what they deliver. Milton does that sometimes, but almost nobody else does.

REGINA BUCCOLA

"ALL'S WELL THAT ENDS WELL YET"

Regina Buccola is Associate Professor of English and a faculty member of Women's and Gender Studies and Creative Writing at Roosevelt University in Chicago. She is the author of **Fairies, Fractious Women and the Old Faith: Fairy Lore in Early Modern British Drama and Culture**, *editor of* **A Midsummer Night's Dream: A Critical Guide**, *co-editor of* **Marian Moments in Early Modern Drama**, *and author of numerous articles. Scholar-in-Residence at the Chicago Shakespeare Theater, she recently co-edited* **Chicago Shakespeare Theater: Suiting the Action to the Word**. *She is also a widely published poet, including the chapbook* **Conjuring**. *I spoke with her in her office at Roosevelt University.*

I grew up in Louisville, Kentucky, where in the summers my parents would take us to really good Shakespeare plays in Central Park. So my earliest memories of Shakespeare are being outside at night in the park with a picnic, watching the plays. One of the earliest I remember is *A Midsummer Night's Dream*, where the fairies coming in through the trees in the park were magical to me. I was probably eight or nine years old.

Then of course I read Shakespeare in high school. There's no one else in my family who's an academic, so I actually weirdly fought against the Shakespeare impulse for a while on the grounds, "Well, everyone does Shakespeare." But then I realized, "Wow, if everyone does Shakespeare, then in these difficult times of getting a job in academia, everyone still needs a Shakespeare person." Probably not until I was in my master's program and thinking about PhD programs did it dawn on me that being a Shakespearean is really an asset, not a liability.

But Shakespeare was already important in my life. I sought out Shakespeare productions on my own and I took Shakespeare courses. I'd also gotten interested in other kinds of early modern drama, including Middleton (I'm currently involved in the Oxford Middleton Project). I teach a course here in non-Shakespearean early modern drama.

I had a great high school teacher named Kathy Breen. I did *Romeo and Juliet* with her, doing a lot of the kinds of things at that high school level that I do now with college students to shake them out of the idea that it is just a tragic love story. We did a lot of work with the verse, and (at an all girls Catholic high school!) she really delved into how bawdy the play was, with the nurse and so forth. So I have vivid memories of her breaking that play open, exploring it as something more than tragic teenage love, hormones gone wild.

I went to Bellermine University in Louisville, Kentucky, where John Gatton taught and still teaches Shakespeare. And now I see him in the conference world; a few years ago, we were in London together for the Literary London conference.

I've kept a similar connection with Clark Hulse, who directed my dissertation at UIC. He has just recently retired, but he is now writing for this essay collection I'm editing for the 25th anniversary of Chicago Shakespeare Company. When I asked him about contributing to the collection, he said, "Oh, I'm retired; I'm not sure." But I knew he loved Edward Hall's *Rose Rage* [*The Henry VI trilogy*] that had toured here, so I said, "You could write about Rose Rage." And he said, "Oh, the hook goes in." He wrote this great piece. I too love the Henry VI plays because Margaret is one of my favorite Shakespeare characters. With the female theater students here, if they're looking for a Shakespearean audition piece, I often steer them toward the *Henry VI* plays, because you've got Joan of Arc, Queen Margaret, Elizabeth, Anne, all these great roles. And they're not as commonly done as the epilogue from *As You Like It* and such.

I have an ongoing debate with one of my grad school pals who loves *Pericles, Prince of Tyre*. It's like a running gag between us. He'll email and say, "I just saw a great production of *Pericles, Prince of Tyre*." I'll respond, "You did not. There is no such thing." I don't really think that, but. . . . Mary Zimmerman's production here at the Goodman a few years ago was fantastic. But I would class that as an adaptation. The text was in there, but she took a lot of well-taken liberties. As a group, all the late romances are highly improbable, but I find *Pericles* the least probable of them all.

I love the problem plays, so *Measure for Measure* and *All's Well* are favorites. I almost always am teaching one or the other of them in any Shakespeare class I do. And I've written a good deal about *All's Well That Ends Well*. Those plays are so interesting because of the complexity of the portrayal of women. *All's Well* is fascinating insofar as you've got a matriarchy at the start of the play, with the Countess ruling. She really intervenes on behalf of Helena to the disadvantage of her son. And eventually this absolute cad is called to account by everyone for his behavior.

These two problem plays are so unlike, say, *The Two Gentlemen of Verona*, where at the end Valentine says, "Oh, you like my girlfriend? Here, rape her. Go ahead, have her." There are very different notions of gender relations in those two plays than in *Two Gentlemen*. Wendy Doniger is also writing for the Chicago Shakespeare Theater Essay Collection, and she and I have had some great conversations about just how bizarre that ending of *Two Gentlemen* is. And of course Shakespeare's not the only one who uses that device

Those problem plays fascinate me because they're incredibly complex. I participated in a post-show discussion of *Measure for Measure* in the mid-'90s during the Monica Lewinsky events. Our panel included a couple of prominent female Chicago politicians. We talked about how much that play spoke to the current situation, how we unfortunately had not come far in certain respects. In regard to the confrontation with Angelo—"Who will believe thee, Isabel?"—we talked about Monica Lewinsky, how disgusting, surreal, and weird it was that she had to produce the garment. We wondered if Monica would have been in Isabella's situation if she hadn't had the dress. Could Bill Clinton have said, "Who will believe thee, Monica?" I love how those plays can be made to speak in the modern era. Those plays in particular grapple with things on the front page of the newspaper even now.

I love Isabella, but I also really love Helena. I'm actually fascinated by both Helenas, in *A Midsummer Night's Dream* and *All's Well*; both of them chase after these men in an assiduous, aggressive manner that leaves you saying, "And you want him why?" That again is really true to life. You see that all the time—and both genders equally. I see young men who do it too. I think, "You are a charming young man—what are you doing with that Kate? Why are you doing this to yourself?" So the two Helenas fascinate me because they're such an interesting mix: assertive, self-directed young women who are shaking free of the patriarchy but who sign themselves up for these absolute cads. Bertram chases after other women and threatens to suborn their chastity; and it's Demetrius who tells Helena, "do not believe/ But I shall do thee mischief in the wood." Plus he wants to force her friend Hermia into marrying him when she doesn't want to marry him.

Sometimes when I don't admire characters, I still find them fascinating in their human complexity. Shakespeare seldom gives us cookie cutter characters. My students will often say of Richard III, "Oh, he's just pure evil." Then I take them to that wacky soliloquy after his nightmare where he's in effect saying, "Who's here? No one. Myself. Do I hear myself? Yes, I do. No, I don't." That whole wacky, bipolar incident he has after the nightmares is fascinating and renders his character more complexly. Granted he's been exultant in his evil up to that point, but he does have a crisis of conscience, even though at the very end of the play he thinks "conscience" is a word that cowards use.

My dissertation director, Clark Hulse, used to talk about Shakespeare's fascinating ability to make offhand references to some random character. In

Henry IV, i, in the lead up to the Gadshill robbery, there's this conversation at the inn where someone is referring to a character that we never even meet on-stage, Robin Ostler, "poor fellow never joyed since the price of oats rose." He used to always teach that. He would say, "That is fantastic! We get this little vignette of this character who's never even on the stage. And you can picture him as sort of a slump-shouldered-oppressed-by-his-life character."

I'm lucky to be in Chicago. First of all, I have a theater conservatory down the hall from me. And I have theater students routinely in class; one of my former students is playing Kate in *The Taming of the Shrew* at Chicago Shakespeare Theater right now. So one of the biggest impacts Shakespeare has had on me is the ability to see firsthand over and over again the human impact of these plays. I get to interact with students who are not only taking my more conventional drama classes, but also doing theater versions of Shakespeare. They're great to have in class because any time you say, "Who wants to read?" every hand goes up.

But there is also the work I do at Chicago Shakespeare Theater. I just did a lecture yesterday before one of the matinees. Seeing all the people who come there and how seriously they take going to the theater is amazing. That's a really great gift, seeing over and over the tremendous impact these plays still have in people's lives, how energized people are by these characters, how drawn to them, and how the characters inform their own lives and their own experiences. That's been probably the biggest impact of Shakespeare for me.

In teaching, I do differentiate some of those other playwrights from Shakespeare. I often point out that Shakespeare in particular is more slip-pery than Middleton and Jonson. And so even though his characters are very complex and recognizably human, when students want to wax biographical about the Sonnets or the plays, I often point out how Shakespeare plays a kind of shell game. A student will say, "Oh, but look at what it says right here, I think Shakespeare is saying…." My response is always, "Yes, but Shakespeare giveth and Shakespeare taketh away, so now let's look at this next set of lines and look what it says right there." Shakespeare is very elusive in his work in a way that I don't think Jonson or Middleton are. They are right there. So in Jonson's hilarious vignettes of London, you not only get a sort of walking tour of his London a lot of the time and the people he knew, but you also get his take on these people; he can be viciously satirical in his portraits in a way that reveals his own biases.

Shakespeare doesn't tip his hand in that way. And I could say the same thing about Middleton. In fact, I have a piece that I'm going to be sending out this summer about *Measure for Measure* and the possibility that Middleton has intervened in there and revised some portions of it. You might see Middleton in the amping up of the political controversy. That persuades me that Middleton may have been intervening, because that's much more characteristic of him than of Shakespeare. Middleton is the man who brought us *A Game at Chess* and had to flee town. So he is much more likely to have his political slip showing as it were, whereas Shakespeare seems to have been very good at not doing so.

Shakespeare seems to me to have probably been someone who held his cards pretty close to his chest. I say to students all the time the reason we lack biographical information about him is that he seems to have kept his nose clean. The reason we have biographical information about some of his peers is that they were getting arrested, getting killed in bar brawls/political intrigue, getting run out of town on a rail because their play was incendiary and offensive to the Spanish Ambassador or whoever. Shakespeare seems to have steered clear of all that. In fact, the only trouble that I can think of that we know he got into was over Richard II and the whole Essex controversy, and that really wasn't his fault. It was his fault insofar as he was a shareholder, but he didn't write the play for Essex; it had been on the stage for years. And he also seems to have just been an extremely savvy businessperson. He's someone who looked at the lay of the land and figured out how he could make money and he did. So I think he was really a smooth operator in a way that a lot of other people in the theatre business were not.

Perversely enough one of my favorite quotations—and it's not merely the quotation, it's the way this phrase is a mantra that recurs in the play— is in the variations on the title, *All's Well that Ends Well*, which in its various permutations are slightly less optimistic. So, for example, I love Helena's "All's well that ends well yet," because on the one hand it's optimistic-ish, but on the other hand it still allows for the fact that there's a lot of ground to cover. Maybe I'm showing my own dark and macabre tendencies, but another one of my favorite quotes is from *Lear* when Edgar is saying to himself, Oh, this is the worst that can possibly have happened. My life is horrible right now, it couldn't possibly be worse, and then his blinded father walks in. So Edgar then says, "And worse I may be yet. The worst is not/ So long as we can say, 'This is the worst.'" Realizing that things can always get worse, he says, "I am worse than e'er I was." That too seems Shakespearean. This notion of life as a mingled yarn, good and bad together, is characteristic of Shakespeare. Even his comedies don't tend to be saccharine. One of the things that has consistently drawn me to Shakespeare is that it's not merely a pat on the head. So for me, the Shakespearean life is a good life.

RALPH ALAN COHEN

"Directitude! What's that?"

Ralph Alan Cohen is the Director of Mission and Co-Founder (with his former student Jim Warren) of the American Shakespeare Center, a theater company in Staunton, Virginia. He was project director for the building of their Blackfriar's Playhouse, the world's first recreation of Shakespeare's indoor playhouse, completed in 2001. He has also directed more than 25 plays by Shakespeare and his contemporaries. He is author of an invaluable book for any teacher of Shakespeare, **ShakesFear and How to Cure It: A Handbook for Teaching Shakespeare**. *He has also twice edited special issues of* **Shakespeare Quarterly** *devoted to teaching. A former professor at James Madison University, he now the Gonder Professor of Shakespeare and Performance at Mary Baldwin College's Master of Letters and Fine Arts program, a program he founded. He also hosts the biannual Blackfriar's Conference for Shakespeare scholars. He spoke with me on a Monday in April, after I had on Sunday seen a wonderful production of* **As You Like It** *at the Blackfriar's Playhouse.*

I just got back from the Shakespeare Association of America meeting in Seattle. Many of us there were aware of how happy we were, of our happy lives. But I belong to another organization—because I work both sides of the fence—called the Shakespeare Theatre Association. These are not people with tenure; these people run Shakespeare theatres and live in the dire circumstances of trying to keep theatres alive. But they are also very happy. So there is something about a life in Shakespeare that really does mostly keep you happy.

I probably first noticed Shakespeare when I was a sophomore at Dartmouth. I went to see the Olivier's *Henry V.* I was very much into film, especially Truffaut, Goddard, and Fellini, and I wondered why the hell they were showing *Henry V.* I was sort of disgruntled as I watched it. But I kept being struck by how wonderful it was. I also was under the misconception that Shakespeare's language was hard, but I had no trouble. There's a moment in the play when the princess says, "Is it possible dat I sould love de ennemi of France?" and Olivier (Hal) says, "No, it is not possible you should love the enemy of France, Kate. But in loving me you should love the friend of France, for I love France so well that I will not part with a village of it." I thought that was the most amazing combination of realpolitik and humor, and an admission of what the whole process is between the two of them, that while it's not really a love story at all, in that moment it's as lovable as can be while still being honest. That was the first time for me with Shakespeare.

In graduate school, I thought I'd be studying Faulkner. I had a good teacher named George Walton Williams who is still very much alive. I saw him in Seattle. He'll be 90 soon. And he made a big impression on me, pointed me in the right direction.

Antony and Cleopatra is my favorite play. I am stronger in that view than ever, even though I seem to love all the plays more each time I am connected to them. But *Antony and Cleopatra* is the broadest, the biggest. I'm a generally cheerful person so *Lear*, which is a huge and great play, is just not my mood. I tend to feel that the world is a pretty good place, even though yes of course there is great pain. *Antony and Cleopatra* has this gigantic sense of size, east and west, life and death, Rome and Egypt, male and female, sex and love, or love and work, or work and play—you can't think of a binary that it doesn't seem to deal with. I love it for that, but I also love it because it has so much humor. It's beautiful humor. Humor during extreme moments of pain. In Shakespeare, there's usually humor at the same time as pain. Finally, I love it because it's random: for example, there's this clown in it at the end when Cleopatra is trying to be all serious about getting dead, and he's funny, and she lets him be funny, and she's funny. So I like it for its surprises. But then all of the plays have odd surprises in them.

As far as being like a character, I would say I am most like Bottom because I want to play all the parts. But I think I'm also very much like— let's see, who's a good insecure character?—I see myself as a lot of Bottom, and a lot of Antony…and for my neurotic side, I'd say a lot of Helena. I'm neurotic along those lines: Helena, Bottom, and Antony.

I don't think we should teach the plays as useful, but they are. They're not really useful in any way you could ever talk about. They're useful in celebrating the random. One thing you can learn from Shakespeare is a kind of an embrace of what's in front of you. He seems drawn to characters who deal with whatever they confront. A favorite moment of mine is from *Twelfth Night* when Sebastian is confronted with a beautiful and wealthy woman he's never met and who seems to think they should be married, and he decides, "Yeah, why not?" I like that.

It's also useful to know that people who care deeply for one another fight hard against each other. It's useful in a marriage to know that when I am angry and upset and yell,—and on that rare occasion when my wife yells back— it is useful to remember that Brutus and Cassius yell at each other, that Antony and Cleopatra yell at each other.

And sometimes Shakespeare is very useful to me in how to speak. It has been useful to me in teaching, of course, because I make a living with it. The American Shakespeare Center has been doing leadership institutes because people came to us and offered to pay us well, so we've had to develop ways of looking at Shakespeare where you learn something about leadership. And it's there. I've learned a lot from that program, from looking at the way people persuade people of things. I'm not saying I can do it, but I can see it and I can understand that when I have done well, there's a model for why I did well. And I can see why and when I've done poorly, there's also a model for that. In some ways in business matters Shakespeare seems to have been a leader. He seems to have had a good sense of when to hang it up too.

What Keats said about Shakespeare's negative capability is amazing. I'm pretty well read in Jacobean plays, and I do really notice Shakespeare's special ability to let things not get explained. And from the glimpses we have of what he may have been like, it does seem he was pretty at ease with himself. You have this sense of his ability to absorb things and not shape them. I'm convinced that with *As You Like It*, for example, he started in one direction, and thought, "This is no good, I'll go in this other direction." And that other direction was just a bunch of people standing around talking in the forest. He was really OK with that. The play becomes wonderful, and it doesn't go anywhere, but he has to end it, so he brings in a god, Hymen, who marries everybody off. It's just ridiculous, nobody else would do it, and it works wonderfully. You have to be a grownup to understand how it works so wonderfully. When I read it in college, I thought, "This is the most ridiculous thing I've ever read in my life." It thought it was so stupid, it made me angry. But the older I get, the more I think, well, that's wonderful. He just lets the play take over.

Maybe I can give you an analogy of someone in the public eye, an artist who is like that. I always thought Howard Hawkes in his films showed a kind of let things happen attitude. Jean Renoir too in his work seems to have thought, "That's a nice moment, we'll keep that." Robert Altman was very much like that too. And everyone seems to have loved Robert Altman. Now the opposite of Shakespeare is Jonson, and that's like Hitchcock, where it's all figured out and you've got a plan.

I feel very lucky to be a scholar and a theatre person. I suppose you could say I am less a scholar therefore and also less a theatre person, but living in the margin, in the place in between, I appreciate that in many ways no one else has as much of both as I do. I feel very lucky. I require of my organization that I direct a play a year. Even if the artistic director might not think this is a particularly good idea, I require that or I'd walk away. I need it. It helps me teach better and helps me know more about the plays. I love the plays, and I really need to work with them.

This whole American Shakespeare Center project is in many ways devoted to getting literary people involved. As I said, I just got back from the Shakespeare Association of America Conference, which is all literary scholars. But we have a conference of our own every two years, the Blackfriars Conference, which people from all over the world come to. We try to get scholars to think about the plays from inside the plays, which they are not necessarily accustomed to. And it's even harder to get people in the theatre to think about the plays in scholarly ways. So we bring together these two very different communities. And they don't speak very well to each other. We try to be a place where that conversation can take place. And that's why, for example, we have rehearsals open to the public. For me the great goal is to get scholars to understand for example, that a speech is there because another character has to be offstage getting dressed up. So last night when you saw Touchstone do the Seven Causes speech, he's doing that in part so that Rosalind can get into her wedding outfit. Knowing such things makes you appreciate Shakespeare even more, knowing that he was thinking, "I've got to kill time while my heroine gets dressed."

As to a favorite quotation or one that comes to mind, some of them I just love to say, like Cleopatra's, "and here/ My bluest veins to kiss— a hand that kings/ Have lipped, and trembled kissing." But right now my little tagline on my email is from *Coriolanus*, and it says, "Directitude! What's that?" I love that line! "Directitude" is a word a servant uses after he's come out of a room Coriolanus was in, where Coriolanus was acting self-important, demanding things. And the first servant says to another serving men, describing how badly Coriolanus has been acting to his friends: "which friends, sir, as it were, durst not... show themselves...his friends whilst he's in directitude." And then other serving man says "Directitude! What's that?"

I've been writing and thinking a lot about directitude lately, because I don't much believe in directitude any more. Maybe this points back to the Jonson/Shakespeare dichotomy, the Alfred Hitchcock/Altman dichotomy. You have Alfred Hitchcock where you have everything planned out and then you have Altman who seems to let his films grow organically. And I like Altman better for that.

But also I find myself more and more surprised and more and more disdainful of directed Shakespeare, despite the fact that I've directed nearly thirty plays for the company. We have a season that is my pride and joy here because we have developed a very good troupe, the people who play in our season from January till April, our veterans, people who are terrific collaborators as well as good actors. They put on five shows, where they are given a maximum of thirty hours for each show. And they do them without a director, with cue scripts. I think those are our best shows. Yes, they have flaws. The people who most see the flaws are people who have come to think that plays have to express a concept and be unified. The people who love them, the people who come for them, like something that we have lost in theatre because of directitude. For the dominant theatrical value system now, these self-directed plays probably fall short, but for another value system that stresses spontaneity, size, color, and variety, they're much better.

I'm interested right now in how we got where we are now in the theatre and how we get out of this trap—because the first real directors didn't occur until the second half of the 19th century. There's been 2500 hundred years of theatre, and we've only had directors for only about 150 of that 2500 years. Why have we moved to this model? And why have actors, who are the most narcissistic of all artists, given up all that agency? I don't quite get it. Especially since from January through to the first week of April, I see work that is better, or better in some ways, than the directed plays we put on.

I'd like to redefine the director's work, maybe use another word. I don't like the word "director" because it's too authoritarian. I'm looking for something more along the Altman lines, where you're there to get a great ensemble of people together and see what they can do. The work that Jim Warren does here when he directs all these plays is not nearly as important as the work he has done teaching actors how to do things. New actors need to be directed. But once you're a veteran, you don't need a director. You need to have been taught by a director. So I think if we could take a word like "guide" and use that more than "director," we'd be better off.

I can't see Shakespeare himself very much telling people how they had to do things, being concerned about how his very experienced actors did each line. I see him giving the meter and the rhetorical figures in their cue scripts : "Here's the metrics. Here's the figures. Do the metrics, do the figures, you will make it good. See you later!"

FARAH-KARIM COOPER

*"OUR DOUBTS ARE TRAITORS,
AND MAKE US LOSE THE GOOD WE OFT MIGHT WIN,
BY FEARING TO ATTEMPT."*

Dr Farah Karim-Cooper oversees the Higher Education program in Globe Education and leads research and scholarship at Shakespeare's Globe. She is Visiting Research Fellow at King's College London and directs the Globe component of the King's/Globe joint MA in Shakespeare Studies. She was the 2013 Lloyd Davis Visiting Professor at the University of Queensland. Dr Cooper is Chair of the Architecture Research Group, which led the research preliminary to the construction of the Sam Wanamaker Playhouse, the Globe's indoor Jacobean theatre. Her publications include **Cosmetics in Shakespearean and Renaissance Drama,** **Shakespeare's Globe: A Theatrical Experiment**, *co-edited with Christie Carson;* **Shakespeare's Theatres and the Effects of Performance**, *co-edited with Tiffany Stern;* **Moving Shakespeare Indoors**, *co-edited with Andrew J. Gurr; and* **The Hand on the Shakespearean Stage: Gesture, Touch and the Spectacle of Dismemberment**. *I talked with her in summer 2012 in the Members' Room of the Tate Modern Museum in London.*

My first exposure to Shakespeare was probably Julius Caesar in the 8th grade in Houston, Texas. But my first important memory was in 9th grade when we did *Romeo and Juliet* and were shown Franco Zeffirelli's film. That film transformed fifteen-year-old me. It was the story, it was the costumes, it was all of it. It wasn't just Shakespeare—it was the worlds he creates. Probably that was when I realized Shakespeare was going to be important, but obviously I didn't realize how important he's become to me.

I went back to Shakespeare when I got to university at California State. I knew I was going to be an English major, and I had some wonderful Shakespeare professors, some wonderful Milton professors too. I was actually leaning towards Milton for a while. One Shakespeare professor in particular, John Brugaletta, got me very excited. But actually all the Shakespeare people at Cal State were amazing, because it's not a research institution, so they were focused on teaching.

I came to England in 1994 to do a master's in Milton. There was a lecturer there who was helping me with my dissertation, which was inspired by Shakespeare and what Milton took from Shakespeare. And that was probably why I got into Shakespeare at the PhD level; it could have gone either way. But that dissertation and my conversations with that lecturer crystallized Shakespeare for me. And there's a Shakespeare Orange County theater company that does productions at Chapman University. When I was an undergraduate I used to see their productions every year. Their *Hamlet* and their *Othello* really moved me. And I wasn't much of a theater-goer. I don't come from a family of theater-goers. But I kept going back to that company. They really did it for me.

Working at the Globe has changed the way I think about Shakespeare. I was starting to write my cosmetics in Shakespeare book before I started working there, but working at the Globe changed what I wrote and my approach to the topic. My book was focused on cosmetics as a poetic trope, as material to woman's history in terms of aesthetic appreciation and its links to arts and poetry. But then I began working at the Globe and advising on productions. When I did my dissertation (before I started actually working there), I advised on the Globe's 2002 *Twelfth Night*. Because of my advice, for the first time they used early modern makeup aesthetics. Before that, the actors had used modern makeup styles, but for *Twelfth Night* they wanted to create a variety of original practices. So that was the first time they used the full white face. I thought, "Wow, my research actually has some kind of practical application that more than one person will read about or will actually witness." Then when I went to see those productions, I thought about how certain moments could be staged and how makeup actually has a theatrical utility, because in my work I had focused so much on the negative attention towards cosmetics within a misogynist context, the prescriptive discourses about women. I hadn't thought about how playwrights were actually using cosmetics not just as a poetic trope, but as makeup onstage to produce illusions and special effects, to make you think there's a ghost in the room or to make boys look like women. That was the point at which theater and my work became unified.

I used to think I had a problem with the history plays because they didn't feel colorful enough. But then when I was working at the Globe we did history plays and I had to really delve into them. I lecture to the actors here, so I had to think about what I should tell them about the history plays. Teaching them changed my mind: I didn't think the history plays could speak to me because I wasn't English, I wasn't a man who's interested in war, and I came from a country that doesn't have monarchies. I just didn't feel connected to them. But that's changed. The history plays do come to life on stage. And when you're embedded in a company and they're working on a production, you have to look at the play in a different way than you would if you were teaching it to undergraduates.

Titus Andronicus is my favorite play. My interest started when I was reading criticism about it and finding that most people thought it showed underdeveloped craftsmanship, that it was too bloody, that it was just underwhelming. Also we now know it was collaborative, so it doesn't seem to have the same value other plays have. I found that all quite interesting. I almost took it as a challenge, because I really loved that tragedy. I think it's compelling — and not just in performance—because of the portraits it gives of families. You could just simply do a meditation on parenthood and the family structures in that play without thinking about politics or any of the bloodshed. It struck me as odd that Aaron is the best parent in the play. He's the only one you see really sacrifice everything or completely dote on his child. And also what happens to Lavinia! As a woman it's very difficult to look at that. But it forces you to confront the horrible possibilities that all women face and to try and understand them. I'm interested in Shakespeare as a playwright who is not interested in oppressive regimes towards women, but is interested in the sort of radical potential his representations of women have. I think Lavinia is a radical character for a number of reasons, but largely because she's able to write and communicate without the appendages that are deemed as necessary. It's a play I think about a lot. And the production we did at the Globe in 2006 was shocking, painful, tragic, and frightening, but also the most amazing production I'd ever seen. So from that production on, *Titus* became my favorite play. It does get you talking. There's family parenting and there's women and then there's race and exclusion. And then it's about what happens when classical history meets early modernity and what Shakespeare might be saying about those interfaces. All those things are compelling.

As far as Shakespeare's female characters, I have a problem with Desdemona. I have a problem with Portia. I love Rosalind because she's so assertive. Shakespeare gives his women a context so they can be in charge, become prominent—even at the end of the play when things go into marriage mode and begin to change.

In terms of his male characters, I'd probably want to have a drink with Hamlet. But I feel odd saying that because I used to tell my female students, who would always say, "I love *Hamlet*," "How many of you would date him?" All the females would raise their hands: "Oh, I'd date him because he's this brooding kind of Ethan Hawke figure." And I would respond, "He thinks you're all whores, so let's talk about that. Why are you drawn to men like that?" Still I too would like to talk to him because he does seem to be that brooding figure, that malcontent you want to understand. He's got this weird amazing intellect, but at the same time he's not very nice to women. His father tells him, "Don't blame your mother," and then he spends a lot of time blaming her. I would like to talk to him about that.

I think Portia is a hypocrite. She manipulates the situation with Bassanio. She's nasty about all the other suitors, racist in the most shocking ways. And she preaches about mercy and then doesn't show any herself. She's very narcissistic and controlling and selfish and self- concerned. So as a character, a human being, I don't like her. I wouldn't be friends with her. But she is assertive, bold, and takes charge of her life, so in some ways is a proto-feminist. You've got to love that.

I'm not a Bardolater, so I don't worship at the temple even though I seem to be working at one. But I love Shakespeare. I love his work passionately, but I'm very able to stand there and say, "Okay, so there's the play *Taming of the Shrew,*" which I can't seem to reconcile with. I don't like it in performance ever. No matter what they try to do with that last scene, it's a problem for me. I have a problem with Shakespeare as a result of that. But I want that problem, that engagement, that dialogue.

When I was in my early twenties, I found the religion that I grew up in oppressive. I didn't want to be a part of it. I was looking around for something else. I studied Buddhism, Catholicism, and lots of different approaches and found that religion doesn't work for me because I don't like dogma. I thought religion was dogmatic. But I was very nervous about not having some kind of central thing that I felt strongly and passionately about. And I'm not saying that I worship Shakespeare, but Shakespeare does give me a sense of something beyond the words. It's a kind of alchemical Shakespeare here at the Globe. And I'm not trying to sound mercurial, but there's something really metaphysical about Shakespeare that I can't quite grasp; I come to the mother ship, I work at the Globe, I teach Shakespeare every day, I work with actors, and something always falls through my fingers. And I think that's what religion does for people. You're always trying to get at something, and it's the pursuit that makes you passionate about it and more engaged with it. So that's how Shakespeare transformed me. I find his work inspiring.

"What is Shakespearean" is a hard question. There are so many conventional answers, like, "It's the characters and their multidimensionality." But Middleton produces multidimensional characters as well, if in a different way. It's the way Shakespeare puts words together—but I love the way Milton does that as well. Maybe it's Shakespeare's meta-theater? Although his plays are transportable, can be moved from different place to different place, you can trace in his plays his intimacy with this part of London and his theater at that time. In *The Tempest* Ariel describes Gonzago: "His tears run down his beard like winter's drops/ From eaves of reeds." This image of icicles or rain drops on a thatched roof dripping could easily be a metaphor taken from Shakespeare's Globe Theatre itself. It's like the chorus scene at the beginning of *Henry V*; you can deliver that chorus anywhere, but it speaks to certain materiality that Shakespeare lived and worked in, breathed in, was intimate with. I don't see that sort of thing in Jonson as often, because Jonson wrote for so many different venues. There's a Shakespearean root that is meta-theatrical. I guess what I'm saying is you can take his plays out of the theatre, but you can't take his theatre out of his plays. I think that is what's different. It's his intimacy with his theatrical world.

I like to think Shakespeare was like Barack Obama, that he had an intellectual presence. Not the politician part, but the intellect, that he was charitable and liberal in his politics, that he was bold, that he was daring and took risks. I'd like to think he had all those qualities all wrapped up in one. In his plays you can trace everything, murder and all kinds of other things, so I don't like to use his plays as a way of seeing who he was. But you hope Shakespeare believed that Shylock wasn't treated very well. You want to believe that you're supposed to feel sorry for Malvolio at the end of the play, and you also want to think that he would have been in the playhouse when the end of *The Taming of the Shrew* was being rehearsed, saying, "No, don't place your hand under his foot," or something like that.

I do have a favorite quotation. *It's from Measure for Measure*: "Our doubts are traitors,/ And make us lose the good we oft might win,/ By fearing to attempt." That quote means something to me because I had a professor, Sally Romotosky, who knew that I was a bit insecure about my knowledge and was scared in public presentations. But she saw potential in my work, and she put this quotation on one of my papers at Cal State. That quote meant a lot to me when I was a schoolteacher and training to do my PhD. I used it as a teacher because it makes you ask, "How do you know unless you try?"

FRAN DOLAN

"YOUR 'IF' IS THE ONLY PEACEMAKER;
MUCH VIRTUE IN 'IF.'"

*Frances Dolan is Distinguished Professor of English at the University of California, Davis. She received her PhD from the University of Chicago, and has previously taught at the University of Miami (Ohio), Columbia University, and the University of Chicago. She has had fellowships from the Guggenheim Foundation and the National Endowment for the Humanities, was President of the Shakespeare Association of America, and has won awards for teaching and scholarship at U.C. Davis. She is the author of **True Relations: Reading, Literature, and Evidence in Seventeenth-Century England** (winner of the 2014 Jon Ben Snow Prize by the North American Conference on British Studies); **Marriage and Violence: The Early Modern Legacy; Twelfth Night: Language and Writing;** and **Dangerous Familiars: Representations of Domestic Crime in England, 1550-1700**. She has also edited six Shakespeare plays. We talked in her office in Davis, where she kindly gave me a copy of her most useful **Twelfth Night** book.*

I think I first read Shakespeare in class, rather than at home, but my response to it was, "Oh, I thought Dad said that"—because my parents were readers. They were not academics, but they were readers, wordsmiths, and quoters. There were all kinds of phrases in Shakespeare that I was completely familiar with from my family's conversation. I first read it in high school, I think, but it seemed strangely familiar.

I went to Loyola University. I had some good teachers in grammar school and high school, but I didn't go to particularly fabulous schools. I was a Latin major in college, but I started taking English classes and really loved the classes in the Renaissance. That made me realize I needed to be a double major because I wanted to take more classes in English. I had passionate, talented teachers. Suzanne Gossett and Bernie McElroy at Loyola University were both wonderful in very different ways. Suzanne let me as a college sophomore take a graduate seminar on Jacobean drama, which I loved. So almost from the beginning I was reading Shakespeare in relation to his contemporaries, which is unusual and really shaped how I experienced Shakespeare. Then as a junior in college I went to school in Rome and was able to go to

London several times and see all kinds of plays on the stage, including *Knight of the Burning Pestle*, things like that that most people don't get to see. It was really these college classes where there was rigor in terms of the discussion of Shakespeare and his contemporaries that introduced me to the Shakespearean life. That was very exciting to me.

I was also a drama reviewer for the student newspaper, but this was Chicago in the seventies and eighties, so there was an amazing theater scene. Steppenwolf Theatre was beginning, with John Malkovich and actors like that, so I went to the theater all the time. That also shaped how I thought about the Renaissance plays that I was studying, because I was always going to the theater and always reviewing. I was writing constantly. It's actually amazing for me to look back and see how much I wrote. As a reviewer, you imagine yourself to have an audience, which is unusual for student writing, and you have to address that audience.

I have a problem with every play that interests me. I was drawn to the Renaissance because it posed problems. I loved Victorian novels, for instance, but I had less to say about Dickens than I had to say about Shakespeare or Webster. I did the textbook *The Taming of the Shrew: Text and Context in the Nineties* because I found that play troubling. All the trouble it caused was where the interest lay for me. So I was drawn to that play because it was difficult. And it does reward me as I come back to it—there's still so much to think about and talk about in that play.

I first thought about *Othello* in relation to plays based on actual crimes. So I wrote a chapter of my dissertation on *Othello*, which wasn't any good, dropped it, dropped the whole dissertation, came back and thought again about how to integrate Shakespeare with the other materials I was looking at. The more I looked at *Othello*, the more what was interesting to me was that it doesn't look like the plays that are based on cases of actual domestic violence. Othello is an exoticized figure, and the play is not set in England. Why does a very mundane story of spousal conflict ending with the murder of the wife take such exotic form in that play? And the more I thought about that and the more I put *Othello* in dialogue with all these other accounts of spousal murder, the more interesting that play became to me.

A lot of the plays that interest me the most I started out worrying like a dog with a bone. Right now I'm working on *Titus*. I first saw *Titus*, actually, at Stratford in Ontario in a production that was unintentionally funny; they didn't know what to do with the play. I think post-Tarantino we're better at figuring out what to do with the combination of violence and humor. But everybody now puts that play in their essential Shakespeare. People teach it because it's enormously teachable. But when I first saw it on the stage

I thought, "Something's going wrong here. This is gruesome and everybody's laughing." And now I am looking at it from a completely different point of view, in relation to materials on agriculture and farming in the early modern era.

I honestly have never previously liked *Merchant of Venice*, but I'm teaching a new class this quarter on law and literature and I started with *Merchant of Venice*, one of the chestnuts of the law and literature canon. The students were so engaged with it, and the discussions were so interesting that it made me completely committed to teaching it again in that class. Somebody brought it up again today in terms of talking about heiresses and their complex legal and narrative stature. Similarly, the more I had to reread *Twelfth Night* to write that book [*Twelfth Night: Language and Writing*] the more I liked *Twelfth Night*. But with *The Winter's Tale*, I'm still mad at Leontes at the end. I'm not that forgiving. And I don't care how much stagecraft you pull out, I'm still not always as charmed as I'm supposed to be by the whimsy and magic of it all. So I have a lot of problems and critique, but they're often deeply interesting problems to me. They're what make the plays interesting.

I once read in a cookbook that I loved: "My favorite plate of green chili is the one that's in front of me right now." And I sometimes think my favorite play is whatever one I'm in the classroom with or really struggling with at that moment, because the more I'm engaged with them, the more I see in them, and the more I get interested in them. It doesn't happen to me that often that I teach a play and think, "All right, never again." There are other books I teach that I think that, but if we're talking about a Shakespeare play and something interesting is happening in the classroom, then that's my play at that moment.

I do love Rosalind. She is one of my favorites. I'm also very interested in Viola; it is interesting that Viola says, "It is too hard a knot for me to untie." Viola has more of a sense of not being sure how she could solve the problems she finds herself in. In fact she doesn't solve them; the arrival of her twin does. I love the incredible agency of Rosalind, and the moment towards the end of the play when she basically says, "I'm going to solve all of your problems by being me. Not by doubling and having my twin arrive, but by just being Rosalind, all will be resolved." That's so moving. It's a celebration of a creative, imaginative female agency. I just think she's incredible. And she gets fabulous rewards at the end as a result. So I love her.

I feel like an advocate for Katherine in *Taming of the Shrew*, even though I have problems with Katherine and with the whole play, as I said. The more I read and reread *Twelfth Night*, the more I agree with people who suggest that with the Malvolio plot, as one critic puts it, Shakespeare sides with the bears. Malvolio is kind of a bear chained at the stake, and in some ways Shakespeare sympathizes with the victim of that kind of cruelty. I've been thinking more and more about that.

I didn't understand how much I had taken from Shakespeare until I started teaching outside the field. My students think it's funny that if I'm in Law & Lit or Children's Lit, I will bring in Shakespeare. They think, "Oh, here she goes again. She's a big Shakespeare professor so she brings in Shakespeare." But those teaching experiences showed me that Shakespeare taught me how to read and how to interpret—and taught me how to think about why one would want to do such things. So today I'm teaching Lemony Snicket, but I started with a question, "How could a story so painful be so pleasurable?" And that's a question I began to formulate in relation to tragedy. Why would we want to read a story that makes us suffer so much? That's one kind of question. Or when I want to say to students, "Look how often you retell a story that looks like this, that has these elements." It's often Shakespeare that taught me the pleasures of a certain kind of character, a certain kind of scenario, a set of conflicts. And then I pursue it in other writers.

Lear is a play that I understand and appreciate more as I've gotten older and as my whole family has gotten older. I have two *Lear* stories. One was when my parents came to see me teach at Miami University. They said to me, "We've got to get to the class early, very early." I said, "You guys, why?" My father had virtually lost his sight at this point, and my mother said, "He does not want to be led into that classroom. So you have to get us in the classroom situated before the students start coming in." I said, "Okay, I completely understand that." You know how when disability is new you don't always understand it, but as soon as she explained it, I understood it. So they're sitting in the back of my class and suddenly I realize I'm asking the students, "Why blind Gloucester? Why not kill him? Why blind him?" And my father raised his hand. I thought I would die! And I was thinking, "I don't know if I should call on him." But one of the students answered, saying, "It's worse. You blind him and you make him wander around being led by other people. You make him dependent." And Gloucester has prided himself on his power. My dad said, "That's what I was going to say. I just wanted to say that." And afterwards my parents said, "Isn't it good that young people have to think about that." And I said, "It is." That's the power of teaching *Lear*.

Another time when we were dealing with a huge family crisis, my mother was listening to *Lear* and a discussion of *Lear* on NPR. They were talking about the Aristotelian notion that you can't evaluate any life until you see how it ends. I said that's very powerful; it's very important in tragedies that lives are defined by their ends. But then I said, "You know, Mom, it's also a literary standard that's too hard on us to apply in life, because we have no control over our ends." And you know, sometimes people no longer recognize you or sometimes we say the wrong thing at the end, so I think that there's a tyranny of the literary that is very hard to live with. I thought how grateful I was to talk about this with her because I can't bear to be held to that standard and I wanted to let her off the hook of being held to it as well. We love literature because we know the ending, but the thing about life is we don't know the ending and we don't control the ending. So I think some of the most meaningful connections I had with my own parents around aging ended up being about *Lear*. I couldn't have scripted it that way, but as I look back I see that's absolutely true. And now when I teach *Lear*, I can't not think of those stories.

I'm teaching Early Modern Drama and the Law right now and we're mostly not doing Shakespeare. But I required the graduate students to choose one Shakespeare that they wanted to bring in, although the assigned reading is all Middleton, Webster, and Jonson. So I think "What is Shakespearean?" is an interesting question. Whenever I teach the non-Shakespearean drama, one of the things I'm reminded of is that it's harder to teach. And it's harder because it was at the time more embedded in its cultural moment. And I love that about non-Shakespearean drama because I think historically. I think historically about Shakespeare too, but I think there are ways in which Shakespeare was not as embedded in his historical moment. I think it's the ways in which Shakespeare wasn't that embedded that's enabled his plays or his words to kind of be isolated from the other writers. Shakespeare's plays are a little bit unstuck in time as compared to Jonson's or Webster's, who are more stuck in their time. And that's not to say Shakespeare plays are universal; it's to say there were things that were very au courant that Shakespeare just wasn't that interested in. And therefore the language is more accessible, or seems more accessible to us —because for instance he's not throwing in as much Latin as Jonson will do, that kind of thing.

I also think Shakespeare had a knack for seeing stories: "Well, a lot of people are telling stories that work like this, and the best version of that story would be this one." I think the self-consciousness with which he observed what was happening in genres around him, on the stage and on the page, enabled him to be enormously skillful at thinking about what made a certain kind of story work. For me that's something distinctly Shakespearean.

I'm interested in false accusation of women. Now, many other playwrights are also interested in the accusation of women. But they don't always make the women innocent. Shakespeare wants the accusation to be false, right? So he hits it that way in *Much Ado*, in *Othello*, in *Winter's Tale*. It's all the same setup exactly. And it's as if he wants to see what are "the resources of kind," as Rosalie Colie put it. How do you take this same situation and give it a comic ending, give it a tragic ending, give it this kind of tragicomedic ending? And that's a deep interest in the operations of form and the resources in literary genre for creating imaginary solutions to real problems, as Fredric Jameson puts it. If the real problem is jealousy and sexual suspicion, Shakespeare says, "Well, what would be the imaginary solutions to it?" And I think that seems distinctively Shakespearean, that kind of fascination with how form operates as a resource for us to imagine our possibilities.

I have many fantasies about what Shakespeare was like. *Shakespeare in Love* remains my favorite, despite the problems I have with it. I would like it to be more complicated than it is, but it's still the best. One of the things I have done at the end of my Shakespeare classes is show the trailer from *Anonymous* and say, "Let's talk about what's wrong about this." We talk about a version of Shakespeare that's both more historically accurate and more useful now: that is, a collaborator, someone who works with other people and is not just alone in a garret; someone who moves across different kinds of careers, using different skills, all connected, but doesn't exactly have one very simple path; someone whose sexuality doesn't fit in a neat box and is a bit of a mystery to us. And I think many of our students no longer exist in the world of the clear heterosexual and homosexual, so that's a good model for them. And they're working in these crowdsourcing spaces or they're renting office space in a place with other people, so some of the models about a more fluid identity and a more collaborative life resonate. I think that's a story we still haven't told about Shakespeare because we don't know how to turn it into— in a word—a movie trailer. And it's not that what we have in most popular representations is inaccurate, although it is; it's that it's not as interesting as what we actually know.

My favorite quotation is obvious for me. It's from *As You Like It*: "Your 'if' is the only peacemaker; much virtue in 'if.'" I love it for its sense of conjectural possibility, but there was a moment in my life when with that line I actually convinced someone to do something that was a leap of faith, so I love it.

FRANCHELLE DORN

"I DREAMT THERE WAS AN EMPEROR ANTONY.
O, SUCH ANOTHER SLEEP, THAT I MIGHT SEE
BUT SUCH ANOTHER MAN!"

Franchelle Dorn is the Virginia L Murchison Regents Professor in
the Department of Theatre and Dance at the University of Texas,
Austin. She received a BA from Finch College and an MFA from
the Yale School of Drama (where she was a founding member of
the Yale Summer Cabaret). For twenty years in Washington DC,
she was the leading actress at Michael Kahn's Shakespeare Theater
Company and a member of the Arena Stage Company. She has
played Emilia in **Othello***, Lady Macbeth in* **Macbeth***, Cleopatra*
in **Antony and Cleopatra***, Paulina in* **The Winter's Tale***,*
Elizabeth in **Richard III***, Gertrude in* **Hamlet***, the Duchess of*
York in **Richard II***, Adriana in* **The Comedy of Errors***,*
Cassandra in **Troilus and Cressida***, Hippolyta in* **A Midsummer**
Night's Dream*, and Mistress Page in* **Merry Wives of Windsor***.*
She has of course appeared in many other plays and has been
featured in movies and on TV. She has won three Helen Hayes
Awards, two Austin Critic Circle Awards, been nominated three
times for the B. Iden Payne Award, and has won two teaching
awards at the University of Texas, Austin. I heard her give
a wonderful lecture in Staunton, Virginia when she was
named Mary Baldwin College's first Doenges Scholar in the
performing arts. I interviewed her at the end of her 2014 run
at the Oregon Shakespeare Festival in Ashland, Oregon, where
she played Margaret in **Richard III** *and Emilia in* **Comedy of**
Errors*.*

I think I first encountered Shakespeare in seventh grade. We read *Julius Caesar*, which I don't think is the best introduction to Shakespeare, but I was very fond of the language from the beginning. When I was around eleven I entered a forensic tournament in Texas and did Lady Macbeth's sleep-walking scene, which I think is impressive, especially since I'd never read the play. It was pretty cool to be able to say those words. I was an eleven-year-old Lady Macbeth.

I'm not sure I remember what my first real Shakespeare role was. I did Greek playwrights in college, not any Shakespeare, so it must have been in graduate school. It must have been *A Midsummer Night's Dream* when I was Hippolyta. I liked being Hippolyta. I got to have a big lance and wear armor. She was very much a warrior queen.

Becoming a Shakespearean actor was serendipitous. When my husband and I left San Francisco, we moved to Washington DC, where the first job I got was at a Shakespeare theater then called the Folger Theater Group. They kept hiring me as an actor. I just took the jobs that were offered me. I've always had an affinity for the language, so it was great fun. I started off playing ingénues, then went on to do more.

I should thank first my seventh grade English teacher, Vivian Hightower. She was extraordinary. And I should also thank Marge Phillips, who taught voice and speech. Last but not least is Michael Kahn, who has been a great mentor for the last thirty years. His is an extraordinary talent and his knowledge of Shakespeare is beyond anyone else's I've ever heard or seen.

All my Shakespeare roles have all been wonderful in their own way. Some of the productions have been more successful than others. I got to return to Lady Macbeth, which was eye opening. That was the first time I worked with Phillip Goodwin, who is one of my favorite leading men in the entire world, a brilliant actor. And Michael Kahn's understanding of that play was just kind of eerie. He said something like—I'm not sure he'll remember the quote, and I probably won't do it justice— "I'm not afraid of witches, but I am afraid of people who think they're witches." That *Macbeth* was eerie and scary and dark and mysterious and fabulous. *Macbeth* is one of my favorite plays.

About ten years ago Philip and I did George and Martha in *Who's Afraid of Virginia Woolf?* So we came full circle doing marriages. For *Macbeth*, Phillip and I worked on our two scenes together a lot, even outside of rehearsal, so it became this intimate thing. When the King arrives and Duncan comes, Lady Macbeth finds it so bizarre to have people in her house. I thought this must be how she feels, living out on the heath with very few visitors, with just that very intimate relationship with her husband: suddenly there are guests—even worse, guests she plans to kill! I love that she's so taut at the beginning, but she's so fragile too. She's the one that breaks down first. And she doesn't really do that much, except give the King's guards drinks.

I ultimately loved playing Paulina in *The Winter's Tale*, but I found that a challenging role. I was probably a bit young to play her at the time, and at first I couldn't quite wrap my head around where she sat as a character. But Paulina is actually nurturing. And Leontes is not a very nice man: he's insane and makes no sense, so she has to dress him down. I remember saying to

Michael, "I don't understand. What have they been doing for the sixteen years?" And finally he looked at me and said, "Fran, it's just a fairy tale." I'm always looking for too much back-story.

I would love to have played Juliet. There isn't a company in the world that would have ever cast me in that role because I never looked like a Juliet even when I was twenty years old. But I find her fascinating and wonderful and quixotic. She's such a depth for an ingénue. And there's one line at the end, "His lips are warm," which breaks my heart every time I hear it. And I think an ingénue that I was never cast as, but probably would have been a good one for me to play, would have been Helena in *All's Well that Ends Well*— because she's a bizarre kind of ingénue. She's strong.

I've been trying to get a friend of mine in Austin to do *Queen Lear* for some time, but that may or may not happen in my lifetime. There have been female Lears, but not a lot of them. I've never been interested in *Hamlet* for whatever reason. I also said to Bill Rauch that I'd be interested in playing *Othello*. Being led down the garden path by one of your best friends—it's a good story. Katherine in *Henry VIII* is a small role, but it's got that great monologue at the beginning. I'd like to wrap my head around that.

As an actor having done so much Shakespeare for so long, I would go through these periods and think, "Okay, enough. I don't want to do iambic pentameter, I don't want to stand up so much, I don't want to learn all these words. I want to sit down at a coffee table and smoke cigarettes and drink coffee." Then once in a while I'd be cast in a play that was like that. And within a few days I'd think, "Well, where's the language? Where's the passion?" So Shakespeare sort of spoils you for any other playwright. Sometimes I just open up the works, read a passage, and it touches my heart and my soul.

Someone asked, "Do you believe that Shakespeare didn't write it?" All I can say is that Marlowe didn't write them, I know that. One friend said it was either written by Shakespeare or someone who called himself Shakespeare. But the genius of that human being never ceases to amaze me. Working on a Shakespeare play is literally like peeling an onion. I also teach Shakespeare, and it almost never fails that a student who's had no exposure at all will find something in it that I haven't thought of. The text allows you to expand in all sorts of ways that you don't even know are possible at the beginning of the rehearsal period. And I love the feel of the language in my mouth. I wish I were as clever as my characters. That he still makes us cry and laugh after 400 years is amazing. How is that?

His detail of character is extraordinary. I don't know how many characters are in the canon. I'm sure there's a number out there. But each of them has a very specific voice. Juliet does not speak like Romeo, Lady Capulet does not speak like Lord Capulet. They are so distinct. And he has such an understanding of the psychology of the characters given that he so much predates Freud. You think, "How does he know that? How does he understand youth and old age and middle age and power and weakness?" It is beyond my understanding. And he allows you to make him contemporary. You can set him almost anywhere. I remind my students: he was a contemporary writer. So I'm sure he would be just fine if he were contemporary today. In my life he just brings a kind of beauty and resonance and fear and trepidation. Still there's always that relief that at least I can leave a character's life; I don't have to stay there in it. Shakespeare is deep, a bottomless well.

My relationship with Shakespeare is the same as an actor or as a teacher. I think I'm a better actor because I teach and I'm a better teacher because I act. As I said earlier, the discoveries that my students make always astound me. Students bring freshness. And as I explain what it is I think I do as an actor, I get clarity about what I'm actually doing. If I can't explain it, I think maybe there's something I'm not doing right in my own technique. And my technique has evolved over time. With my syllabus, I like to hand out my outline for studying acting, which has evolved over the last 25 years. In doing Margaret in *Richard III*, I didn't know who she was going to be. I'd seen a few Margarets, I'd heard a few Margarets, and I relied specifically on the text. But if you just play what he writes, you're in very competent hands. I have to remind my students and myself of that.

For me the Shakespearean is exquisite language with extraordinary passion. Because he is a poet and there are few real poets in the world, he is all the truth and all the beauty all the time. There's no one else like that. I think that is what is Shakespearean.

When you study about the King's Men, you think they were a raucous group, out drinking and such. But it's hard to imagine that Shakespeare wasn't quiet, contemplative, and spending a lot of time alone. I can't imagine that his inspiration came from noise—maybe from fear or from self-doubt, but not from a lot of people around. And he must have gotten a real cramp in his hand. I think, "Someone wrote this? Took a pen and wrote it all?"

For a favorite quotation I'd choose, "I dreamt there was an Emperor Antony. O, such another sleep, that I might see/ But such another man!" Playing Cleopatra was heaven, because she's so extraordinary. The production was not the best production, so it's the one role I wish very much I could have gotten to play again.

As Shakespeare writes her, as opposed to the historical Cleopatra, she starts off as a brat. She is spoiled. She wants what she wants. She is the epitome of hedonism. Then, as Shakespeare writes her, she meets this guy who doesn't put up with it and says, "No, we're going to stop. And then she has that extraordinary fifth act, which is the greatest love story. He's dead by then.

I always tell my students that if I hadn't been an actor, I would have been an ax murderer. What Shakespeare allows me to do as a human being is release whatever the crazy stuff is that makes up Fran Dorn; I can put all of myself into this language and never fill it up. There's no limit. There's sound and fury signifying nothing, but if you actually invest in it, you can go any-where. It was wonderful to be able to be all those facets because Cleopatra has every facet of a human being. She'll always be my favorite. And I think I did a pretty good job with her.

DOMINIC DROMGOOLE

"WHERE ARE MY TEARS?
RAIN TO LAY THIS WIND,
OR MY HEART WILL BE BLOWN UP
BY THE ROOT."

Shortly after graduating from Cambridge, Dominic Dromgoole
became an assistant director then the artistic director of the Bush
Theatre in London. After being in charge of new plays at the Old
Vic, he became artistic director of the Oxford Stage Company
(now known as Headlong). In 2005 he became artistic director of
*Shakespeare's Globe, where he has directed **Coriolanus**, **Antony***
*and **Cleopatra**, **Love's Labour's Lost**, **King Lear**, **Henry IV***
*(parts 1 and 2), **Romeo and Juliet**, and **Hamlet**. I spoke with*
him in his office at the Globe Theatre. I was especially grateful for
his willingness to talk with me about his Shakespearean life because
he had indeed already written a wonderful book on the subject
*(**Will & Me: How Shakespeare Took Over My Life**). This book*
is full of feeling, humor, and intelligence, an exhilarating story of a
Shakespearean life. I especially recommend the account there (fuller
than the account here) of why he was first moved by the quotation
*above from **Troilus and Cressida** (a play he has both acted in and*
directed).

Shakespeare reaches in every corner of your life, doesn't he? There's very little that isn't exposed or revealed or responded to by Shakespeare. Shakespeare is about resistance to or absence of hierarchies—he's trying not to say one thing is better than another. Shakespeare gives so much respect to each individual that crosses his stage and gives so much individual life to each one of them. It's as if they are each as important as each other, whether you're Francis the drawer in *Henry IV* or whether you're King Henry IV. He explodes the idea that one thing is more important than the other, or that one thing requires more weight or should be more favored than the other. That's the biggest lesson. So you try to live a life without hierarchy, so that eating a Big Mac from MacDonald's can be as enjoyable and as thrilling as dining in a Michelin starred restaurant. Each in its own way can be as enjoyable or as relieving as the other. And in *Henry IV,* Eastcheap is really better than the

King's palace, which is lonely and sad, while in Eastcheap you've got vitality and support. That absence of hierarchy runs through all the plays.

Everyone is always asking, what are your favorites, what's your favorite play, what's your favorite character, what's your favorite that, and I just say you can't really approach Shakespeare in that spirit. You can't have a favorite because the lesson of Shakespeare is to try and enjoy everything. Of course, when you direct plays, the amount of time you spend on them ingrains them in you more thoroughly and makes them more completely a part of yourself, but that doesn't mean that if you approached another play in the same way, you wouldn't get the same value off the other play. And sometimes a casual acquaintance can be as revealing and thrilling as a long relationship.

I come from a family who worked in theatre and television. My father worked with a lot of new playwrights. And I ended up working with a lot of new playwrights because I began by working at a new writing theatre in Shepherd's Bush. Then in this situation, you realize, "Well, Shakespeare is a writer." And what writers do is write to appeal, and to reveal, and to be enjoyed. They don't write for themselves. They don't write for academics. They don't write for other artists. They write for an audience. And Shakespeare did that more than anyone because his theatre, the Globe, was one of the most successful and popular theatres of any time. That sort of insight allows you to strip away a lot of pretension and nonsense. Shakespearean wasn't writing for a thin coterie; he was writing for the world. And so he uses cheap jokes, he uses comedy exposition, he likes talking dirty, he likes being appreciated by the groundlings just as much as by the sophisticates.

So with Shakespeare there is always contrast, always dark beside light: inclusivity—not refining experiences down to pure patterns, but trying to be as inclusive of all life as possible, which is his big distinction from the great and classic French and the great and classic Germans, this ability to put the completely banal beside the very lofty. And there is his capacity to include mess in art rather than excluding mess, to see mess and art as congruous, allowable. He didn't seem to revise. He's full of mistakes, full of errors. There's a lot of nonsense, even some very bad writing, but he was always after a bigger prize than tidiness. He didn't want to write the well-fashioned artifact; he wanted to write life, and life requires a bit of messiness. You never know, but Shakespeare might have been quite fastidious and tidy in his own creative process, because he allowed so much mess onto the page. In my head, I can imagine he was quite well-ordered. And he went in a rush, he wrote fast, like many great writers, like Chekhov and Coward. Coward is the great and authentic genius of the last hundred years in the English theatre. He wrote *Private Lives* in two days (though he had been thinking about it). He started *Hay Fever*, which is a beautifully constructed masterpiece, on a Friday evening and finished it by Sunday lunchtime. And he'd never thought of it before. It just poured out of him. Writers of that degree of talent write fast. As Shakespeare did, writing his plays while living two lives, a London life and a Stratford life, working in the theatre, acting, learning lines, reading extensively. To get to the theatre plays of that size, you have to move quickly.

I played Pandarus in a student production, and I loved playing it. One line spoke to me very privately about where I was at the time in my own head and in my own emotional setup. It's when Pandarus is looking at *Troilus and Cressida* while they are in a state of great emotional turbulence, and he can't empathize or get involved. And he hates himself because he can't get involved, which is a classic student crisis. It was really revealing to me because it laid out so simply what I was feeling, when in a private moment Pandarus says, "Where are my tears? Rain, to lay this wind, or my heart will be blown up by the root." And it was very powerfully clear to me about where I was then, though not actually where I am now. That revealed to me how deep Shakespeare could dig.

BARBARA GAINES

"LECHERY LECHERY, STILL WARS AND LECHERY!
NOTHING ELSE HOLDS FASHION."

"IT IS REQUIRED YOU DO AWAKE YOUR FAITH"

Barbara Gaines is the founder and Artistic Director of the Chicago Shakespeare Theater, a winner of the 2008 Tony Award for Outstanding Regional Theater. Gaines has directed more than thirty Shakespeare plays, winning Chicago's Joseph Jefferson Awards for Best Director and Best Productions as well as three Laurence Olivier Awards (the highest honor in British Theatre). She serves as a member of the Shakespearean Council for the Globe Theatre in London, has received several honorary doctorates, and was awarded the Honorary OBE. I talked with Barbara Gaines in her office at Chicago Shakespeare Theater, where she was in the midst of directing **Timon of Athens** *for Spring 2012. Her schedule was such that we talked while she ate her lunch. The conversation was necessarily brief, but I found her sharply intelligent, charismatic, and warm. And the theater itself, on Chicago's Navy Pier, is impressive as well.*

I was probably thirteen when I discovered Shakespeare. Somebody gave me a copy of the Sonnets. I just read it and liked them.

As a student at Northwestern University, I had one of the great Shakespeare professors in the world, Wallace A. Bacon. He taught Frank Galati, Mary Zimmerman, and so many other people. But I knew Shakespeare was going to be the most important thing in my life when I started teaching it, which was in 1983. I was an actress before that, but I had some surgery on my knee and couldn't walk, and I needed to make a living. So I started a class with professional actors here in Chicago. They were all pros, people I'd worked with, and we worked on Monday nights. Then it was so popular we worked on Monday and Tuesday nights. Twelve actors became 40 over two nights. I worked with them, and they taught me a lot about acting. I taught them what I knew about Shakespeare. And then all this [*gesturing at the space around us*] happened from those classes.

Both a teacher and a director need to be able to communicate. As a director, you try to inspire your actors to do their best work, and I would think a teacher tries to do the same thing.

Professor Bacon at Northwestern was probably the greatest angel of my life because he made us understand the inner life of the messengers and the commoners as well as of the kings and queens. So he was the greatest teacher I had.

And then of course the actors were my teachers. These are friends of mine, sensational professional actors here in Chicago, and they have taught me so much more about the text. They are and were my constant inspiration. I can say that my inspiration wasn't someone else's production. Peter Brook's productions always inspire me, but the main thing for me is the inner life of the characters and how I connect the inner lives of those characters to what's happening now. I'm continually in the present. I never thought of anyone in a Shakespeare play—a king or a scrivener—that they didn't live now. How the characters live on in the present is my continual source of energy, because everything in Shakespeare without a doubt relates to this moment in time. That's what I work from. So I'm constantly reading. Political science is a great interest, as well as biographies and history. I'm very interested in tying all that together.

I really do see Shakespeare as connected to current events. History hasn't changed. In the Renaissance, you have the War of the Roses, but check out the Middle East! There you have the War of the Roses in action now.

But, yes, the comedies give me a pain in the neck. I just don't understand them as well as I understand the others. I don't understand *Two Gentlemen of Verona* at all.

Timon is not that hard! The hard thing about it was just getting the script in shape (because it's a first draft), cutting out a lot of excessive characters that have no meaning. But directing *Timon* is thrilling. My favorite play is *Troilus and Cressida*—because it's the story of mankind. Right there in three hours, it's the story of all of us. I'm haunted by war and the waste within it. I've directed *Troilus* three times and I hope to do it three more times. It started this theater. It was our first show, the miracle play that made it all happen for us. When I first collected money to do Shakespeare plays, the first play I chose was *Troilus and Cressida*. It was first play we did in a theater. It still haunts me. I could do it every year in a different world capitol. It's riveting.

I really don't think in terms of favorite characters. But *Troilus* I'm haunted by, *Lear* I love. I love *King John*, I love *Pericles*. I identify with all of them; that's why I can't pick one. One of my favorite characters is the scrivener in *Richard III* who only has a few lines to say in the play but he's the soul of the play. I love these lines of his:

> Why who's so gross,
> That seeth not this palpable device?

Yet who's so blind, but says he sees it not?
Bad is the world; and all will come to nought,
When such bad dealings must be seen in thought.

This is a man that lives his life signing death warrants for Richard III. And he's the only person in the play who says it's horrific, who says what's going on. He's able to nail the horror and yet all he does is sign or write the death warrants. He's fantastic, actually. He's the keen and shrewd observer of this serial killer.

But I love all of them. There's not one of them I don't love, though I don't understand Proteus. (See, I'm back to *Two Gentlemen*.) He's young, I guess.

I think my soul is more evolved because I have lived inside of Shakespeare's world. There is just a greater evolution of understanding. Shakespeare certainly is the greatest school of human understanding. It's just the depth of the soul. Ben Jonson was a satirist. He gives simple, very simple answers, simple and cut and dry, no nuance, ultimately no depth of character, no depth.

As to what Shakespeare was like, I would put you in touch with the First Folio introduction by his friends and fellow actors, Heminges and Condell, who wrote, "Who, as he was a happie imitator of Nature, was a most gentle expresser of it. His mind and hand went together: And what he thought, he uttered with that easinesse, that wee have scarse received from him a blot in his papers. But it is not our province, who onely gather his works, and give them you, to praise him. It is yours that reade him. And there we hope, to your divers capacities, you will finde enough, both to draw, and hold you: for his wit can no more lie hid, then it could be lost. Reade him, therefore; and againe, and againe: And if then you doe not like him, surely you are in some manifest danger, not to understand him." So he was probably a happy and gentle man.

Of course, there are many quotations I love. I can't choose one so you have to print two. "It is required you do awake your faith," from Paulina in *The Winter's Tale*. Those are words to live by. And then "Lechery, lechery, still wars and lechery! Nothing else holds fashion," from *Troilus and Cressida*. That's the world. You can't let war and lechery keep you from awakening your faith. Hopefully good will transcend evil.

Shakespeare is about whatever you need it to be, whatever you need at the moment. If it's about theater, it's about theater. If it's about something terrible going on in your life, it's about something terrible. You see what I mean? Shakespeare changes. Shakespeare morphs as life morphs for you.

RUPERT GOOLD

"So doth the greater glory dim the less.
A substitute shines as brightly as a king
until a king be by and then his state
empties itself, as does an inland brook
into the main of waters. . . .
Nothing is good, I see, without respect."

*After graduating in 1994 from Trinity College, Cambridge with a degree in literature and being a Fulbright Scholar in Performance Studies at New York University, Rupert Goold became a trainee director at the Donmar Warehouse, then an associate at the Salisbury Playhouse. He was Artistic Director of the Royal and Derngate Theatres in Northhampton, Associate Director of the Royal Shakespeare Company, the Artistic Director of the Headlong Theatre Company, and (currently), the Artistic Director of the Almeida Theatre Company. He has directed opera, musicals, revivals, new plays, farce, pantomime, and, of course, Shakespeare. He notably directed Patrick Stewart in **Macbeth**, winning The Evening Standard's Sydney Edwards Award and the Olivier Award for best director. He subsequently won additional Olivier, Critic's Circle and Evening Standard awards for **King Charles III**. His projects include well-regarded films of **Richard II** and of **Macbeth**. He has also co-authored three adaptations for the stage (**The End of the Affair, Faustus,** and **Six Characters in Search of an Author**). I talked with Rupert Goold in the summer of 2012, at the offices of the Headlong Theatre in London.*

M y first memory of Shakespeare is of a picture book I had, not Lamb's *Tales from Shakespeare*, but like it. I can still picture some of the illustrations, very '70s, quite bloody and sensual. I'd love to find that book again because I can't remember who illustrated it. It left a huge impact on me, particularly in the pictures of *Macbeth, Romeo and Juliet, Twelfth Night, Dream*—a lot of the shows I've gone on to direct. I probably did read the stories as well, was aware of them at some level.

Probably the first show I saw which made a huge visual impression on me was Antony Sher's *Richard III*. I must have been about twelve. I think my parents took me to the Barbican. I remember it leaving this big impression, but also I remember not understanding very much of it and probably being a bit disappointed by that. Now I feel very passionate about trying to make Shakespeare as accessible as possible, and not just for a young audience. Many of the people who love Shakespeare and work in Shakespeare take for granted their understanding of the text and their literary study of it. I was from a bookish family, interested in theater. I think at school I was in a production of *Romeo and Juliet* when I was 15 or so. But it wasn't until I went to university that I really could say that I understood a Shakespeare play when watching it. So I think that we sometimes take that understanding for granted. Still, the Sher *Richard III* at the Barbican left a real impact on me. After that I probably saw a couple of others while I was at school.

I've done quite a lot of Shakespeare. It's interesting. Here at Headlong we don't do anything but new writing or new versions, but we do run a sort of an emerging directors program geared around Shakespeare. We've done three in the last three years. I think Shakespeare and obviously some of the other great classics, the texts we all know well, are the best vessels for directors to try to find their own identities. So if you're an aspiring, ambitious director, there's a sense that what you might do with *Othello*, for example, might mark you out as a director more than what you might do with just any play.

Jonathan Miller's book *Subsequent Performances* had a big impact on me. I think it's out of print now, actually, but it really celebrated the idea of radical reimaginings of existing texts rather than the idea of some sort of oeuvre performance paradigm for these texts. I saw Miller's colonial *Tempest* in the 80's when I was at school; he represented a sort of swashbuckling, charismatic, witty approach that I felt became sort of marginalized. There's always been a kind of split in England, which sits as a sort of midpoint between the classicism/conservatism of the American aesthetic towards Shakespeare versus the recherché, kind of hauteur approach the further east you go into Europe.

Theater is meaningless without actors, and actors, especially stars, tend to dictate the identity of the work. There's always been a suspicion about directors in this country. What do they do? Do we really need them? With directors like me, who do fairly conceptual rereadings of some of these plays, people say, "Oh, it's attention-seeking and unnecessary or ill-thought through or just unnecessarily flashy." I suppose Peter Hall has particularly espoused the spare, almost reactionary position on verse. It's very much a British tradition, Brooks' aesthetic of *The Empty Space*, which is the great British book on theater. The idea is that you put the actors in the space, you don't adorn them with anything, and they say the words simply and clearly with respect for the verse. That is really the pure Shakespeare, but I suppose I've always been on the Miller side. It's a big garden; you can grow some strange flowers! I have a clear methodology in the way I approach Shakespeare, which is respectful and comes out of my academic training. I don't think I'm vandalizing these plays, but, in any case, the plays are very robust.

One of the differences between the academic study of literature and the professional realization of plays is that really as a director your job is to make something homogeneous and live and not dull. So the plays that I might have found problematic when I was studying them, like *The Taming of the Shrew* or *The Merchant of Venice*, plays that have intellectually difficult thematic issues are actually less problematic than the plays that are dramatically inert or that have bad scenes in them. The one that I've always really had struggles with is *The Tempest*, which is the first one I did at the RSC. I found that it was discursive, had a lack of action and was static and, yes, sterile in a way. So that was absolutely one I haven't liked. But when I take one of these plays on my approach is to think the good scenes will sort of take care of themselves— you can find different ways of doing them, so you shouldn't worry about them too much. Where your production energies need to be focused on are the weak points of the characters and the scenes that traditionally one finds tedious or dull. More particularly for me my whole conceptual design for *The Tempest* was based on the first lords scene where the lords just talk on and on. Everyone always says it's terribly dull. So you have to find ways of spicing that second scene up.

I think the most complete, the most flawless Shakespeare play is probably *Macbeth*. The one that I think I could watch again and again is *Hamlet*. And the one that I like to direct most is *Henry IV*. Those are the three I think that stand up. I'm also really fond of *Twelfth Night*.

As far as characters I am drawn to or would like to imagine meeting, it would have been interesting to see what Juliet would have grown up into. I find her and her sort of intellectual development so exciting, especially in the second half of that play, but of course you only get an image of a 14-year-old's development. In life I'm naturally an Antony, so I love Cleopatra and how she seduces Antony. I hold her quite high. I'm first thinking of the girls here. And with the male characters, it's terrible clichéd in a way, but I really emotionally relate to the *Henry IV* plays. I had a very Falstaffy figure in my youth who sort of led me astray, so I'd like to meet Jack as well. I think the profundity of the play is that you do reject those figures. I didn't really reject my Falstaff, but for my health I had to reject his lifestyle.

Shakespeare is such a brilliant writer that the characters you think you're going to find hard often don't turn out to be that hard. I hadn't really warmed to Portia until I did *Merchant of Venice*, and then I felt very differently. I think there are certain thankless roles to act. I've always thought—even though I've seen some great actors, maybe even had a great actor do it when I directed it—that Laertes is a really tough gig. It's a thin instrument compared to the sound of the rest of the orchestra. And Banquo is a sort of tough gig as well. He just suddenly gets going and then he's gone.

This is slightly woolly, but I've struggled with having any religious conviction in my life. I've been exposed to it and tried, but I just can't quite get beyond the evidence issue. But I've done an enormous amount of ecclesiastical work (around *Paradise Lost*, Graham Greene adaptations, directing "The Last Days of Judas Iscariot," and so on). My wife's Catholic, my children are Catholic, I'm very drawn to Catholic sensibility, and I think it's about a greater yearning for the sublime in a kind of romantic Keatsian way. I do find that in Shakespeare. I find a bounty there that's sort of inspiring. There's something about being an artist that when you recognize one like Shakespeare being so far above you, it's actually reassuring, allows you to be more comfortable just being yourself. So there's a kind of distance that is nice.

I came from Cambridge, did a literary degree. I don't think academia is at all an inappropriate or incorrect way to produce directors or actors. There are many wonderful directors who came from practice and many charlatans who came from my background. But I was brought up through college by doing it a lot. You get much better at Shakespeare by doing a lot of it. My background is sort of Anglo-middle class literary, but that's who I am. And I feel that's okay. Some people have a background in basketball or farming. It's just brought up in them. Yes, I was privileged in being exposed to Shakespeare and taught by good teachers, and I never take that for granted, but it is my background, my cultural heritage. Shakespeare is our national poet. I'm sure if you were a conductor of Mozart or Wagner in German or if you were a French philosopher, that's part of what you are. Thinking of Shakespeare as our national poet is reassuring.

I was going to write a book about Shakespeare (and maybe one day I will), talking about these very, incredibly intense personal experiences around a lot of the plays I've directed, deep encounters with either actors or others, right from my student days to now. I never take Shakespeare plays on casually. I don't know whether I'll do one for two or three years, but if I do I'll make sure I really know why I'm doing it, not just who are the right actors for it, what is my production concept, but what's going to happen to me in it. So I had a desperate, horrible time doing *King Lear*, which feels entirely appropriate because it's a desperate, horrible play to go through. But it was a really incredible experience, in and out of the rehearsals, so I always feel like something's going to happen when I start one of them. I'll fall in love or have a breakdown—something will happen.

Shakespeare and Chekhov are the two really plural humanists. With Ben Jonson or Marlowe or Beckett, you feel there is a worldview being imposed on you and the world is being read by this world-view, however extraordinary it may be. I've been working with Shakespeare for years and actually I think there is something bourgeois and rather timid and compromising and middle class about him. Certainly the evidence about him after he retired suggests that line. But he knit that mix together into a great celebration of toleration and cautiousness, which is very English. So I think there is that in him. There is an anxious schoolboy from Warwickshire that's part of him. I think he was probably incredibly un-PC, that he really has a life-affirming and celebratory vitality, a pretty with-it view of the world. Again, I think the Hal story is instructive. I recently saw Mark Rylance talk on Newsnight about what contemporary politics could learn from Shakespeare. He made the very good point that what Shakespeare teaches us is about being ready for life, that wisdom is predicated on experience and rites of passage through experience. And *Henry V* being our paradigm exemplar hero in Shakespearean literature, had to go through a familiar problem: the misbehavior in his youth. And now we tend not to allow that early experience to our people in positions of authority. Rylance was saying rightly that of course you could probably say the same about Martin Luther King as about Prince Hal, that if we knew totally about his lifestyle he probably would have been discredited. Shakespeare would never be so small-minded to think that we have to be born perfect to be perfect. In fact, quite the opposite: we're all born flawed and we go on these journeys to become better people. So he understands error in a compassionate way, more than most writers.

There are so many great quotations I could choose. One of my favorite passages in Shakespeare is the "special providence in the fall of a sparrow" speech in Hamlet, but I won't choose that because everyone would probably pick that. I do really like Portia's speech just before she comes back to Belmont in Act V:

> So doth the greater glory dim the less.
> A substitute shines brightly as a king
> Until a king be by, and then his state
> Empties itself, as doth an inland brook
> Into the main of waters. . . .
> Nothing is good, I see, without respect.

The poetry in it is beautiful. And I think every time you think you know anything about life, in particularly about Shakespeare, when you travel a little bit further, you realize you knew nothing. So we're all like Portias in the world, stuck in our ivory bound towers, ready to go on trials that will teach us we're back at the beginning again.

STEPHEN GREENBLATT

"So I have heard and do in part believe it."
"Simply the thing I am will make me live."
"The worst returns to laughter."
"The rest is silence."

Stephen Greenblatt is Cogan University Professor of the Humanities at Harvard University. He previously taught at U.C. Berkeley. His books include **Will in the World: How Shakespeare Became Shakespeare** *(a Pulitzer Prize finalist and one of the most-read books on Shakespeare);* **Hamlet in Purgatory; Practicing New Historicism; Marvelous Possessions: The Wonder of the New World; Learning to Curse: Essays in Early Modern Culture; Sir Walter Ralegh: The Renaissance Man and His Roles; Shakespearean Negotiations: The Circulation of Social Energy in Renaissance England** *(winner of the MLA's James Russell Lowell Prize), and* **The Swerve: How The World Became Modern** *(winner of the Pulitzer Prize, the National Book Award, and the James Russell Lowell Prize of the Modern Language Association). He is co-author (with Charles Mee) of a play,* **Cardenio** *(inspired by Shakespeare and Fletcher's lost play of the same name). He is a founding co-editor of the journal* **Representations** *and has edited six collections of criticism. His honors include the Distinguished Humanist Award from the Mellon Foundation, and the Distinguished Teaching Award from the University of California, Berkeley, the Holberg Prize (for outstanding scholarship), Yale's Wilber Cross Medal, a Mellon Distinguished Humanist Award, and the Erasmus Institute Prize. I talked with him in his office at Harvard in May 2017.*

My earliest memory of Shakespeare must have been an eighth-grade class taught by Miss Gillespie in which she had the I think extremely foolish idea of teaching *As You Like It*—which I hated. I can still remember the words "Sweet my coz, be merry" with some unpleasant feeling. But then I encountered Shakespeare again in what must have been my junior or senior year of high school in a class taught by someone named John Harris, sort of life-changing, a class in which it was just *King Lear* for a semester. He was a wonderful teacher and a wonderful man. So I had one of those experiences that most people like me and like you probably have had as well: at some point you get a teacher, usually in high school, if you're lucky, sometimes earlier (and even but not so often later), who just suddenly reaches you. He's gone, poor man, but he was a great, great teacher. He seemed to me to know everything. At the same time, it was my first experience relative to understanding Shakespeare of modesty, of hermeneutical modesty; I can't remember any longer what moment in the play we were talking about, but he had thought a lot about it and simply didn't understand it, didn't understand what was being said, or what the relationships were. And he had brooded about it a lot. I was amazed because he seemed to know everything. It was kind of a deep moment for me, of realizing that not knowing sometimes is as important as knowing.

I didn't take a Shakespeare class as an undergraduate—I don't think it was required at Yale when I was there. I didn't have as far as I remember a Shakespeare class, but I must have read some Shakespeare. I went to Cambridge on a Fulbright to do a second B.A., but I don't think there was a Shakespeare requirement there either. Or there wasn't a Shakespeare paper, as they would put it, on the Tripos, the exam. I read and saw various plays, but they weren't part of my study. And when I went back to Yale as a graduate student to get my Ph.D., then I did take a Shakespeare class. I had a quite wonderful Shakespeare class, quite important, from a marvelous teacher and eventually my dissertation director, Alvin Kernan, who was a significant Shakespearean. He's long in years, but he's still alive I believe, in retirement at Princeton. He wrote several quite important Shakespeare books. He taught a wonderful graduate Shakespeare class. Looking back on it, many of the people in the class—who would have included my colleague Marge Garber, Larry Danson who teaches at Princeton (or maybe recently retired), Marianne Novy who became a Shakespearean feminist—went on to teach Shakespeare. But I did my Ph.D. dissertation on Sir Walter Ralegh, not on Shakespeare at all.

So that was that, and then I went to teach at Berkeley. I still wasn't thinking about myself as a Shakespearean. I thought of myself as a Marxist literary critic. I was teaching lots of different things, including Renaissance classes, and I worked on my Ralegh book. After I wrote the Ralegh book, I continued really thinking the issues that the Ralegh book was about, having to do with how a life gets shaped, what the relationship is between the life someone leads— imagine someone fashioning a life—and literature. And out of that I wrote *Renaissance Self-Fashioning*. It was only in the very end of *Renaissance Self-Fashioning*—which is a book of six chapters, starting with Thomas More—when I was working on *Othello* that something clicked in a very powerful way. I hadn't wanted to spend a huge amount of time working on Shakespeare, but my own literary imagination was excited in an unusually intense way by what I was reading and thinking about. I'd seen plenty of Shakespeare plays, had gone to Shakespeare plays endlessly. I was in England on a Sabbatical year in the early seventies and I went constantly to the theatre. It was not that I didn't have lots of theatre experiences in which Shakespeare figured, but it was really only at the very end of *Renaissance Self-Fashioning* that I thought, "Hmmm, something is released in me or triggered in me by thinking about Shakespeare and writing about Shakespeare." So I spent more time doing that. Then Shakespeare became exciting and fun for me and I began to work more on Shakespeare. It probably happens to most people who work in Early Modern Studies; if you're working in English at least, Shakespeare is the big elephant in the room, even if you're not working on him. (Or Milton, if you're working on a slightly later period.) And eventually you have to figure out that you're either just going to avoid it completely, or you decide you're a little piece of rock floating around in orbit around an enormous sun, and then you get pulled in more and more towards that huge sun.

Maybe I jumped slightly ahead of myself with talking about *Othello*, because there was something else that happened, it must have been in the early 70s. Because of my interest in Ralegh and because Ralegh wrote *The Discovery of Guiana,* a man named Fredi Chiappelli, who was then head of UCLA's Center for Medieval and Renaissance Studies, invited me to a conference that he was organizing, called "First Images of America." I decided to write something about the fantasy that Indians didn't have any language— an obviously counterfactual and counter-intuitive fantasy. I wrote a long piece that involved lots of research and that was a lot of fun, reading Hakluyt and a lot of other people. And there too, when I finally got to *The Tempest,* that's where all the pieces came together, where I felt somehow the deepest issues were being engaged. I guess early on those two plays, *Othello* and *The Tempest,* were kind of central for me.

I've had problems with all the plays in one way or another, if by problems you mean provocations to keep going, to not let it go, or feeling that you're not let go by it. That is the principal experience of thinking about Shakespeare, of studying Shakespeare. It is part of the magic of a life lived grappling with Shakespeare. I remember one of my tutors in French Literature at Cambridge; I don't remember his name any longer. He was a specialist in Rabelais, quite an important figure in Rabelais studies. He was retiring, and I remember having a tutorial with him and asking him, "Professor So-and-so, what are you planning on doing after your retirement." And he said, "Oh

I'm not sure what I am doing yet. The only thing I know for sure is that I am never again reading a word of Rabelais." And I thought, "Oh man." I actually thought at the time, "This is not great news!" If it gets to you, if you have made the right match for yourself, then it's precisely about not exhausting the subject, about there remaining problems for you. So, in my case I'm invested in lots of them, in *Lear, Merchant of Venice, Twelfth Night,* and *Hamlet,* but many many more than that too. *Winter's Tale,* I've come back over and over to think about. *Romeo,* I could almost unfold the list of all the plays. I also quite love *Much Ado*—and *Measure for Measure* (slightly off the center of the canon).

I am fascinated by the general Shakespeare phenomenon of the characters—and there are lots of them—who seem to have a life that's lived slightly independently of the play that they're in. The most famous ones obviously are Falstaff and Hamlet, maybe Shylock too. But they are by no means the only ones. I think there are lots of Shakespeare characters who have this weird effect that they seem at least in one's imagination to exist outside the orbit of the play that they are in. It's a making real of something fantastic or purely imaginary. It's a weird achievement and is a characteristic Shakespeare achievement. And it's true of odd characters like Barnadine in *Measure for Measure* or the loathsome Oswald in *Lear.* So it doesn't have to be good characters or characters that have a lot of time given to them. I don't know how he does it. I've spent a lot of time thinking about it, but I couldn't tell you how he manages to do this. It's quite powerful.

It's interesting to me that I can't think off the top of my head a Shakespeare character I'd like to have a drink with. I'd like to have a drink with Shakespeare. But no Shakespeare character immediately leaps to my mind as someone I would really love to talk to. If I were forced to play the game I could think in a predictable way of Viola maybe, or Benedick, or maybe Beatrice. And Imogen seems very charming to me.

Of course, I don't have a simple answer to this at all [what have you learned from Shakespeare?] or even a complicated answer, but I would have said if one is reaching for basic understanding of how Shakespeare could affect you, it would be in multiple ways. First, I would have said, "Not to look away, to actually look at the people you encounter in the world—in a kind of unflinching way." The current Pope said recently that when you give money to people on the street panhandling, look at them, look at their faces and speak to them. I'm not sure Shakespeare would put it, how should I say, in the charitable mode, but I think Shakespeare was in the hortatory mode of Pope Francis. It's not necessarily about charity, but it's about looking and taking in and not looking away. Putting aside any policy questions, that's part of the lesson of *King Lear* and lots of other plays: just looking and not pretending you don't see what is there. Then you're not like the politician with glass eyes who pretends he doesn't see what he sees. ["Get thee glass eyes,/ And like a scurvy politician seem/ To see the things thou dost not." *King Lear*] So that's one thing. Then, I'm not sure I learned this from Shakespeare, but having a kind of loathing of cruelty would be another. Laughing when you can laugh. One can list a lot of things of this kind, but whether one gets them from Shakespeare or not, I don't know.

I don't have an answer that's my own or particularly new [as to what is the "Shakespearean"]. Yeats's phrase "the emotion of multitude" will do, that there's a particular kind of multitudinousness in Shakespeare that's unusual. That particularly marks him? Maybe? But he's not the only person in the history of the world to have had this. I think Homer had it too. But Shakespeare has a very powerful sense of a very full universe, with intensely insistent and realized humans and natural presences. Something like "the emotion of multitude" is the best I can do right now.

[In regard to what Shakespeare may have been like as a person] In writing *Will in the World,* in writing not in the book, I actually wrote for each of the chapters a kind of spiritual exercise, as it were. I wrote a kind of letter or a statement in Shakespeare's voice. I wrote absurdly in a way: "This is what I felt when my father did this, this is what I felt when I walked out to Shottery, this is what I felt when I crossed the London Bridge for the first time." I wrote it out. Obviously, I didn't publish it, and I wouldn't publish it. But I think at least for that particular project I had the opposite instinct or impulse from Borges (as much as I admire Borges), from Borges' famous argument that Shakespeare precisely has no personality, no identity, he's God or whatever, and God doesn't have a personality. I had both the opposite desire and the opposite feeling that you actually had to be able to say inwardly what you think this person was like as a person. You certainly should be able to say that if you were trying to write the book that I was writing. But if you're trying to connect to this author in the deepest way you can, you should actually be connecting to a human being, and should be able attempt to channel, as we would do if we talked long enough, what each other's personalities were like. So I did it. But having said that, I didn't publish those things. There are things that you feel, how should we say, inside that you work your way toward, but they would be somewhat absurd to write them and publish them.

The closest I came was writing something for a joke, so maybe I did out myself a little bit. For the International Shakespeare Association meeting in Stratford last summer I was on a Shakespeare/ Cervantes panel, to commemorate their deaths in the same year, at almost the same time, the same month anyway. And so I wrote a letter from Shakespeare to Cervantes in which Shakespeare talks a little bit about himself, the kind of person he is, and why he finds Cervantes interesting to read. Shakespeare was probably reading Cervantes at the end of his life—it's kind of amazing to think about. I wrote a "Dear Michael" letter with Shakespeare not anticipating that Michael was necessarily going to receive his letter let alone understand his English. But he was trying to say why reading Don Quixote was a revelatory experience for him and what feeling of connection he had with Cervantes. It had to do with all kind of qualities, a certain excitement at language, certain ways of getting excited at language, a certain fascination with madness, a certain fascination with how human beings try to mitigate their aggression and cruelty but only partially succeed in doing so, a certain way of situating yourself in relation to very powerful people, and so forth and so on. Then of course in a way the great thing was not the revelation of connectedness, but the revelation of something else: what it would have been like for Shakespeare to read in effect the first great modern novel, perhaps the greatest modern novel, and realize that there's a whole other form that's radically different from the form he worked in his whole life—Shakespeare basically working in the form of the short story. Shakespeare always has to end it; he has to get through it, in three hours. If you think of the Shakespeare who wrote *Antony and Cleopatra*, who clearly had somewhere in his head the sort of Tolstoyan dream of *War and Peace* or Cervantes' dream of doing some enormous thing, you realize that the form in which Shakespeare worked couldn't even begin to allow him to make good on it.

I'm not sure what quotation I would like, but I will say in no particular order, "So I have heard and do in part believe it." Or maybe "Simply the thing I am will make me live." Or "The worst returns to laughter"—a happy one, maybe appropriate for our particular moment. Or "The rest is silence."

Plays of & William Shakespeare

THE Globe Theatre, 1613

ANDREW GURR

"*THIS DISTRACTED GLOBE*"

Andrew Gurr was born in Leicester, raised in New Zealand, and educated at the University of Auckland and at Cambridge University. Before his retirement, he taught at the Universities of Wellington, Leeds, Nairobi and Reading. He has written a number of books essential to anyone seriously interested in Shakespeare and his era, including, **Shakespeare's Opposites: The Admiral's Company 1594–1625, William Shakespeare: The Extraordinary Life of the Most Successful Writer of All Time, The Shakespearean Playing Companies, The Shakespearean Stage, 1574–1642, Studying Shakespeare: an Introduction, Playgoing in Shakespeare's London,** *and* **Hamlet and the Distracted Globe.** *He has co-written* **Rebuilding Shakespeare's Globe and Staging in Shakespeare's Theatres,** *published numerous articles and essays (including "In-jokes about Spear-Shakers," referred to in our conversation), and edited a number of plays by Shakespeare and by John Fletcher. He was chief academic advisor for the rebuilding of the Globe Theatre in London and an advisor on the building of the Blackfriars Playhouse in Staunton, Virginia. He won the 2008 Sam Wanamaker Prize for pioneering work in Shakespearean Theatre. We talked at a crowded London Globe Theatre Café on a late July afternoon.*

When I was 12 or 13-years-old, I went to a production in New Zealand by the Royal Shakespeare Company. I was just bowled over by their *Henry IV Part 1*. It was just one of those things that was a good theatre experience.

Although I hardly ever went to the theatre, my family took me to the cinema at eight o'clock every Saturday night. I remember my first actual physical thought came when I was taken to the cinema version of Verdi's *Otello*, during which the hero cut his throat and then sang his dying aria. And I can remember being outraged by this, thinking, "This is not what would have happened"— which response is of course the effect of cinematic realism. That started me thinking about doing theatre in various ways. And Shakespeare was part of this.

We saw some very good theatre in my days as a student at Auckland, which, when I ended up studying nothing but English, made me feel that Shakespeare was a good choice.

I got a scholarship from New Zealand that took me to Cambridge. My object had been to write the great New Zealand novel—but after six months I decided this was a total waste of time, and all I could think of to do was a PhD, which was slightly too professional a training for most students from New Zealand at the time. I was just beginning with the routine of doing a postgraduate degree rather than just an undergraduate degree, and I talked to a lot of PhD students at Cambridge. All of them were doing theses on poets nobody had ever heard of, from the 18th century mostly, and they were dead bored with their subjects. And I thought if I'm going to spend three years full time, it's got to be something that interests me. What is the top subject? Obviously I had to do Shakespeare. So I did a thesis on Shakespeare. That was really the deciding moment, which followed from seeing what was good about Shakespeare and going from there. You want to study somebody you know will last.

I had some rather random help as a postgraduate student at Cambridge. I was wished on Muriel Bradbook quite early on, and she was great. She was a real delight and had a wicked sense of humor. She was a great lady of that period and as a woman was held in a very firm minority since it was Britain and totally masculine and all that. I also felt very much in the minority as a colonial at Cambridge. She was the only person in the whole of Cambridge who arranged meetings of postgraduates. We never met one another otherwise. She was wonderful that way, quite supportive. I met Anne Righter, Anne Barton as she now is. She had just gone through. She was the great American student. And she was actually offered to me as an example because she had not only read all of Shakespeare but had read all of the 600 plays written and published up to that point. This accomplishment was offered to me as a quiet lesson in what I ought to be aiming to do.

My wife and I both came from New Zealand at the same time, but she did the undergraduate degree at Oxford while I did the post-graduate degree at Cambridge. We met whenever we could and went to the theatre as much as we could. And she actually was an actress. She acted at Oxford. She played Isabella to Ken Loach's Angelo. So we always went to the theater. I actually hadn't a particular delight in the theater at that time, but she just wanted to go to everything. It was just after John Osborne's *Look Back in Anger*. It was a great time for London theatre, with two absolutely distinct traditions available. You either went to the "Anyone for Tennis" kind of play or you went to something that was sordid and serious. We fell absolutely for a number of plays. We loved Jellicoe's *The Knack*. That was a lark. We got long memories out of these plays.

We went to Stratford and saw everything. Some were good, some were awful. And one or two plays absolutely bowled us over there. The first one that bowled us over was Clifford Williams' *The Comedy of Errors*. It was absolutely stunning. It was so good actually that when we went back to New Zealand, both of us with our two children in 1966—a long time ago now—we saw a local amateur production of *Comedy of Errors* that was clearly totally based on the Clifford Williams we had seen in London. We discovered that Ngaio Marsh, the novelist, lived six months in London then six months back home in Christchurch, in New Zealand, and she staged versions of the plays she had liked in England. So she staged her version of Clifford William's *Comedy of Errors*. And it was not only lovely enough to see Williams' original, which was absolutely mind-blowingly funny—we had always thought Shakespeare was a bit serious, but that was absolutely hilarious—but so was the copy of it, which was obviously a copy. That experience was instrumental for me.

Beyond that I think there were two or three productions that really changed my thinking about everything. And they were all Peter Brook's. We saw his *King Lear* at Stratford. We drove all the way from Leeds to Stratford. It took five hours to get there and five hours to get back! It was dire. But the play itself was glorious. And then when we were on leave from Africa—we had gone to Africa—we saw his *A Midsummer's Night's Dream*. Those two actually transformed your consciousness, not just of the play, but of life generally.

His *Lear* made me think about *King Lear* being in its way incredibly nihilistic. I think now you can probably call it a dystopia. The idea of a united kingdom is a utopia, but what you get in *Lear* is the disunited kingdom. (It was propaganda for King James in a way.) It was such a consummate work of absolute destructiveness, especially in the way Brook pared it down. One of our friends was in the play, as a spear-carrier. His one line was, "Edmund is dead, my lord." He said the actors referred to the production as "the all leather show," because they were all required to dress up in leather, in sort of Anglo-Saxonish leather. But they'd all have to go out and roll in the fields first, because they looked too smart in their leather. That gave me an insight as to what it was like to act in a play. Our friend, Gordon, gave us a lot of illustrations of what the actors did, what Peter Brook did with the actors, and also Brook's way of creating a context, an environment for the play.

And the *Dream* did the same thing in quite different ways because it was hilariously funny, but it kept hinting at things. It blended and separated Hypolita and Theseus and Oberon and Titania, and it played the whole game of love up through the reconciliation at the end. It seemed to me to throw a whole new light on the play. It was absolutely refreshing in that it made me think more clearly about the usual things I thought about all the time. I had always said that *A Midsummer Night's Dream* was such a marvelous collection of clichés—because I knew it so well, had seen it so many times—but this was a revelation, to see it in that absolutely fresh fierce light, with that bareness that Brook is so good at. And all of that made me above all feel a renewed clarity, despite how totally complex the world is. If you can see something infinitely complex with absolute clarity, then you've really got somewhere intellectually. That was a revelation to me.

In some respects, I've thought *A Midsummer Night's Dream* was the ultimate play. And it has this wonderful metaphor in it. You know when Theseus has his speech about the lover, the lunatic, and the poet, and how imagination destroys everything, Hippolyta says, "Ah, but they all had the same dream." And that is the perfect metaphor for the theatre. You individually have the dream, but whole audience has the same dream. So there is therefore more than just the individual mind doing its individual thing. And it seems to me you have something collective as well as individual about theatre. It was all part of my process of learning what theatre can do.

I've done two editions of the two versions of *Henry V.* There is a sense in which *Henry V* is kind of the ultimate cul-de-sac, and it seems to have been so for Shakespeare, in that he himself was so divided about it that he built that divide into his play. And therefore he even allowed the quarto version, which is only half of the play, to take its place on stage. So *Henry V* has become in a way crucial to my thinking about Shakespeare.

As far as plays ----that I find difficult, I have to admit I think I understand the late plays and nobody else does. I used to think that nobody could really enjoy *All's Well that Ends Well*, but I now think you can, and I've worked out why. I saw a brilliant production last year at the National Theatre directed by Marianne Elliot. All the women are the heroes and do all the work, and all the men are absolute idiots. She did the play in such a feminist context, and it was the only time I've seen the play absolutely make sense. I carefully avoided seeing the Globe's *All's Well*, because I don't think it could be, would be the same experience. I've developed a distaste for a lot of the more popular productions of Shakespeare in recent years because I get to feel too strongly that I can see how the plays work, and the directors often get it wrong. It seems to me there is a negativism or perversity that distorts some recent productions one way or another. I've more and more come to value Shakespeare's plays as plays where the author clearly knows far better what he's doing than do the directors. The idiocy of trying to do *Henry V* in the modern day is a long-lasting grievance of mine. Often it's still got to be a Peter Brookish production if you really want to focus anything. It's sad in a way. I've spent 60 years going to Shakespeare plays, and I have experienced an awful lot of déjà vu over this 60 years.

In a sense, Falstaff is everybody's favorite character. Falstaff is perhaps built from the Shakespeare/Southhampton relationship, with the older man entertaining the younger man. That of course can make Prince Harry the villain, in the rejection of Falstaff. I don't think there's any particular character I'd pick as a favorite, but if I had too, I'd probably say Rosalind. *As You Like It* is such a wonderful play.

I've spent pretty much the last forty years right here, getting the Globe built. That's been a heavy commitment. I used to defend myself against Sam Wanamaker. You might politely say he was a very heavy presence here. But you could always distract him by quoting Shakespeare. That was vital.

Shakespeare can live with incredible complexity. And every step in every play is the resolving of an absolute crisis. For example, *Measure for Measure*, that brilliant play, is so neatly and artfully resolved that it can give an idea of how to work in committees. I used to run the academic committees that were sorting out the design of the Globe. (This went on for years; in fact, it is still going on. I have another of these meetings in a few weeks.) I worked on the Quaker principle, which is totally psychologically devious, where you sit everybody down and you make them stay until they all agree. I sustained this until the very last minute of the very last meeting, where there was an absolutely urgent conflict, and we had to vote. We only had one vote in nine major meetings over the ten years or so. If you continue whittling away, if you continue arguing, it will eventually become obvious, at least to a majority of the people, that there is no place to go but forward in a certain direction.

One of the early lessons we learned is that if you try to make a single small change to the design, it would have an immediate domino effect. If you change one thing, you had to change everything. So we learned early on that you had to be thinking about all the alternative possibilities. The really wonderful thing about Sam's project was his trying to get everybody to agree on single precise events. As long as you had theories, you can keep all sorts of possibilities. But when you have to build something, it's an absolute problem-solving exercise. That's what architects have to do. They have to solve problems. And we had brilliant architects. And brilliant designers. But they all had to agree in the end. And that agreement came about because of an attitude of problem solving. It was a very slow process but I learned problem solving from a variety of techniques. It was always in a sense Shakespearean, in that you always know that the solution in Act V is extremely problematic, but nonetheless it always does sort things out. Everybody is satisfied.

The finding of problems is energizing and utterly unsatisfying, but the solving of problems is massively satisfying. You have to get to an end—that was the Shakespearean principle I was thinking of all the way.

There are masses of evidence in Shakespeare of sticking with the problematic but finding a way through. *Henry V* is the ultimate case. It seems to me the difference between the Folio of *Henry V* and the Quarto of *Henry V* is that in the Folio Shakespeare indulged himself by giving both sides of the question: Is Henry good? Is Henry bad? Is Henry safe? etc.: the heroic Henry who was a massive achiever, as against the absolutely selfish Henry who destroyed all his friends and allies getting to where he wanted to get. And in a sense Shakespeare gave up on *Henry V*. He gave the company a manuscript that gave both sides of the question, the good and the bad. And what the company then did was the Quarto version, which was staged. We can't possibly have an absolutely ambivalent *Henry* on stage. You can't have it both ways. You've got to go for one side or the other. And obviously you've got to go for the heroic Henry. So they rewrote the play, or they stripped down the play, to just the heroic side. And Shakespeare accepted it, despite having written the Folio version of *Henry V,* the one point where he himself decided to stick with his ambivalence.

I love to see productions of *Henry V* that totally ignore features that are in the play. You know that bit where Henry gives the order to kill the prisoners, and immediately on comes Gower saying that the king has decided because of the attack on the baggage train and the killing of the boys that he will have revenge by killing the prisoners, the gallant king. And that's such an obvious misrepresentation of what actually happened. The order for every soldier to kill his prisoners was an immediate and violent response to a threat on the battlefield. The fact the Shakespeare builds in Gower's misunderstanding of the reason for the order is a lovely case of facing both ways. Henry was ruthless, Gower is saying, but Henry had reasons to be ruthless, he was feeling revengeful, etc. He's finding excuses as it were. That seems to me to be Shakespeare sitting on the fence, when he knew damn well that in production you couldn't. So he allowed the company to do the Quarto version, which streamlines it down and gives a much more simple-minded version of the play.

I've seen a lot of productions of *Henry V*, and I've never seen a production that actually succeeds in presenting Henry in a coldblooded light—except Peter Hall's, where Ian Holm, who is a brilliant actor, played Henry as absolutely ice cold all the way through. They did an absolutely marvelous version of the wooing scene in which both Katherine and Henry knew absolutely well that the marriage was inevitable, that it was politically vital. And so they both went through the motions. Hall played it up by having Alice, Katherine's maidservant, be all whoopy and weepy, while Katherine and Henry were both getting bloody impatient with this woman. That was the closest I've seen to a play that gave a cold-blooded Henry, who knew absolutely what he had to do and did it for the sake of retaining his crown. That's a perfect illustration of the way in which Shakespeare on this one occasion, having come to the end of a sequence of four plays, realizing this is the last play, just could not avoid keeping his sitting on the fence position, but was so aware it was an impossible thing to stage that he allowed the company to remake the play into the quarto version, a much simpler play. And every director since then has totally lost that point. For example, the "Once more into the breech" speech is about an attack on the breech that did not work, which was a failure. And Shakespeare builds that failure into the Folio version of the play. But Olivier, for example, made that speech into part of his totally heroic *Henry*. This is one of the clearest problems, where actors get in the way of the play. It's like all those productions of *Richard II*, where you cast your favorite tragic hero as Richard, and you forget all about Bolingbroke. (Mark Rylance at the Globe did a good version of *Richard II*.)

I have the feeling that Shakespeare wanted to be a great poet, but in 1594, for whatever reason, he was coerced into becoming a playwright instead. And therefore he didn't rate his plays as highly as he did the poems he might have written. He wrote *The Rape of Lucrece*, then a few months after it was published, he was enlisted into The Lord Chamberlain's Men. I think that was a decision that was made for him. It made him loads of money, much more money than Daniel, Jonson, or any of the others who chose the way of poetry rather than playwriting. Quite seriously, I don't think Shakespeare valued his plays nearly as much as we do. It's sad in a way, but it seems to me there is a lot of evidence for it, like the fact that he never bothered about publishing his plays.

I think he found it easy to write his plays. There are some seminal plays (like *King John, Hamlet*, the *Henry IV* plays) that are clearly rewrites of Queen's Men plays that the company had acquired. Quite clearly he had such talent at writing that he didn't mind what he was doing. But there are hints in the Sonnets about his choice of going for money rather than fame ("the dyer's hand" and all that). In some ways I feel sorry for Shakespeare in that he felt he was not really given the opportunity to write the great poem. But God, when you read Heywood, Drayton, and all the others about the United Britain and all of that, you feel rather glad that you don't have to plow through another post-Spenserian great poem. We have reasons to be grateful that circumstances conditioned what he did, but I think it's increasingly clear that he always felt slightly that he was writing with his left hand when he was writing prose, and was therefore flippant and light hearted.

I've just done an article in *Notes and Queries* about a reference in *Henry IV Part 1*. It's about the moment when Worcester is trying to talk to Hotspur about their dangerous plot, and he says he's going to open up a book and read Hotspur "matter deep and dangerous,/ As full of peril and adventurous spirit/ As to o'erwalk a current roaring loud/ On the unsteadfast footing of a spear." That's the simile he uses to describe this perilous undertaking. The inevitably pedestrian reading says that walking over a gorge over a sword perilous was standard in some early mythologies. But why a spear and not a sword? It is of course because the "the unsteadfast footing of a spear" is a shaky spear. I have traced several different images of shaking spears as an image of what actors do, you know "the spear shaker." (And there was also False Staff, which is an analogy.) It was his fellow actors who when they issued his early plays in 1597-8, after the writing of *Henry IV*, hyphened his name, "Shake-speare." That was an in-joke about him being a spear shaker. And "the unsteadfast footing of a spear" is throwing this joke back at the actors, and only the actors would pick it up because they were the ones who used the spearshaker image. So it's an in-joke for the actors.

The word "Spearshaker" was first used by Peele in *Edward I* in 1590. And there's a similar play on Shakespeare's name in Greene, "the only Shakescene in the country," which is part of the same game. That was the kind of a joke he was prepared to play with his fellow actors.

My favorite quotation would be "this distracted globe." When Hamlet talks about "this distracted globe," he is not only talking about the skull on his head, the head on his shoulders, but he's also talking about the image of Hercules holding the globe, which was supposed to be the new image of the new company, the reason why it was called the Globe. In this reference to the Globe as being distracted, it's not only Hamlet's head that his driven him to distraction and made him mad. The crowd in the yard at the Globe Theatre is also clearly distracted by these tricks that he's offering them in the play. For me, "this distracted globe" is the ultimate quotation. That one phrase has at least four or five distinct meanings.

Hamlet is my constant play. You live with it all the time. A while ago I read about "the chair of state"—which helps explain why Marcellus says, "Something is rotten in the state of Denmark." When Claudius is giving his speech in Act 1 Scene 2 about how Fortinbras is threatening the state, "thinking by our late dear brother's death/ Our state to be disjoint and out of frame," clearly the chair on which he is sitting is not at all disjoint or out of frame. So that's a reference to the chair of state, or the state as it was called for short. I love when Marcellus much later says something is rotten in the state of Denmark, meaning the nation, but also referring to the throne that Claudius sits on. And being rotten means that the chair of state might look absolutely stable and secure, but actually be unstable.

Bart Van Es did an interesting little piece in *Shakespeare Quarterly* in which he suggested that Shakespeare was not so much an actor, but much more a writer, that there's no evidence of his being an actor until certainly well into the 1590s, and that the idea that he joined the company as an actor rather than as their writer is a very difficult thesis to maintain. Bart was trying to emphasize that Shakespeare's vision of himself was as a poet, and I go along with that—because really Shakespeare had to make the choice. Samuel Daniel was the most obvious model for him because Daniel was writing about—guess what—Richard II from the beginning of his great verse history [*The Civil Wars*]. And of course Shakespeare knew it and copied from it from 1594 onwards. So he was deliberately doing a kind of diminuendo version of the great poem that Daniel had written. And Shakespeare may very well have wanted to write it himself, but Daniel got in first. And the difference in Shakespeare's version and Daniel's is fascinating, because in a sense Daniel went the other way. He had Queen Anne's patronage in 1603, but he never really made money out of it, whereas Shakespeare was making money after money after money from 1594 on. And he even invested in the company in 1599.

I'm reminded of another device I've been interested in, which touches on the issue of how bonded Shakespeare was with his company. When he wrote *The Merchant of Venice*, Richard Burbage had moneylenders knocking on his door—and probably knocking on his head—because Burbage's father James had put all his money into building The Blackfriars. And the Blackfriars had been banned from use by the Privy Council in 1596. And so the moneylenders, who James Burbage had got all the money from, would have been knocking at James Burbage's door until he died in February of 1597.

When Shakespeare was writing *The Merchant of Venice* and creating Shylock, Burbage, who must have played Bassanio, was most aware of the pressures that came from moneylending. It's clear that Shakespeare had good reason for writing *The Merchant of Venice* at that time, the beginning of 1597, when Richard Burbage, who'd inherited the Blackfriars and its debts from his father, was most beleaguered by moneylenders. So Burbage was in a way doing method acting in playing the role. And in the play everything works out— because of Portia. Portia is a victor in the whole thing, she rescues Bassanio, she rescues everybody, she sets it up so they all go off and get married, etc. It's a wonderful version of a totally romantic and unrealistic conclusion to the crisis with Shylock. "It's a mystery," as the Henslowe character says in "Shakespeare in Love." That moneylending connection is an illustration of how conscious Shakespeare was of the whole company, and Burbage in particular, being in big trouble.

And that is the other reason why in 1599, they decided they had to build the Globe. The Burbages had no money; they just provided the timbers from The Theatre. Shakespeare and four other sharers put up a hundred pounds each. The reason why they did it and nobody else was that they had already had that bad experience with moneylenders from the Blackfriars in 1597. They didn't want to deal with moneylenders again. No more Shylocks for them! So I feel that's part of the illustration of Shakespeare becoming slowly, almost involuntarily, bonded with the players. When he became a householder in the Globe in 1599, that was the first absolute commitment he had, putting his money and his belief in the company rather than just doing what circumstances made him do. I think circumstances made him become a playwright in 1594, and he had major doubts.

The long closure of the theatres because of the plague in 1605-9 was a major loss to everybody, and he must have had a lot of time to go back to Stratford then. But he came back to London again. He was evidently in London writing *The Tempest* while Jonson was writing *The Alchemist*, both for the same company, opposite plays that would do well together. I think that after *The Tempest*, 1610, 1611, was when he went back to Stratford for good—because by then some of the older sharers had stopped acting. Armin gave up acting; I think Heminges had given up acting by then and was working as a company manager. Condell was still acting later on, but the younger generation like Lowin and others were in by then.

I think that the point where he gave up the company was 1613, when the Globe burnt down. He was asked for money to help rebuild it, opted not to, and got out. I think that was when he gave up, because there is nothing he evidently wrote after 1613. *The Two Noble Kinsmen* and *Cardenio* were collaborations, and you can write collaborations without actually being on the job. Ernst Honigman has the idea that one possible cause of his retirement was the death of his mother, who was one of the business managers of his affairs in Stratford. Susanna was growing up fast and was his main executor in a sense. There was Anne his wife as well still living in Stratford. But his mother, Mary Arden, died in 1608. And that might have been when he thought he had better go back and look after all the money he had invested in Stratford. His granddaughter Elizabeth was obviously an important figure for him too, and it is interesting that she was called Elizabeth, after the Queen.

There is an incredibly complex piece of archeology going on at New Place. It will be fascinating to find what they put together out of it. There's so little actually known about New Place. I'm beginning to become rather fond of the 18th century guy who bought it then pulled it down. Think about what it would have been like had it survived! He got so fed up with the tourists knocking on his door, which is absolutely understandable.

JEAN HOWARD

"NEVER, NEVER, NEVER, NEVER, NEVER."

Jean E. Howard is George Delacorte Professor in the Humanities at Columbia University, where she chairs the Department of English and Comparative Literature. Her books include **Shakespeare's Art of Orchestration**, **Shakespeare Reproduced: The Text in History and Ideology** *(edited with Marion O'Connor),* **The Stage and Struggle in Early Modern England**, **Engendering a Nation: A Feminist Account of Shakespeare's English Histories** *(with Phyllis Rackin),* **Marxist Shakespeares** *(edited with Scott Shershow), and the four-volume* **Blackwell's Companion to Shakespeare's Works** *(edited with Richard Dutton). She is a co-editor of* **The Norton Shakespeare** *and General Editor of the Bedford contextual editions of Shakespeare. Her most recent book,* **Theater of a City: The Places of London Comedy 1598-1642** *won the 2008 Barnard Hewitt Award for Outstanding Work in Theater History. A past president of the Shakespeare Association of America, she has received Guggenheim, ACLS, NEH, Folger, Huntington, and Newberry Library Fellowships. I talked with her in her office at Columbia University.*

My earliest exposure to Shakespeare was at Brown University. I wasn't taught Shakespeare in high school. So I was a sophomore or a junior when I took Elmer Blistein's "Complete Works of Shakespeare." And he meant the complete works. In one year we read all Shakespeare's plays without exception. It's a style of teaching nobody does anymore. Most people do ten plays a term, and even then some people think you're doing too many. But we did the entire canon, a play a day. That was my introduction to Shakespeare. It was also at Brown that I saw my first performance of Shakespeare, *As You Like It*, which I remember to this day because they had Hymen come in on a pair of stilts, this giant figure of the god of marriage towering over everyone. It was great. I remember that moment very well. I came from a very small town in northern Maine, a farming community where there was no local theater, so I never saw anything before that.

After that, I went to England. I had a two-year Marshall Fellowship from '70 to '72 and I was in London, thank goodness! The Marshall lets you go anywhere. I picked London as my first choice, University College London.

It was when Frank Kermode was there. I got to live in a big city, and that's when I started to go to the theater seriously. I think it was the first fall I was there that I saw Peter Brook's *A Midsummer Night's Dream*, the famous one at the Aldwych. And I saw Judi Dench in *Twelfth Night*. I saw the most astonishing group of plays. Of course, that entire complex below the Thames wasn't open yet, so we used to go to see the Royal Shakespeare Company at the Aldwych Theater in the Strand. And the Old Vic was very important. Ah, to sit up in the gods at the Old Vic! There was other Shakespeare around, and it was just twenty pence to go to the theater. I used to go sometimes two and three nights a week and I never had been to live theater except college theater.

I went to England to be a Miltonist and what I did at University College was an MPhil in Milton. I worked particularly on *Samson Agonistes* and essentially closet drama. At the time I wasn't approaching *Samson Agonistes* because it was drama; I just loved it as text. But when I left England after two years with my MPhil in hand and I went to do my first year at Yale, I switched from being a poetry person to being a drama person—all because of two years of theater in London. It was absolutely transformative. So then I went back and worked with Maynard Mack at Yale and did a dissertation that became my first book, *Shakespeare's Art of Orchestration,* on how the plays are prepared, scripted, and orchestrated for performance.

Yes, Mack was known as an 18th century person. He did all those editions of Milton, Pope, and all, but he also did that series of famous essays. Remember the one about the questions in *Hamlet* and then *King Lear in Our Time*, that short volume? And he'd done one called "The Jacobean Shakespeare," which he called a humble addition to A.C. Bradley. And he planned his entire career to write a book on Shakespearean tragedy; it's the book he never wrote, which is a great pity. When I went to Yale, he was the Shakespearean and Gene Waith was the non-Shakespearean drama person, and I worked with them both. And they were very, very informative—both of them—on my thinking. Mack was simply a great scholar and a very interesting, provocative teacher. For his graduate seminars, he used to do something that I've done a modified version of all my life. He divided the class up into four groups and he would assign each group a task, like to pick out the best essay on this play and tell us about it or—this one is the killer—to act a scene. And then another group had "freedom, high-day, freedom," which meant they could do anything. And he smiled at us the first day, he said, "You think this is going to be the easy one, but you're going to find out this is the hard one." It was a very interactive seminar. He didn't sort of lead it in the old school way. He made people do things with other people collaboratively in a dramatic way. You performed with others. And it taught people to be collaborative, which I think is important in graduate school. Everything can be, especially in those days, competitive. Gene Waith didn't teach Shakespeare but taught the range of drama. I studied plays with him that started with *Gammer Gurton's Needle* and went up to the Restoration. He did wonderful Beaumont and Fletcher. And he was also teaching contemporary drama; I studied Osborne and The Angry Boys in Britain with him. He was doing John Arden and all kinds of contemporary dramatists that nobody else at Yale was touching. So I got quite a good range of dramatic instruction at Yale.

In teaching my graduate seminars I often give the students tasks to do; they have to come in with something. Sometimes it's to lead a class with a set of questions or a short proposition paper. I also often have my students in graduate classes learn to do the tasks they're going to have to do in the profession, like practicing giving a short MLA-style paper where we think about presentation as much as content. Sometimes I have them do book reviews, which they're going to have to do, to learn how to be generous and not mean critics.

Troilus and Cressida is the hardest play for me. I never think I know how to teach it. I have taught it, but I don't have a good way to teach it. I teach it as satire of heroic conventions and so forth, but I find it so alienating that I really have trouble thinking that I'm a good teacher of it. That's my hardest one. I can see because it poses such challenges that it doesn't open you up. I feel it's a failure on my part; it's not the play's fault that I don't have a way in.

My favorite comedy to teach and think about is *A Midsummer Night's Dream*. I think it's magical. I have never known a class that didn't love it. And it so perfectly captures what I think is the heart of Shakespearean comedy, this sense of a dream world that you go into where mysterious transformations can occur. And he built that play in such a marvelous way. It's perfectly constructed! And it has the play of voices between different social groups, which becomes the characteristic of that whole middle part of his career. I think he found it in *A Midsummer Night's Dream*, then he perfected it through the history plays and the great comedies. So I love teaching and thinking about *A Midsummer Night's Dream*.

And I'm drawn tremendously to *King Lear* and always have been. If I was picking out a tragedy as my favorite, it's that one. It's very painful. It's just so elemental. And so much of the bitterest family dynamics of the world are in that play. And then it's made into politics so that the familial and the national meld perfectly. And I find that quite an astonishing feat.

As to characters, I love Rosalind above all: that self-consciousness and wit, with the ability to completely give way to her emotion. She's so smart, so intellectual, and yet so head-over-heels in love. I find that sensibility remarkable in her performative skills. If we have to do favorite Shakespeare characters, of the women characters it's Rosalind, whose intelligence, poise, emotion, and passion, I find the most compelling.

I am very drawn to Shakespeare. I'm talking 35, 40 years. I started teaching in '75 and it's now 2012, and I've taught Shakespeare almost every year for that time. So the modes of thought and emotion, structures of feeling, are so deeply inside me that I can't even say how they affect me, do you know what I mean? I certainly don't go to Shakespeare for any lessons. It's not about lessons. It's about sensibility and feeling the deep structures. Our most profound narratives are about ourselves. And I think you do interiorize some of that, but I at least can't talk about it in any particularly meaningful way.

Two words come to mind: capaciousness and contrapuntal. Capaciousness in that the emotional range and the social range is so great in Shakespeare. I find it is a characteristic he shares with some of the other dramatists of the period, like Webster. But the capaciousness of his vision—and I think of it largely as a social capacity, to register people from the Costards of the world up to the kings with a complete range of expressive devices—is really unusual. And then the contrapuntal for me refers to the way in which every proposition is tested by another proposition in Shakespeare. Sometimes he's just catching the contradictions of the age. But sometimes it's about a kind of balancing of viewpoints that leaves the reader, the theatergoer, to figure out what they really think. That is again a characteristic of the age, but magnified in Shakespeare.

I never really think about Shakespeare's personality, though I've read all the biographies. I like to think of him as a figure of negative capability, someone for whom the age registered its most complex thought and feeling. And I think of him as very capaciously open and that's about as far as I'm willing actually to think about the biography of Shakespeare.

People might think I'm having a depressing day, but the quotation that comes to my mind is "Never, never, never, never, never," which expresses the complete finality of death and oblivion, that you don't come again. The way that is registered at the end of *King Lear* is particularly moving. Maybe as you age what "Never, never, never, never, never" means becomes more real. I don't think it's nihilistic or despairing; it's a fact. And the end of that play shows somebody not wanting to register that fact, but the play registers it, and that's where the tragedy is captured.

NICK HUTCHISON

"NIP NOT THE GAUDY BLOSSOMS OF YOUR LOVE,
BUT THAT IT BEAR THIS TRIAL AND LAST LOVE."

Nick Hutchison is a director, an actor, and a teacher. His directing work includes **Twelfth Night** *(McCoy Theater, Memphis, nominated for nine Ostrander Awards);* Wilton's **Vintage Christmas** *and* **The Taming of the Shrew** *(Wilton's Music Hall);* **Much Ado About Nothing** *and* **Love's Labour's Lost** *(Folger Theatre, Washington DC);* **Crimes of the Heart** *(London);* **The Importance of Being Earnest, Love's Labour's Lost** *and* **Much Ado About Nothing** *(American Shakespeare Center, Virginia), and* **Pinter Short Measures** *(Cheltenham Everyman). For drama schools he has directed* **Dolly West's Kitchen, Playhouse Creatures, The Knight of the Burning Pestle, Pericles,** *and* **Our Country's Good** *(RADA);* **On the Shore of the Wide World** *and* **The Art of Success** *(Mountview), and* **Every Man in His Humour, Our Country's Good, As You Like It, The Taming of the Shrew,** *and* **Pericles** *(BADA).*

Nick's acting work covers television, film, theatre and radio, working with, among others, the RSC, the National Theatre, and the Globe. He has played Hamlet, Romeo, Macbeth, Orsino and Benedick among many Shakespearean roles. He has been frequently seen on TV and film, including the movies **About A Boy, Miss Potter,** *and* **102 Dalmatians.**

Nick lectures on Shakespeare for Shakespeare's Globe, and across Europe and the USA. We talked in a London pub.

Shakespeare opens you to different ways of seeing things. Shakespeare tends not to see in black and white, tends to distrust people who see things in black and white, like Angelo and Isabella in *Measure for Measure*. He's open to other ideas and other thinking. I say to students that Shakespeare believes that the people who see things as black and white are the kind of people who fly planes into tall buildings. So Shakespeare opens you to being more receptive towards other people. What I love about Shakespeare is (we've just been working on some *As You Like It* scenes) that he doesn't patronize the lower classes. He doesn't idealize them, they're not glorified peasants—it's not Marie

Antoinette. But they're not patronized either. When you try and patronize them like Touchstone does Corin, they turn on you—and with considerable integrity. And despite all we talk about living in a patriarchal society, he flagrantly thinks that women are a force for good, and that women are more emotionally mature and powerful than men.

I say to all the actresses I teach and direct that if you're playing a female role in Shakespeare and you've decided that you're a feeble victim, you're playing it wrong. The standard line is that we don't know what Shakespeare thinks because we don't know if he was Catholic or Protestant, blah blah blah. But we do know what Shakespeare thinks about some things. He thinks that good is better than evil and that is better to be kind than to be unkind. He thinks that love, and by love I don't think he means romantic love but serious love, is the ideal. He thinks that patience and endurance are essential.

I don't really care what happens to bread when you put it in your mouth, whether it turns into the body of Christ or not the body of Christ. I do care about the moment where you see someone you thought was dead moving. That's why I find *Pericles*, *Cymbeline*, and *The Winter's Tale* almost unbearable. We all know that the dead don't come back to life, but in *Pericles* for three hours we can see how great it would be if they did. Shakespeare gives you the emotional capability to take that on board.

I'm not interested in cultural icons, I don't want my Shakespeare to be up there on a pedestal. I don't care that he's a money-grubbing bastard. I don't care that he wants to live nicely in a big house because I'd like to live nicely in a big house. I love that he's a practical writer. I love that he kills Lady Montague because he's run out of actors. I love that he sends Hamlet to England because the actor playing Hamlet needs a break. That's the guy I like. I suppose what my Shakespearean life has been about is how his company did it, how they put the plays on, realizing the practical side of Shakespeare. It gets you away from all the iconography and to the man who just happened to write spectacularly good plays.

We banter this horrible word relevance around all the time, but if they're not relevant they're not worth doing. It strikes me that they are completely relevant and not in a down-with-the-kids, let's turn it into rap-speak kind of way. The truths enunciated are eternal. You do meet teachers who are trying to persuade their students that Romeo and Juliet's love is purely platonic even though they marry. But I don't remember as a teenager being so excited about the concept of platonic love. I had other issues to deal with at the time.

We named my elder daughter Beatrice. It means she who blesses and we are spectacularly blessed with her. Again it goes back to the lack of sentimentality, the lack of Hallmark card stuff in Shakespeare. Don Pedro says to Beatrice, "out of question, you were born in a merry hour." And Beatrice says, "No, sure, my lord, my mother cried; but then there was a star danced, and under that was I born." Childbirth hurts, but what you get out of it is a dancing star. My wife would punch you in the face if you said childbirth was a metaphysical experience. It hurts. Shakespeare's not allowing Don Pedro to romanticize childbirth; it's damn painful, but then you get Beatrice.

Adrian Noble said, "You really won't get the late plays until you have children. And you won't really get the late plays until you have daughters." I kind of laughed at the time but now that I'm older and have daughters I realize how right he is. And Shakespeare knew what it was what it would be like to lose a child like Hermione does. I find his characters' trust in the reformative power of love very moving.

I think I decided Shakespeare was going to be a part of my life, not necessarily a professional part of my life but an integral part, when I was very young. I had an incredible drama teacher when I was at school, Robert Avery. In my first year at school, when I was about 13, he put on *King Lear*. (There were older kids, 16- or 17-year-olds in it.) It was fantastic. I remember listening to the Lear speech about "Let's away to prison" and just thinking that's the most beautiful thing I'd ever heard. From then on, I really loved Shakespeare. We did an extraordinary, very modern, very fascist, production of *Coriolanus*, loads of leather, which some parents walked out of because they were so shocked. This instantly put me onto Shakespeare's side!

Patrick Spottiswoode got me very involved in the Globe when I was 26 or 27, meeting Sam Wanamaker, running some of the first workshops at the Globe, and being in the first workshop company. I immediately felt the Globe was a special place. That's when I first started to understand about the stage and the way it works, the way that Shakespeare writes for actors. I really started to get interested and went out of my way to make Shakespeare my special subject.

I'm working with the Young People's Theater at the moment, which is 16- and 17-year-olds. You'd think that you're teaching and not very much would come back the other way. But recently we were looking at a little scene from *Cymbeline*, and I was talking about Cloten. There was a Dutch kid in the class and he came up to me and said, "I know you'll know this, but do you know what Cloten means in Dutch?" I said, "No." He said, "Would Shakespeare have known Dutch?" and I said, "Highly likely he would have known Dutch people because there were so many Dutch merchants in London and he was living in Silver Street, in the middle of I believe a European area." He said, "Well in Dutch 'Cloten' means 'balls.'" I didn't know that!

The first Shakespeare I directed was *Much Ado About Nothing* in Virginia, which was an extraordinary experience. I was still mostly working as an actor, but Ralph Alan Cohen and Jim Warren gave me the directing job. I'd directed before, but I'd never directed a whole Shakespeare play. It was glorious to have the chance to shape the whole thing. I also did *Love's Labour's Lost* for the American Shakespeare Company, which I loved doing. It was a fantastic cast and it's my favorite play. *Love's Labour's Lost* is an extraordinary piece, a) because it's written by such a young man and b) because Shakespeare takes a format, comedy, and makes it not end happily. This makes the play amazingly powerful. The boys think they know what's going to happen, that they're in a comedy, but suddenly Mercadé appears, they're not in a comedy any more, and they don't know how to deal with that. The women do, of course, and the men don't. The princess of France is one of my favorite characters because she has integrity stamped through her like rock. The speech to the king at the end where she just says marriage is "a world-without-end bargain" strikes me as one of the most beautiful. The point is the same in *As You Like It*, the understanding that marriage is not about young love. It's about Hymen's "blessed bond or board and bed." It's about whom you're having breakfast with in 50 years.

The production I did of *Much Ado* at the Folger in 2005 was the happiest professional moment of my life. I'd seen the work of and become friendly with Kate Eastwood Norris, who played Beatrice for me, and we hatched the plan to do it together and pitched to the Folger. Apart from being away from home, which I don't like, every day I was thinking, "I can't believe I get up and I go in and in the morning I get to look at folios and quartos, which you just call up, and in the afternoon I get to direct a sensational cast in the most wonderful play."

I also loved directing *Pericles* because it's such a difficult but such a beautiful play. Suddenly seeing through it, the clouds shift, and you see how this play works. I'm skeptical that it's a collaboration with Wilkins. It's a magical play. One of the things I love about Shakespeare is that when he's at his simplest, he's at his best. I can't hear Thaisa's line when she meets the daughter that she thought had died in childbirth, Marina, and she has four words. She just says, "Bless'd, and mine own!" that line chokes me up because it's just so simple. There's nothing more to say. I love that the greatest wordsmith we've ever had knows that words can only do so much.

I saw Simon Russell Beale last year in *A Winter's Tale*. I love his acting. I remember sitting there thinking any minute now he's going to say, "Oh, she's warm" and I'm going to explode into tears. And he did and I did. Part of the joy can be knowing what's coming. It's like, oh this is going to hurt, but this is gorgeous. I've never acted in a Shakespeare play where I've really felt the magic I've felt when I'm directing. I think that's partly because as an actor you're so concentrated on what you're doing, whereas in directing you take the whole thing on.

I'm a huge fan of Adrian Noble. I was in his *Cymbeline* at Stratford. I remember doing a monologue in *Cymbeline* and by the time I was finished with it I was so far down the line that I'd lost sight of where I'd started. And he just said to me, "What's the overwhelming emotion you're playing in this monologue?" And I said, "I suppose it's amazement." So he said, "Why don't you try playing it amazed?" I went, "Yeah, that's a thought"—because I'd spent so much time sort of doing all this other stuff. The other director who I think is a genius in terms of his take on the text is Peter Hall. The older I get the more I go with his description of himself as an iambic fundamentalist. Shakespeare writes in verse for a reason. If he didn't, he could just write the whole thing in prose and make it all easier.

One of the things that stuck with me was the first piece of Shakespeare I saw at Stratford. We had a school trip and saw Trevor Nunn's famous *Comedy of Errors*, the one with Judi Dench and Mike Williams. I just sat there going, "Well, if that's Shakespeare I want in." It was so funny and so cool and so unbelievably well-choreographed. Nunn turned it into a semi-musical. At the end, what is the rhyming couplet? "We came into this world like brother and brother/ And now let's go hand in hand, not one before the other." They turned it into a five-minute song during the course of which they all ran down to the front of the stage, and then into the audience, dancing with the audience. I thought, "This is it. If this is what Shakespeare can do, I want to be a part of this." You name a joke, they got it in. It was fabulous. Purists could say it's not how Shakespeare did Shakespeare, but I think Shakespeare would have stood and applauded to the rafters.

When I direct a Shakespeare play, I like to find a passage, a little touchstone to give the whole cast. In *Love's Labour's*, my favorite, my touchstone phrase is, "A jest's prosperity lies in the ear/ Of him that hears it, never in the tongue/ Of him that makes it." That seems to be the key to where Berowne goes wrong. He thinks being funny is good in its own right, while Rosaline and the Princess realize the damage you are causing with your oh-so-clever aristocratic wit, that is not just damaging to other people but damaging to you. Rosaline describes this kind of wit as "wormwood" in your brain. When I did *As You Like It* my touchstone line was, "Men have died from time to time and worms have eaten them, but not for love." And in *Pericles*, Thaisa in the last scene, says, "Did you not name a tempest,/ A birth, and death?" For me, that's what that play is all about. For *Shrew*, I used Petruccio talking to

Baptista, saying, "And where two raging fires meet together,/ They do consume the thing that feeds their fury." It's important that he says two raging fires because he's bracketing himself with Katherina, saying, "We are alike." It's not, "I need to extinguish her raging fire." It's, "We will extinguish each other." I think that she helps him as much as he helps her. It seems useful to have something that you can always brush up against and say, "Does that help?" And the touchstone would vary from production to production.

What makes something Shakespearian, from my point of view, is not to do with feeding words into a computer or going de-dum-de-dum-de-dum. I would characterize it as a generosity of spirit. If the writing doesn't have generosity, then the characters don't. And if the writing doesn't have generosity, then I would have a problem with it being Shakespeare. It's no coincidence that the *Thomas More* section that we think is Shakespeare is about trying to think what it's like to be an immigrant. In that instant, there is generosity. In *Coriolanus* he doesn't have that prettified view of the masses, nor does he think there shouldn't be a hierarchy. But ultimately he needs everybody to have a generosity of spirit; that's what I see in him. But, I have to say, you don't necessarily see it in his life. You look at Katherine Duncan-Jones' *Ungentle Shakespeare* and her discussion of the whole Stratford enclosure thing, and you think, "Okay, he's not necessarily the cutting edge of the resistance." But hell, he's got it in the plays. We can't all live what we believe.

As to a favorite quotation, I think it has to be from *Love's Labour's Lost*, from the Princess of France. There are so many great phrases in her last speech. The part that makes me cry the most is when she says, "If this austere, insociable life…/Nip not the gaudy blossoms of your love,/ But that it bear this trial and last love." Shakespeare was interested in what will go on. He doesn't think it's clever to die young. He doesn't think it's clever to be *Antony and Cleopatra*, messily and clumsily committing suicide. What he cares about is to "bear this trial and last love."

MICHAEL KAHN

"IT'S TOO CORNY TO SAY, 'THE PLAY'S THE THING.'"

Michael Kahn is the Artistic Director of the Shakespeare Theatre Company in Washington, D.C., which under his leadership has grown from residence at the Folger Shakespeare Library to the Lansburgh Theatre to the Sidney Harman Hall. He has directed plays on and off Broadway and at regional theaters, and opera at various venues. He held the position of Richard Rodgers Director of the Drama Division of the Juilliard School from 1992 to 2006. With the Shakespeare Theater Company and in conjunction with George Washington University, he created the Academy for Classical Acting, a one-year graduate program in acting Shakespeare and other classical texts. He has also been on the faculties of New York University Graduate School of the Arts, the Circle in the Square Theatre School, and Princeton University. He has received the Saturday Review Award, multiple Vernon Rice Award nominations, a Tony Award nomination, a MacArthur Award, a Joseph Jefferson Award nomination, two New Jersey Critics' Awards, the Daily News Critics' Citation, and multiple Helen Hayes Award nominations and wins. We talked in a quiet room he found for us downstairs at the Sidney Harman Hall.

My mother was a Russian immigrant, and she read, but she was self-educated for the most part. She had read *A Tree Grows in Brooklyn*, which was a popular novel, and in that novel, the Irish immigrant mother reads Shakespeare to her daughter. My mother worked. She had a dress shop and she would come home at about 5:00 or 5:30 at night. Basically the only time I spent with my parents was after dinner and before going to bed. And inspired by *A Tree Grows in Brooklyn*, my mother would read me Shakespeare— not *Tales of Shakespeare*, not Charles and Mary Lamb, but actually Shakespeare. Therefore, for a couple of years I heard all Shakespeare's plays. Obviously I didn't understand them. I was four or five, maybe a little bit older, but not a whole lot.

By the time I was going to school I don't think my mother was reading to me; I think I was reading. So I knew the characters and some of the stories. But I didn't think about them. We had these three very tall, heavy, leather-bound volumes of Shakespeare, with extraordinary illustrations. Those were around the house all the time.

I was brought up in New York, and when I was in my teens, I was taken to the theater a lot. I saw productions of Shakespeare in New York City by Maurice Evans and Judith Anderson and people like that. So, I guess I wanted to be in the theater since I was about four or five.

But it wasn't until college when I actually directed Shakespeare. I directed *Pericles*, very badly. I had a very good Shakespeare professor in college at Columbia named Andrew Chiappe. He never published, but he was very famous. His classes were huge lectures. And he was also my advisor. He was a Jamesian kind of gentleman, but he took an interest in me. And he sort of championed me even when the school newspaper didn't like *Pericles*. He spoke against that reviewer in his class. He said of the reviewer, "You bit the hand that feeds you."

It's funny that Shakespeare was always in my life. But I didn't plan to be a classical director until I was in college and realized that I wasn't that interested in the plays I was seeing on Broadway. In college I discovered how interesting doing a play of Shakespeare was and then it became something that clearly interested me. It wasn't how I started because I started out as an avant-garde director, doing everyone's new plays. Once I realized that Shakespeare was complex and interesting and challenging, I found myself really excited by it.

In my late 20s, I was asked by Joseph Papp to direct *Measure for Measure* in Central Park, and I have been doing Shakespeare ever since. So— even though there was a hiatus in my doing Shakespeare—I found and still find that the complexity of the text and of what Shakespeare is asking us to think about is more interesting than almost anything anybody else writes for the theater.

I'm asked about my favorite play a lot. I used to say, "Well, I like all the runts of the litter like *All's Well That Ends Well*." But although I've never done all of it—the full two parts of it as two parts—I would say that the breadth of *Henry IV, Parts 1 and 2* is miraculous to me, that it covers, really, life. I did put them together once to make an evening of *Henry IV*, which was extremely satisfying. I think the richness of both parts, independently, is unparalleled. So that's my favorite, if I had a favorite—only because I think there is everything in those plays that anyone could imagine in terms of human existence. There's class and family and power and war and…. It's an extraordinary, extraordinary play. And someday maybe I will do both parts independently. It's very hard to do *Part II* unless you are doing *Part I*. For the audience, you really need *Part I* to make *Part II* alive enough. So you don't usually program *Part II* in a separate season.

I find the autumnal quality of *Part II* to be amazing. It has a real dying fall, as Orsino says in *Twelfth Night*.

Because we are in Washington, I'm asked all the time about political figures in Shakespearean terms. I would be asked, for example, if Bush II was Prince Hal? And I used to say, "Well, he might have been Prince Hal, but he certainly wasn't Henry V in the best sense of the word. And while he was Henry V in the worst sense, behaving illegally, he didn't have the stature of Henry V."

Do I identify with any Shakespeare characters? You know, as a director, I find that in order to work well, I have to identify with all the characters. I can't direct an actor in a role if somehow I haven't investigated being that character in some imaginative way. But I don't wake up in the morning and say 'I am this,' or 'I am that.' I don't really feel myself as a Shakespeare character, probably because I have too much respect for the ability for Shakespeare to create such complex characters that I don't see myself as endowed as some of those characters. But when I work I am all of them, at some time. I have to be.

I say to my actors at the first rehearsal, "I understand everything about this play probably better than you do today, but by the end of the rehearsal you will know your characters better than I ever will, though I will probably still know the play better than you because my job is the play and your job is the person." So I think the actors' job is to uncover and inhabit the character as written, filtered through their own experience. Mine is to uncover the play, present the play, obviously filtered through my own experience. It has to be out of my own experience, but still as true as far as I can tell to what the play-wright's intention was. That doesn't mean the interpretation doesn't change. When I do a play ten years later the interpretation will change because there will be parts of the play that will reveal themselves to me more strongly than they did ten years before, or my own experience has made me understand something that I didn't quite understand before. So the actor is meant to be his character or her character, and my job is to fit that into a sort of orchestration of the whole event.

Certainly I'm surprised that I was fortunate enough to do this kind of material when I was young. When I come back to a play, I'm somewhat humbled by how little I knew about it the first time around. When I was young, I was supposed to do *King Lear*, but it didn't happen. And I can't imagine what I would have done with it without having the experience of either my parents aging or myself aging or some awareness of senility, much less of awareness of evil and of children. There are some plays that experience helps you understand better. And some plays really should be done when you are young. In a way, you should do *Romeo and Juliet* the first time when you are young because it doesn't really work with a nostalgic point of view. The director of *Romeo and Juliet* is much better to be in the thick of it. And in a way that's probably true about *Twelfth Night*, although I didn't get to do *Twelfth Night* until I was older. And since it is the most perfect comedy ever written, I enjoyed the unbelievable skill of the play's construction. But now when I come back to plays, I of course see them as an older director. I see them more as about the play than I do as about myself. When I was a young director, I saw the plays more as about myself and about what I would do with them. Now I'm more interested in what the play inspires me to investigate.

Does a play change anybody or do the experiences of life change people? I suspect the largest changes that have influenced me are from my life. But what I discovered in Shakespeare that has been profound for me is his building of character out of contradictions. And if you could see that in a play, then you could accept human beings in a different way. On good days I am more tolerant of people's ambiguity—well, contradictions—than I would have been if I hadn't done Shakespeare. And I am more aware and willing to live with ambiguity because that is the truth of Shakespeare. Those things have affected me profoundly in how to see life. But life has helped me to recognize those qualities of Shakespeare. I can't know what my life would have been like if I had basically been doing Broadway comedies or musicals or television. I assume it would have been different, I think less rich, but who knows?

Of course, working with Shakespeare makes you appreciate language, but I think what it has taught me most is about character and to live with some amount of uncertainty. I think the most subversive part of Shakespeare is that he's not a moralist. I appreciate scholars, but a scholar's job is to make a case for a point of view; otherwise why would that book be published compared to another one, even if the point of view is that Shakespeare is ambiguous? And I don't know whether scholars, who are obviously brilliant people, change their minds during the course of an investigation of an author over a lifetime. I know that artists do. What I thought about a play in 1960 and what I think about a play now is usually considerably different. The play is the same, but as a result of experience and immersion I can see the play, hear the play, or bring something to the play so that it speaks to me in a richer way. I would be disappointed if I came to a play ten years later and I repeated the production—though I would certainly remember in terms of skill the things that worked and the things that were for me still true.

For instance, when I did *Measure for Measure* the first time, my first big Shakespeare for Joe Papp, it certainly was a black comedy, with Angelo sort of a Tartuffian character in a black comic world. When I came back to it years later in Washington, especially during an NEA controversy, I was aware that Angelo was a man trapped in a job he shouldn't have, in a society that was in serious trouble, and was unable to handle all that except in a kind of fundamentalist way. And people turn to fundamentalism in situations that are too difficult, so that some set of immutable rules, Draconian rules—whatever you want to call them—seem attractive. But why does Shakespeare have Angelo forgiven at the end of the play? I don't like some productions now because of how Isabella doesn't speak at the end. I don't like all those productions that have dark endings. It's called *Measure for Measure* for a reason. There are people who come from very extremist points of view, either religion or morality but those extremist points of view are tempered by reality and eventually by human understanding. So I wanted to understand why Shakespeare forgave Angelo. And in thinking about that I began to see how difficult it was to be Angelo.

In the same way, there is a little video of me on Big Think that talks about how when I first did *Henry V* (which was during the Vietnam War) I saw it as a kind of anti-war play. I saw all the wrong things that Henry did, but I didn't quite know what to do with the heroic speeches. I had to undercut them. By the time I did it again, still not thinking that it celebrates war in any way, I saw how it does explore the difficulties of being a leader. You do bad things. You do good things. You are heroic. You are petty. You are idealistic and you are very much a part of realpolitik. So I have learned that and am somewhat more tolerant because of that—of politics and people. I'm not tolerant of extremists: I wish they would see *Measure for Measure*. But I am more understanding of the difficulties of people in such difficult positions. Being sympathetic doesn't mean I agree with them, but that I am sympathetic or empathetic in terms of what difficulties this man was thrust into.

I finally understood *Othello* when I did it the last time. I did it before, with the Othello as the older man that Shakespeare writes, with an actor who was willing at that time because he had done it before when younger. But I began to realize that Othello and Desdemona have had had no experience in relationships. With Othello, there is no mention of another woman—except maybe when Iago says he thinks Othello slept with Emilia, which is very debatable because they don't seem to know each other terribly well in the play. Directors latch on to that all of the time, but it is really not in the text except for one sentence said by a psychopath. Othello and Desdemona have had no experience at having a relationship, and there is a large age difference, and then they are shipped off to an island in the middle of a war, or not quite a war, just an island, a sort of all-male island. Desdemona has no friends except Iago and Emilia, and Cassio eventually. Othello has never been with a young wife and he's aware that he's older. And he's easily preyed upon. So the play is less to me about jealousy as a tragic flaw. (I was brought up on all the tragic flaws; I was also brought up on Shakespeare and world order. I'm not sure I believe in any of that stuff any more.) I don't think that jealousy was necessarily Othello's tragic flaw. I think he was placed in a situation where his insecurities forced him to be jealous because somebody else was preying on those insecurities. So it makes for a very different production if you see this general as a human being, not just a raging, jealous maniac, but somebody, who, in spite of himself, because of his past, because of his present, falls into jealousy. And it eventually gave a much, much truer portrayal for me and for the audience. I understood Othello; he was no longer a symbol of some humor, but was actually a man in a difficult situation that he had no equipment to handle. And I don't think Angelo had the equipment to handle his situation either.

When I did *Richard II* last year I understood that Richard II was a classic narcissist. So I read a lot about narcissism and I began to see his insecurity, how his self-image needs to be so elevated because it is so easy to destroy. That allowed Michael Hayden to play that part in a real way that made Richard's mood changes make sense. That understanding came from just being older and knowing more and more about psychology. It continually fascinates me that Shakespeare is absolutely true psychologically without having any formal psychological training. I would have thought that Freud could have learned as much from Shakespeare as he could from dreams. Shakespeare clearly learned it from life. Shakespeare was obviously a wildly empathetic person to be able to understand as much as he understood.

I guess what is "Shakespearean" as opposed to something else is that Shakespeare's exploration of the world is done in incredible language. So you have a pretty specific form in which many things are investigated. You have passion in a form; you have murder in a form; you have exploration— but you also have a poet—and you don't get that many other places. I'd guess Shakespeare's ambition really was to understand the world—or man's nature in the world, or quite frankly man's nature in the universe—but he did it in a form that's highly organized. So my answer to "What is Shakespearean" is probably and particularly the tension between the form and the passions of the characters.

Shakespeare's ambition was huge as to what is possible to be done on the theatrical platform, and most of the time he achieved it. But not all the time. I don't think every play of Shakespeare is a great play. It is easy to make a case—though maybe he didn't write it all—that *Cymbeline* is not a great play. *Pericles* is not a great play. *Two Gentlemen of Verona* is just a charming play.

I'd be happy to make a case for *Coriolanus* as being great. But my audiences don't like *Coriolanus*. Every time I announce I'm going to do it, they get a chance to say what they don't like about it very much. I do it anyway. I had a good time with it the last time I did it. Then there is a play like *Love's Labours Lost*. I saw it when I was young in a production directed by Laurence Olivier and it wasn't funny or anything. I did it in a kind of modern version a few years later and it was a big hit. So, you know, in that case, was it that Olivier's production didn't bring out all that was in the play? Or did my production add something to the play to make it more palatable, to enjoy the wordplay, and give it a different kind of life? I don't know. But I do know that the greatest plays of Shakespeare are the greatest plays ever written.

But the play that almost always bores me is *The Tempest*. The first act is putting Miranda to sleep. (It is very hard for me in watching the play not to feel like Miranda.) The second act is introducing the villain. The third act is introducing the clown. It takes forever. And yet when I saw it in Italian by Giorgio Strehler, I thought it was an amazing production. Without really good direction *The Tempest* can send me to slumber-land. And I've done one that wasn't so good.

People always ask, "Did Shakespeare write them?" and my facile answer is, "I'm not changing the name on the theater or our stationery." (But the other thing is that I want to stop reading about the Earl of Oxford.) I cannot believe, since Shakespeare's plays were successful in his lifetime, that on somebody's deathbed there wouldn't be a little note under his pillow saying, "Well, believe it or not, I wrote *Hamlet*." It is just not in human nature to keep that a secret for a lifetime and then have it kept after you're dead. It is not possible; somebody would have said something.

And I think it is a crummy class-thing to say that a middleclass person couldn't know all those things. Mozart did, Picasso did. Why couldn't Shakespeare be a genius? Why does he have to be somebody else? But I honestly don't care, because whoever wrote them was a genius. I've done all the plays, and sometimes I think more than one person wrote them anyway. But partly I think he was like Picasso, interested in changing styles. His curiosity was great.

And I know all of the theories about why Shakespeare stopped writing. I think he might have written himself out, which playwrights do. And secondly, he may not have wanted to write for the theater that had then become popular. I don't think he really enjoyed doing masques. I think the masque in *The Tempest* is fun to read when all is said and done, but I don't think he wanted particularly to write about shipwrecks and pirates and exotic Indians wandering around. He was writing about people's souls in different forms, and once that was no longer what people wanted, he stopped.

As to a favorite quotation, please pick one for me, because I literally go dead when I am asked that question. I could find one maybe, but I don't have one right now. It's too corny to say, "The play's the thing." Actually I do believe it is—but then again, no, I don't.

PETER LICHTENFELS

*"THERE ARE MORE THINGS IN HEAVEN AND EARTH, HORATIO,
THAN ARE DREAMT OF IN YOUR PHILOSOPHY."*

*Peter Lichtenfels, since 2003 a professor of Theatre and Dance at
the University of California, Davis, is a professional theatre director
and writer on Shakespeare and contemporary performance. At UC
Davis, he created exchanges with Shakespeare's Globe London, and
the Shanghai Theatre Academy, and directed* **Romeo and Juliet**,
A Midsummer Night's Dream, *and* **Cymbeline**, *among other
plays. From 1981-1991, he was the Artistic Director of the
Traverse Theatre in Edinburgh and Theatre Director at the
Leicester Haymarket Theatre. Between 1991 and 2003, he combined his professional theatre directing with an academic post at
Manchester Metropolitan University, the only university conservatory program in the UK. He has just completed a co-written book,*
Negotiating Shakespeare's Language in Romeo and Juliet
*(Ashgate 2008), accompanied by a full critical edition on the web
(http://www.romeoandjulietedition.com/). His 2008 production
of* **A Midsummer Night's Dream** *for the Dramatic Arts Centre
in Shanghai won "Best Production" by the Shanghai International
Arts Festival.*

I think the first time Shakespeare really dawned on me was in high school.
I grew up in Canada as an immigrant kid from Germany. In high school,
maybe grade nine, we had to read *Julius Caesar*, which was the first play
everybody did in those days; it was about civic duty and how not to kill your
leader. I immediately connected Shakespeare's language with the language of
the King James Bible, a little bit which we read each morning before classes
began. Shakespeare was not a totally foreign language.

I read Shakespeare plays at university but never with the thought
of directing them. At Queen's University in Kingston, I had intended to
study intellectual history and English. But a senior theater major who
was detailed to look after me that first week at university asked "Why
don't you take a theatre course?" I needed one more course, I thought
theatre would be an easy diversion from my real studies and signed up.
During the first or the second week of term, we had to go to the
theater. It was my first time—I had never been before. Right there

and then it was clear to me that was what I wanted to do with the rest of my life.

We were required to go see a play in Toronto, which was 180 miles away. It was Peter Brook's RSC production of *A Midsummer Night's Dream*, the first professional play that I saw. I loved it. Though it was in a huge "airplane hangar" of a theatre, and the set was the size of a squash court, I was "transported." That was my first Shakespeare. After graduating I moved to Edinburgh, saw a memorable *Macbeth* directed by Yukio Ninagawa, at the Edinburgh Festival. It had a totally different rhythm, and artistic sensibility, but not any less breathtaking.

In those moments of rapture and decision I only ever wanted to be a theatre director. I was incredibly lucky to get work at the Traverse Theatre in Edinburgh for about twelve years, doing new plays by new writers. It was an amazing place of which I also became Artistic Director. And at some point I needed to move away from only working with young playwrights, reading new plays all the time. I wanted to begin a conversation with playwrights from the past. That was when I began to read Shakespeare seriously. I must have been around thirty-three years old.

In 1992, I came to UC Davis for the first time as the Grenada Artist in Residence. I did *Tartuffe*, and it went really well. I started working with Liz Carlin, the voice teacher in the Theater Department at that time. And I started working on Shakespeare with the students, I think it was *Richard III*. She was instrumental in teaching me how to begin reading the language. Then I spent the next four, five, six years reading the language and finding ways of opening it up, ways of speaking it and ways of reading it. That more than anything changed me. I became fascinated with the many, many ways you can unpack the language.

I worked on *Romeo and Juliet* with my partner (Lynette Hunter) for 13 years. After 13 years I could still ask questions of the language, and the language still repaid my attention. It hadn't died in any way. I love the language, the way it creates spaces and the way it opens your imagination—in the ways it slows you down. Working with Shakespeare's language is a practice. When I work with the students, I work mostly with the words. Students need to learn how to unpack the language, open up their reading.

For me the "Shakespearean" is always the language Shakespeare. The words bring something forth into the palpable, into affect, which the actor brings into their body, finds way of materializing it, and then lets them disappear as other take their place. It is always a process. If the actors are good, the process continues with the audience.

I'm sure the people in Elizabethan times didn't speak in Shakespearean language either. The artifice of Shakespeare's language heightens it, distills

it, and makes you be attentive to the language. I love other Jacobean playwrights, but the level of the language that they're working on doesn't have
that space or expanse that Shakespeare's language has. Even when you stick
with it, it doesn't release as much as Shakespeare's.

Another joy about Shakespeare is the sense of being in a world, and of the
world at the same time. This is one reason he is always in fashion.

Park Honan's is the Shakespeare biography I like best. I like it because,
in a way, it is not a biography. He just asks, "What kind of school was he at?"
And then looks at what the schools taught. He then looks at farming, and so
on. And so he builds up a picture of Shakespeare that, for me, is much more
evocative than the kind of biographic fallacy of "he was like this" or "he
was like that." I am fascinated that Shakespeare hides himself. The way he is
always, yet never, there.

Politically, in terms of the plays, he has conservatism. His plays serve as
the popular understanding of Britain coming into its modern history. He
wrote for the people that had money, and (perforce) in Elizabethan England,
leisure time.

As far as favorite plays, I'm very fond of *Henry IV, part 2, Hamlet, King
Lear,* and *Romeo and Juliet*. Of course, my favorites change. When I direct a
play, I do that play because it has something to do with my body. So *Henry
IV, part 2,* for me, is a meditation on ageing, where the spirit is young but
the body gets older. It's funny, wistful and has sadness about it. But there are
some plays that I'm not inordinately fond of, like *The Tempest*. I don't know why.

I don't really think in terms of favorite characters. As a director, you have
to love them all. But I do, for one, really like the Scrivener in *Richard III*, how
he is compromised because he doesn't have power. And I like the townspeople
who have to go to Baynard's Castle, where Buckingham tries to cajole them
into crowning Richard, and they say nothing. I love that act of resistance. So
those two come to mind.

A quotation that resonates with me comes from *Hamlet*, "There are more
things in heaven and earth, Horatio,/ Than are dreamt of in your philosophy."
It is famous, and overused, but it resonates with me because there are many
kinds of intelligences and many kinds of knowledge with which to learn.
There's traditional knowledge, passive knowledge, rational knowledge, knowledge through touch, knowledge through words. I relate to the multiplicity of
ways of communicating. For example, I probably learn more about a person
through just a gentle touch on the shoulder than I do speaking to him or her.

RUSS MCDONALD

"I WAS ADORED ONCE TOO."

Russ McDonald was Professor of English and Comparative Literature at Goldsmiths College, University of London. Previously he taught at University of North Carolina (Greensboro), where the Carnegie Foundation named him 2003 North Carolina Professor of the Year. He also spent a decade directing the Teaching Shakespeare Institute for secondary school teachers at the Folger Shakespeare Library. His books include **The Bedford Companion to Shakespeare: An Introduction with Documents***;* **Shakespeare and the Arts of Language** *(Oxford Shakespeare Topics);* **Shakespeare's Late Style***;* **Look to the Lady: Sarah Siddons, Ellen Terry, and Judi Dench on the Shakespearean Stage***; and* **Shakespeare and Jonson***. He is co-editor of* **Shakespeare Up Close: Reading Early Modern Texts** *(a volume of essays in honor of Stephen Booth) and, most recently,* **The Bedford Shakespeare***. I interviewed him in London, in the Members' Room of the Tate Modern Museum.*

My first experience with Shakespeare was in high school reading *Julius Caesar*. It was an advanced class, so I had to read another play on my own. I chose *As You Like It*. I didn't like it. I didn't understand it. Part of the problem I think is that there's so much prose in that play and without having any help, it's hard to get. So that was pretty negative. *Julius Caesar* was okay. We had to memorize speeches. It was an old-fashioned mid-twentieth century style pedagogy and it wasn't good.

And then my life changed in my senior year in high school. I was in Houston, at an inner-city high school. It had been a great high school, but it wasn't a great high school when I went to it. We had a terrific 12th grade English teacher, Avis Hartley, who was so demanding, so intolerant of any foolishness, and so inspiring. I thought she was about 80 at the time; she was probably about 40. She's dead now. It was a tremendous class in that we started with Richardson's *Pamela* and then we read *The Canterbury Tales*, Jane Austen's *Emma*, a whole slew of things, up through George Eliot. And in that year we read *Twelfth Night*, *Macbeth*, and *Antony and Cleopatra*. That changed my life altogether.

Then I went to college at Duke. In my junior year I took a year-long Shakespeare course with George Walton Williams, who is still alive. He turns 90 in October. I had lunch with him last month. That was a wonderful experience. Williams' Shakespeare course more or less determined that when I went to graduate school I wanted to work in the Renaissance.

I also had a great teacher in Renaissance Drama in graduate school at Penn, Robert Y Turner. He didn't publish very much, but he was a tremendous teacher. And he actually didn't teach Shakespeare. So I wrote my doctoral dissertation on Ben Jonson rather than on Shakespeare because I wanted to work with him. That's common: a lot of students choose the teacher and then love whatever subject the teacher works on.

I don't read Shakespeare's plays for content. I don't worry very much about Shakespeare's politics, sexual politics, or other problems like that. This is a very traditional, conventional view, but it seems to me that in all the plays for everything we find offensive there's a balance that cancels that offense or at least makes us aware that it may be offensive and that there are other points of view as well. *The Merchant of Venice* is a good example, or *Taming of the Shrew*, or any of those plays that have political crudeness.

I go in phases. Right now I'm tired of *The Tempest*. But then I'll see a wonderful production of a play. At the moment my three favorite plays are the two *Henry IV*'s, *Coriolanus*, and *Twelfth Night*. *Twelfth Night* is an easy choice. Stephen Booth, in a wonderful line, said that *Twelfth Night* is the most beautiful manmade object in the world. I started to try to direct a production of *Twelfth Night* when I was in college and gave it up immediately. But I was in a production of *Twelfth Night* in college. I was the clown, which is a great part. I do think *Twelfth Night* is nearly perfect in spite of all the confusions about Viola's talking about her singing but never singing, and Fabian coming along to take the clown's place in garden scenes for reasons that are never explained. Those sorts of things must have had to do with the construction of the company, the furnishing of actors, boys' voice changes, and other physical practicalities. I love that play.

I love the two *Henry IVs* because they are such an imaginatively rich meditation on failure and disease and old age. I tell my students that they're not old enough to read them, but that they can go back to them in 20- or 30-years' time. And *Coriolanus* I love because of the paradox that his great talent is also the thing that destroys him. *Coriolanus* seems to fit that tragic paradox that Shakespeare uses in every play: the thing that does the hero in is what makes him great. I also love *Macbeth*, perhaps for musical reasons. I remember in high school walking down the hall repeating to myself, "Is execution done on Cawdor? Is execution done on Cawdor?" because there's

a strange musicality about it. Much of *Macbeth* is like that. That duet between
Lady Macbeth and Macbeth around the murder is almost like singing. The
extravagance of *Antony and Cleopatra* is also poetic. I did see the great production at the National Theatre, the Peter Hall production with Judi Dench and
Anthony Hopkins in 1987, and she was tremendous. I go back to those.
Also, *Midsummer Night's Dream* never fails. It can be done terribly and still
be okay. It's not a popular choice, I suppose, but I love *Romeo*; it's just so
poetic. I love the sound of it, the extravagance of it. It's like *Anthony and
Cleopatra* in a way, sort of matched plays about couples and both of them
over the top when it comes to verse.

Someone who didn't really know Stephen Booth asked him if he had seen
Pericles, and he replied, "Have I seen it? It's the official play of the People's
Republic of Berkeley." And it is a wacko but charming play. I love it. I've seen
it about fifteen times. It's fantastic. The reunion scene, the scene with Marina,
is just overwhelming.

As a character, of course Falstaff is great, but some of the minor characters are also memorable and thrilling. Pistol is a good example, especially in
the second *Henry IV*, the swaggering, all that stuff about swaggerers. Justice
Shallow is another wonderful character. And I think Sir Andrew Aguecheek
is one of the great characters in all of Shakespeare—just the sense of dimness
and hopelessness and yet optimism—that amazing combination of contradictions. And also, his line, "I was adored once too" may be the greatest line of
Shakespeare. Who could have adored him, his mother? What must she have
been like?

There are little bits with different characters. Doll Tearsheet has a couple
of fantastic flashes in *Henry IV*. You see Pistol, this cowardly, disgusting man,
and she then gets right at it, saying to him, "You a captain! You slave! For
what? For tearing a poor whore's ruff in a bawdy-house!" It opens a window
onto an episode that is then whisked away.

Shakespeare's plays are a source of inexhaustible pleasure. I can return to
the plays either in the theater or on the page and enjoy them almost unfailingly.
Perhaps it's partly a function of my Oedipus complex. I came from a sort of
Puritan background. My father was an electrical contractor who had no time
for the theater or art or anything else, and so of course that's what I gravitated
toward. For me the plays provide endless joy—intellectually, emotionally,
musically, poetically—all different ways.

Almost ten years ago, Lukas Erne published a book called *Shakespeare as
Literary Dramatist*. His argument is that we've gone too far in arguing that
Shakespeare was only a man of the theater, that he didn't care at all about
his plays being read. I think he's right that Shakespeare must have had some

interest in being read. Half of his plays were read in Quarto in his lifetime. Half of them weren't, and we aren't quite sure what the explanation for that is, but still I think that they are great works of art on the page as well as in the theater. I go to the theater three nights a week or so. I go to almost everything, and I almost never get tired of seeing Shakespeare plays. But I don't think that that cancels the power they have when you sit down with them at your desk and you're by yourself in a quiet room.

Shakespeare plays are a dream to teach. They teach themselves if you've any skill at all in opening them up for students. Students love them, and they are infinitely rewarding in that respect. So every time I go to see a play I think, "I get to open this up now, unlock this for somebody else." And that is a tremendous source of satisfaction because what you're doing is giving somebody the keys to great pleasure for the rest of his or her life. I used to take American students to England for a two-week theater course. And now sometimes when I'm on the train to Stratford, I will see a former student, and it's one of the great moments when they say, "Well, I'm back here because I was just drawn to it by your course." So teaching Shakespeare allows the delusion that you've changed people's lives!

I've got about eight answers to what is Shakespearean. I'll start with one. I've been inveigled by two American professors into co-editing a festschrift for Stephen Booth. He is the smartest man in the United States, I think. I admired him when I was in graduate school. I learned how to read poetry from that book of his called *An Essay on Shakespeare's Sonnets* (not the edition he did of the Sonnets—I think this book was his dissertation for Douglas Bush). I wrote a piece for that that I think answers this question. I think the difference is texture. That is, there is more going on in a Shakespeare play, both in the verse and in the narrative, than in the work of most other playwrights. That line I mentioned about Doll Tearsheet is a good example. It takes you into another world for just a second and then draws you back. You're already in another world, you're already in a fictional world, but then it removes you to a further fictional world and it whisks you back to this one. And that exercise is very Boothian. Booth loves thinking about the mind moving back and forth, the mind excited by puns, for example, or rhythms, or that sort of thing. Another good example is Aguecheek's "I was adored once too"; you have to flash for a moment about why. What could this refer to? Or in *The Taming of the Shrew* when Biondello is telling Lucentio to take Bianca to the church and marry her while he still can. Lucentio wonders if you can get married that quickly, and Biondello says, "I knew a wench married in an afternoon as she went to the garden for parsley to stuff a rabbit, and so may you, sir." There is a whole little play in Biondello's little story! So the pleasure of entering a fictional world, which you are in when you are watching or reading the play, is then multiplied as you keep moving into other imaginative spaces and then getting moved back. So I think that texture is one thing. Jonson has that sometimes, but not quite as much. There are wonderful, wonderful things in Jonson's plays. Some of them like that, but not quite with the consistency. Also, the same thing is true of the poetry, that is—to use a Stephen Booth word—the eventfulness of the verse.

I haven't done this in a while, but I like teaching the very first tetralogy [*Henry VI 1.2.3* and *Richard III*] because it's so unexplained in terms of poetics. It's full of rhymes, rhythms, retorts, figures, tropes, turns—all that stuff. Shakespeare begins to restrain himself past 1594 or so. I just adore *Richard III* partly because of the eventfulness of the language.

I've been assigned by the *TLS* to review two new biographies. There's about one a week, you know, even though we don't have any information as to what Shakespeare was like. It's impossible to know. Look at Wagner. He produced some of the greatest works of art in Western culture and he was a monster. Shakespeare could have been a monster. I doubt it because he got along with his company; he worked with that company for fifteen years, so I think that he was agreeable enough, but who knows? Well, you know Stephen's great line on the Sonnets: "William Shakespeare was almost certainly homosexual, heterosexual, or bisexual. The Sonnets provide no information on the matter." So I don't really have any idea what Shakespeare was like.

I should emphasize my theater loyalties as well. I saw the great Peter Brook *Midsummer Night's Dream* when I was a senior in college and that was tremendously moving. And when I graduated from college I went to Europe for six or eight weeks before I went to graduate school. I went to Stratford intending just to go to a play and then take off, but I stayed for a week and saw everything, some things twice. I saw the great John Barton *Twelfth Night* with Judi Dench, and I saw that *Merchant of Venice* that she was in that she didn't like at all. And she was also the Duchess of Malfi. In those three parts. Judi Dench was just overwhelming. I can still hear a few inflections from the way she delivered lines. And there was a *Much Ado* on that week as well. That week really turned me around, alerted me to how magical those texts could be on the stage. I'd been in one of the plays and had seen a couple, and I'd seen the Peter Brook, which was powerful. But seeing all those in a row opened my eyes.

BARBARA MOWAT

"WHY SHOULD A DOG, A HORSE, A RAT HAVE LIFE, AND THOU NO BREATH AT ALL?"

Barbara Mowat has been director of research at the Folger Shakespeare Library, executive editor of **Shakespeare Quarterly***, chair of the Folger Institute, and editor (with Paul Werstine) of all of Shakespeare's works (in the Folger Shakespeare Library editions). Before coming to Folger Shakespeare Library, she was Hollifield Professor of English Literature at Auburn University and then dean at Washington College. She has served as president of the Shakespeare Association of America, president of the Southeast Renaissance Conference, chair of the MLA committee on the New Variorum Shakespeare, and a member of the advisory board of the International Shakespeare Conference (Stratford-upon-Avon). Recently she has published,* **The Dramaturgy of Shakespeare's Romances***, a lively and helpful guide to how* **Cymbeline***,* **The Winter's Tale***, and* **The Tempest** *work. She talked with me at the Folger Shakespeare Library in Washington, D.C.*

I encountered Shakespeare in a meaningful way the second term I was a graduate student at the University of Virginia. I had had one undergraduate course in Shakespeare, which I did not particularly like. I had some high school experience, which was absolutely dreadful: the teacher didn't understand the language and therefore we didn't understand the language. I started out as a math and science major. But I made the switch to English at the University of Virginia, where I took the Fredson Bowers graduate seminar. Bowers is a giant among bibliographic and textual scholars at the University of Virginia, but his course had nothing to do with editing or text. We spent the first semester on the first two and a half acts of *Hamlet*. We were responsible for the Kittredge notes for the entire play. Then the next semester we did some other plays. He encouraged me to send the paper that I wrote for that second semester to *Shakespeare Quarterly*, and it got published. And that was the start of my Shakespeare life.

My favorite Shakespeare play has always been *Hamlet*, and I think it will always be *Hamlet*. It has the incredible depth of his tragedies. And it has the beginnings of the distinction he started making between the intellectual, rational villain and the emotional, imaginative hero, which you get a little bit with Hamlet and Claudius, enough so that you can see where this distinction is going to go. The play also has a lot of humor, a lot of lightness, a lot of thought, a lot of questions, and fascinating characters. There may be greater tragedies— *Macbeth*, *Lear*, or *Othello*—I don't know. And some of the comedies are fantastic. But when it comes down to it, *Hamlet* is the one that I would always go to. If I only had one, that would be it. So among characters, too, Hamlet is the one.

Among the women, I find Portia really interesting. I find Rosalind really interesting. I find Viola interesting. Those would be the ones.

When I chose to go into English literature and then out of that chose to go into Shakespeare Studies, I found my career. That is where I have been ever since. And so it has had a huge impact on my life. I edited the *Shakespeare Quarterly*. I've edited all of Shakespeare's plays. I've been almost 24/7 living with Shakespeare.

I do not believe that we can tell from the plays a lot of what Shakespeare actually thought about anything because he speaks through the characters, but the primary message that comes to me through the plays is compassion.

It is good to be reminded of compassion, of the centrality of compassion. I think about the scene when Gloucester's eyes are put out. There are some things that happen toward the end of that scene that are often cut in modern productions, where they want to make it more grim. But there is the servant who loses his life defending Gloucester. And there are the servants at the end who are willing to risk their lives to help Gloucester find his way. Shakespeare is so careful about that kind of thing. I also have discovered in how he shaped his comedies that he is always extremely careful as he approaches the end of his comedies to put in something that reminds us that this is a play, that we can't count on this in real life. I find that very helpful. And I found what he does with parents and children extremely helpful in raising my own children.

There is a quality about the way that his language deals with the world that I find constantly enriching. If you've got those lines moving around in your head, it just has to keep you grounded in a special kind of way.

Shakespeare is a storyteller and Jonson is a plotter, and that makes a huge difference. Shakespeare's relationship, the play's relationship with the audience is gentle, encouraging, and friendly. There are not very many plays in which he just pokes fun at things. But there are some, like *Troilus and Cressida*, where it is very hard to find any characters to sympathize with. And there is some of that in *Coriolanus* as well. But even there you get the compassion coming through.

From the things that we know about his personal life, particularly his investments and his personal dealings with people, he can be portrayed as a very

unpleasant person. But it is hard for me to connect that with what we
see in the plays, so I don't try! I don't think it can be done. Henry James said,
"If you want to know me, know my work," and I think that's true with Shakespeare. Whatever he did in his life, that's on one level, but what we know is
what is in the plays and the poems.

Your life does change when you are teaching Shakespeare's plays or writing about them; a certain amount of yourself gets into it. And you need a bit
of distance in your thinking in terms of "OK, this is how I understand this?
But how do I explain it to somebody else?" And editing *Shakespeare Quarterly*
became really a new way of teaching because a lot of the people who were
submitting essays were graduate students, people who did not have someone who could read their stuff for them. In editing *Shakespeare Quarterly*,
I learned a lot about Shakespeare and a lot about the changing approaches to
the plays. I saw that for a couple of years everybody was working on one play,
and then for a couple of years everyone was working on a different play. And
I got to talk to all the people in the reading room at the Folger too.

One thing I've really enjoyed is helping out in the theatre, giving notes,
ideas about casting, and that kind of stuff. That is another advantage of being
at the Folger—we've got the theater here.

It's still hard for me to even believe that these words on the page can
get transformed into this three-dimensional, noisy, exciting stuff. It really is
amazing to go from the page to the theater. And of course, he knew that when
he was writing. Shakespeare wrote for actors to memorize and to perform,
and actors love him for that reason. Actors can tell that he wrote with them
in mind. I think you can sense that when actors are on the stage. They are so
comfortable and so excited.

The biggest change for me came when I started editing the plays because
you work with the play word by word. We looked up every word in the *OED*
to see if there was any possibility that it had a different meaning in the 16th,
17th century. I found that there were passages that I had previously mistaught
because the editor of whatever edition I was reading hadn't thought to look a
word up, so I thought the word had its modern meaning when it didn't.

The other thing that I've found is that every play is so different—though
they are all clearly Shakespeare's. I was talking to a lawyer last night who
wanted to be convinced that Shakespeare wrote all his plays—you know this
question. He wasn't arguing against Shakespeare's authorship, he just wanted
to be convinced. And all I could say is that the words are the same, the images, the phrases, the sentence structure. It's a single voice. Despite that, every
play is unique. So with every play it has been so exciting to get in there and
to take it word by word, period and comma, figure out if a word had a special

meaning. And I learned that most of the words had at least three meanings. The amount of wordplay that goes on has absolutely amazed me—with almost every word. There are so many levels of meaning.

I have a friend who is writing a book about teaching children—his children and children in general—how to memorize Shakespeare. He does a lot with the line, "I know a bank where the wild thyme blows." He suggested the line meant the scent of the thyme is blowing across the field. I wrote him a note and said, "Or it's being blown by the wind, or, most likely, it's bursting into flower." (The word "blow" in connection with "flower" usually means bursting into flower.) And today I was thinking it probably means all three of them. Your mind can pick up all of those meanings. You have the scent, the flowering, and the wind, and probably each one of them is intended. And so every single time I go back to whatever play it is I'm working on, I'm always ready to be surprised.

There are a couple of quotations from *King Lear* that are sad and sound hopeless, but for some reason in moments of deep grief and loss, the quality of the lines give me comfort: "Is man no more but this?" and "Unaccommodated man is no more but such a poor, bare, forked animal as thou art." That is one. And the other one is "Why should a dog, a horse, a rat, have life,/ And thou no breath at all?" Again in the presence of death and loss, he is able to say the things we can't say.

Or in *Romeo and Juliet* one that I just adore is, "O, that I were a glove upon that hand,/ That I might touch that cheek!" That captures the power of being in love so simply, and in almost all one-syllable words ("upon" is the only one that has two syllables).

Shakespeare had the power to articulate things we can't articulate. I always taught my students—and I think I'm still probably right about this—that the reason he puts Juliet up in a window and Romeo below is so there is no physical contact, so that everything has to be conveyed through language. That is why that scene is so incredibly powerful. Of course, in movies now they have him crawl up the wall and all over her, but I don't think that was intended. If you've got to put it all into language, then everything has to be said. That is Shakespeare's gift to us.

ADRIAN NOBLE

"Thou Met'st with Things Dying, I with Things New-born."

*Adrian Noble studied English at the University of Bristol and began his professional career as a director at Drama Studio London, then moved to the Bristol Old Vic, to the Royal Exchange Theatre in Manchester, and to the Royal Shakespeare Company as assistant director, then as director He worked for the Peter Hall Company, the Manhattan Theatre Club and elsewhere, before becoming Artistic Director and Chief Executive of the Royal Shakespeare Company from 1990 to 2003. He has also directed London West End musicals and numerous opera productions. Since 2010 he has been Artistic Director of the San Diego Old Globe's Shakespeare Festival. He is the author of **How to Do Shakespeare**, an entertaining and enlightening book that is used by students, actors, directors, teachers, and scholars. He is married to Joanne Pearce, an acclaimed actress, on stage (with the Royal Shakespeare Company and elsewhere), and on television and in the movies. As he mentions in the interview, in 2008 Joanne Pearce took leave from acting to enroll as a history student at Oxford University. I talked to him in late spring 2012, where he was directing **As You Like It** for the San Diego Old Globe.*

First of all, my grandma, for whatever reason, bought me this cheap edition of Shakespeare from Woolworths. That was one thing. And the second occurred when I was in what we call the sixth form. I was doing my A levels, so I was 16. I had a chance encounter with a teacher from my school (who wasn't my teacher). I bumped into him in the street, and he asked me how my studies were going. Obviously, I wasn't totally forthcoming, and he said, "Well, what's wrong?" and I said, "To be honest I'm not sure I'm doing the right subjects." He was a teacher of English who, by the way, went on to become a music critic for the *Sunday Telegraph*. He took it upon himself to introduce me to literature, which I knew nothing about. We didn't have any books in our house or anything like that. My parents weren't ignorant, but they were working-class people who had done okay. He gave me some short stories to read, because they're quick. He gave me "A Diamond as Big as the Ritz" by Scott Fitzgerald. Then I read and liked *The Great Gatsby*. I realized that literature was a rather exciting way to go. So I changed subjects quite late on in my first year (we have two years in the sixth form in England). I dropped geography, changed to English, and encountered Shakespeare.

And at the same time, the third plank—there were three planks—was the opening of the Festival Theatre in Chichester. Laurence Olivier was running it. And obviously they did Shakespeare, so I saw Larry play Othello. I started to study Shakespeare at school and I started to read this edition that I'd been bought. I started going to see the movies that occasionally came to our cinema, *Henry V* and *Hamlet*, again Olivier. And I became intoxicated by Shakespeare, by the language in particular. I would say all the speeches; I'd learn a lot of them by heart in my bedroom. I think in taste I was quite undiscerning, so in my view, a very famous production of *Othello* was of equal merit to the Polesden Lacey Players in *Midsummer Night's Dream*, who were amateurs. I thought the amateurs were just as good as the National Theatre of Great Britain. So that was my introduction. Then I went on and did Shakespeare at university.

I started doing some acting in school, not Shakespeare or anything like that because we didn't do Shakespeare plays in school. I loved acting, so I had this vague idea that I might be an actor. So when I went to university, I started acting. Then I went to Stratford for the first time with my flatmate, Graham, and I saw these productions. I thought they were marvelous. And as I've said on many occasions, it was very clear to me that that's what I would like to do: I'd like to join the Royal Shakespeare Company. I had no interest whatsoever in joining the National Theatre. It was very, very, completely clear that I wanted to go to the RSC, if ever I was good enough. That was when I was an undergraduate. And I ended up doing it. I ended up running it.

This sounds rather naive, really. For example, I didn't really know there was such a thing as a director. I didn't know that job existed until I was 20. I had no idea there was such a thing. Why would I? Well, I knew there was such a thing as a director; it was the chemistry teacher who organized the plays! But I didn't know what they were professionally.

I didn't direct any Shakespeare at university. I only acted. I had little parts in one or two Shakespeare plays. And I stopped acting at university because I decided I wanted to be a director, and I thought the drama at the university was a bit pretentious, actually. So I stopped doing it, and I worked with children in a black area of Bristol, largely a West Indian population. I worked with children for the last year as a kind of drama hobby.

And then I went to drama school. And interestingly, the drama school I went to offered a quite wonderful directors' course. I can't imagine a better directors' course, and in a way I owe everything to them. But the principal was of the view that Racine was much more important than Shakespeare. He thought Shakespeare was grossly overrated. So we did very, very little Shakespeare. But it was a marvelous course and it gave me the intellectual framework and the practical tools to direct classical plays.

The real breakthrough for me was when I ended up at the Bristol Old Vic. My drama school had been so idealistic that they taught everything about the theatre, especially the European influences of Brecht and Stanislavski, but they taught nothing about how to get a job. So for two years when I left I worked with kids in what you might call the projects, sort of like slum areas of Birmingham. And then I won a bursary to go to the Bristol Old Vic. In a way it was kind of straightforward from then on. I was extraordinarily lucky that a gentleman called Richard Cottrell, who was the director of the Bristol Old Vic, gave me these shows to do. He had a clear view that he wanted the Bristol Old Vic to be a classical theatre company. That was his clear brief. And over those three years we assembled the most amazing company of actors: Peter Postlethwaite, Daniel Day-Lewis, Lindsay Duncan, Miles Anderson, absolutely extraordinary actors. That was our company. Plus other people like Simon Callow coming in. Fortunately Cottrell recognized that I probably had the skill to do classical work. So he just chucked them all at me: *Timon of Athens, Titus Andronicus, View from the Bridge, The Changeling.* Just stacks and stacks and stacks of plays.

But *Titus Andronicus* was the turning point. I didn't know much about Shakespeare at all, but I read up on it, and found it rather curious that it was a huge, huge hit, that and *The Spanish Tragedy* at the time. I thought, "That's interesting. I'll try and work out why it was." And we made it into a huge hit. Thelma Holt tried to transfer it to London, but we couldn't because of the physical nature of the production. It was undoable. But it was a big hit and it got national attention. So I sort of realized that maybe I had a bit of a talent there, but ideally I still wanted to go to the RSC. So after 2 ½ years I resigned from the Bristol Olympic and applied to the RSC and got in as an assistant director.

Of course, you could say it was fate, because people don't do that now. If people nowadays did what I had done, they would expect their very next job to be running the RSC. But back then there was a clear path from being an assistant director to being a resident director to being an associate director. But by the end of the '80s, directors weren't interested in that path, which of course has serious consequences because if you do tread that path, by the time you become an associate you know what you're doing, you know about Shakespeare, you know how it works. But if you just come in up there, you know bugger all about it.

There are a number of Shakespeare plays I quite deliberately haven't done. I haven't done *Merry Wives of Windsor*. I've done the Verdi opera, *Falstaff*, which I think is actually better. It's a wonderful, wonderful opera. I couldn't get *Twelfth Night* right at all. I didn't get that right. I messed that up. And in Stratford I didn't get *The Tempest* right, but I got it right here, I think. I was pleased with what we did here and I'm going to do that production in England.

I find some of the Roman plays difficult. I find *Coriolanus* difficult to get my head round, though I think Ralph Fiennes's film was marvelous. We had dinner just after I saw it and before it came out, and I said to him that it seemed to me that he found a clear connection between the intensity of the experience of war and the need for heightened language, that he melded the two things together, which meant that it didn't sound like ordinary people speaking in a funny way. Do you see what I mean? In his film, it sounded like you needed to express yourself in that way because the danger and the political stakes were so intense that heightened language was the right form of communication. By the way, I think Baz Luhrmann did that as well in *Romeo and Juliet*.

I've been hugely drawn to the late plays, and that's why I was so pleased about *The Tempest* last year because I hadn't gotten that one right before. It's very hard, but I understood something about the magic that I think made it work. And *The Winter's Tale* is the great one for me too—a fantastic play, perfect. It's the best.

I suppose there are certain characters I am drawn to. Falstaff, of course, but that's partly because of Robert Stevens. You sort of marry a character to an actor in your mind somewhere, and I love that character and I love Robert. Somehow they are completely, invisibly linked in my mind and imagination.

If you're doing a Shakespeare play, you have to create a world in which the actions and events are logical. You also have to identify the nature of the events, which of course are different from play to play. That's what I mean by conceptualizing— not just saying, "Oh, I'm going to set it in a concentration camp," which is usually intellectually lazy.

I found it relatively easy to move from Shakespeare to opera. When you're working with Shakespearean actors, you have to make the form a natural extension of the means of expression. And that is what you have to do with opera as well, for like Shakespearean actors, opera singers have a strong sense of form. There is the bar and it's absolutely non-negotiable. And there are conventions that you use to direct in opera; one has to embrace them and make those conventions a living form. That's what I was saying about the nature of the event. You have to identify the nature of the event.

As I said in my book, Shakespeare invented musical comedy in Act 4, Scene 2 of *The Winter's Tale*. It is what people thought was invented in America in the 1930s and 1940s. Actually it was invented in London at the beginning of the 17th century; the whole notion of the interrelation of song and narrative and character is absolutely clear in the sheep-shearing scene in *The Winter's Tale*. And if you approach that scene like a musical comedy scene, it becomes massively exciting to work on.

And from my point of view, I moved from that. I did an opera when I was very young, *Don Giovanni*, which actually went very well. But then at the end of the 80's I was asked to do Purcell's *The Fairy-Queen* at the Aix-en-Provence festival. We did Shakespeare's text, and I took a bunch of actors over, Roger Allam, Gemma Jones, and others who I subsequently and still work with. That was sort of an early 17th century take on Shakespeare. It was quite interesting: at the end of Shakespeare's *A Midsummer Night's Dream*, lessons are learned by the exposure of the high-class lovers to ordinary working people. And at the end of Purcell's *The Fairy-Queen* there are lessons learned by the lovers by exposure—not to the working people—but to the gods. And it tells a lot about the very late seventeenth century society when Purcell wrote it that he and his audience felt they could only learn from the gods; they couldn't possibly learn from the bottom.

The next big thing I did was with the same music director, Bill Christie, a Monteverdi opera. If there's a musical cousin to Shakespeare, it's Monteverdi, because Monteverdi starts from the word rather than from the note. In Monteverdi as in Shakespeare, you need to get the word right and the thought leading to the word right; you need to recognize the relationship between the thought and form. In Shakespeare, for example, you need to notice the line endings, and it's the same in Monteverdi: you can see your way in terms of the phrasing, the choice of melody, counterpoint, etc., etc., etc. You can see the way the characters think, and it all comes down to the word. In the beginning there was the word, both in Shakespeare and in Monteverdi. Then of course that started a lot of the opera that I did in the '90s and the 2000s, up to now.

Shakespeare obviously has influenced me in the sense that I've spent substantial periods of my working life doing Shakespeare and being involved in companies whose purpose is to present the works of Shakespeare. I was married in Stratford, in Holy Trinity. The Royal Shakespeare wind band played at my wedding and these actors—Simon Russell Beale, Roger Allam, John Wood, Sinead Cusack—either sang or spoke at my wedding. So it was completely a Shakespeare wedding. And my children were virtually born in the theatre, spending a lot of their childhood years inside the Royal

Shakespeare Company. So Shakespeare has permeated my life.

Shakespeare has influenced me as an artist *primarily* because he's a humanist. If you reject that notion, I think you're wasting your time as a Shakespeare director. That means there's a value put upon the individual, on the human being. And the perspectives that he has on life are, I find, particularly rich, whether it's a perspective on politics via the individual or the absurdity of our lives, the comedy of our lives—as in *Romeo and Juliet*, with all the absurdities that we get up to in love. So his humanism affects me profoundly, and I'm not saying just as a person but as an artist. That's very, very, very important.

In a classical play all items, all the themes, characters, plots, and sub-plots inform the central theme; that's enriching and exciting, and gives one a particular way of looking at art. So that's very important and difficult. And Shakespeare's more difficult to do than everybody else; therefore, you have to be at the top of your game. (No, I should say, Restoration comedy is more difficult, which I avoid like the plague because it's so hard.) But Shakespeare is also very difficult. It's as if you're a racehorse trainer or a jockey and you choose steeplechasing, right? You've got to be able to jump seven foot fences, you know, that's what you have to do, and if you can't do that.... So as a director, you've got to be at the top of your game to succeed in Shakespeare. It's a constant challenge. I don't know quite what to read into this, but I remember in the '80s and 90's when I did a long sequence of Shakespeare plays, I'd ask myself, "How can I possibly do this play?" Then I'd wonder, "How did I ever direct that last one if I didn't know what I now know?" That was a curious feeling, but I kept feeling it endlessly.

It's clear from his texts that Shakespeare wrote antithetically. Shakespeare used metaphor in a very particular way and Jonson doesn't in any way at all. There's a closer connection between Marlowe and Shakespeare, but Jonson has such a strong individual whiff. It's like comparing Dickens to Anthony Trollope; you can tell within eight words who's written the novel. But I think finally it's an attitude towards the world. Shakespeare has this rather non-judgmental view of humanity, whereas I think Jonson is very judgmental. And there's so little of Marlowe—that's kind of the tragedy—but it's wild, wild. Like all the middle stuff of *Faustus*, you'd rather just flush it down the toilet; it's absolute crap, page and pages of crap. And then he's got some of the best writing in the English language and you wonder how? What is that about?

I find the whole thing about who wrote Shakespeare's plays silly. What's clear is that one person wrote them all. The moment you spend any time directing or acting Shakespeare, you know that one person wrote all of those plays. There are bits that he didn't, and it's very, very clear the bits he didn't.

Actors usually know the bits he didn't before the director, actually, and scholars always know. But I'm not a scholar and I get rather nonplussed by a lot of scholarliness. I don't read scholarly writing on Shakespeare at all. I find there are other contextual things that are more interesting.

The really astonishing thing is that Shakespeare had, as with Mozart, the ability to get it right the first time. That is absolutely jaw-dropping. We know he didn't do lots of rewrites, and actually he couldn't have done; there wasn't enough time to do them. But I think he was evidently a very practical person. He understood the craft—no actually he didn't just understand the craft, he invented it. Drama didn't progress in a straight fashion; it takes off vertically in the early 1590s. And of course it wasn't just him, there were others. It was obviously a very exciting time, particularly with Marlowe, who was one of the great groundbreakers.

So Shakespeare invented drama as we know it. But I think to a degree he also invented a way of looking at history, which has pertained up until about the last 30 years, which is that we examine the interrelationship between the individual and the objective political events. We look at the way the public affects the private and the private the public—that is really how history was written and taught until the last 30 or 40 years. I'm slightly attuned to that because my wife as a mature student went to Oxford to read history. So I could test this theory out on her and she said absolutely, that is exactly what has happened. There's no question that Shakespeare invented how we look at history. Part of the whole post-modernist thing is to have a different view on that, as with post-modernist takes on literature and all the humanities.

One of my favorite passages in Shakespeare is in *The Winter's Tale*, when the old shepherd says to his son: "Thou met'st with things dying, I with things new-born."

ROBIN GOODRIN NORDLI

"HOW WILL THIS FADGE?"

Robin Goodrin Nordli is a classically trained actress in her 19th season with the Oregon Shakespeare Festival. She has performed in 52 productions of 28 different Shakespeare plays. She holds a MFA from the American Conservatory Theatre in San Francisco and has worked professionally as an actor since 1984. In 2000 she created her wonderfully entertaining one-woman show, **Bard Babes,** *about her experiences playing Shakespeare's female characters. She has performed* **Bard Babes** *around the country and for the Holland America Cruise Line. She has performed at many regional theaters, including The Mark Taper Forum, The American Conservatory Theatre, The California Shakespeare Festival, Berkeley Repertory Theatre, and Arizona Theatre Company. She has taught and lectured at a number of institutions, including UCLA, Beijing University in China, National Taiwan University, and Southern Oregon University. She has won a Dramalogue Critics Award for her performance as Imogen in* **Cymbeline***, a Bay Area Critics Award for Rosalind in* **As You Like It,** *and a Backstage West Garland Award for Maxine in* **Tongue of a Bird***. She is also the recipient of the Oregon Arts Commission Individual Artists Fellowship for 2009. I talked with her at a coffee shop in Ashland, Oregon, where she was rehearsing an adaptation of* **The Merry Wives of Windsor***,* **The Very Merry Wives of Windsor, Iowa***.*

The first real connection I had with Shakespeare was when I was fourteen. I auditioned for my first play in high school, *The Taming of the Shrew*, and got cast as Bianca. The director, Mrs. Lukowitz, was fabulous— she just said, "Okay, I know Shakespeare. You just need to figure out what you're saying and find a way to mean it. That's the only thing you have to do. Don't go on a head trip about it." I'd go to every rehearsal whether I was in it or not, and the language was just so interesting, informative, and deep. As a kid I'd always loved poetry and this was just an extension of that into theater. It was fabulous. Her approach of "figure out what you're saying and find a way to mean it" carried me for a long time. By the time I got into graduate school, a lot of people in my class were intimidated by Shakespeare or put it on this pedestal, but I'd grown up with it being just a really great story with incredibly wonderful language. That was an asset. So I think she helped me enormously. Mrs. Lukowitz lives in Florida now, and when I did Portia in *Merchant of Venice* here several years ago, she came. It was a great full-circle opportunity.

When I got into graduate school, I realized how many Shakespeare festivals there were. Then when I graduated I was going off and doing a lot of those and I thought, "Okay, this is a huge part of my life." For a while it was the meat and potatoes of what I was doing theatrically.

Bill Ball was at the end of his career running the American Conservatory Theater in San Francisco when I was there, and he was enormously helpful. And what a great guy! The whole thrust of the place at that time was so language based. That for me took it all to the next level.

Ironically the first role that comes to mind as far as difficult isn't one I'd probably be considered for: Leontes. Leontes is a tough role—how he behaves in the first act and the transition from that. I have actually played a lot of the male roles in Shakespeare, nineteen. I'm going into the twentieth right now. I'm about to do *Merry Wives* as *The Very Merry Wives of Windsor, Iowa*, playing Master Ford, but in a lesbian relationship with Mrs Ford. And I've done Grumio twice in the *Shrew*, two different versions of *Shrew*. Sometimes I play them as men, but sometimes they're women incarnations of those roles, which I think can be extremely rich.

I will tell you the most influential performance I ever saw, and not because it was my favorite one. I was 15 and had just done Ophelia in *Hamlet* in high school, and my mother gave me a ticket to go down to Chicago—I'm from a suburb of Chicago—to go see a woman play *Hamlet*. And I thought, "How bizarre!" At that time, I'd never heard of that. It was fascinating because I'd never seen a female character have such control over her life or her story. She suffered the consequences of her actions, she made decisions, and everything was in front of the audience. And I thought, "Wow." Usually if you're Lady Macbeth, you go crazy offstage and you just come on with it. Or half of your story is told while you're not there. But with the woman playing *Hamlet*, everything happened to her onstage, and I thought, "That's amazing."

Fast forward. I go to ACT, I graduate, and eventually I find out—like 15 years ago—that Bill Ball had directed that production. And it was Dame Judith Anderson who had done it. And she was 73 at the time! It was an "Oh, my God" experience. So I've always wanted to do *Hamlet*. It's on my list. (They always say when you play Hamlet you play yourself, that Hamlet is you, whoever you are.)

I think Richard II would be really interesting too. I know Siobhan McKenna did Richard III up in Stratford. I do think those male roles possess a huge other challenge, so when you talk about difficulty I think part of me goes to those.

I've had many roles I loved. I would say Imogen in *Cymbeline* was the first time in a play I had the sensation of driving the boat. It's got its problems; it's not the greatest language. Some of it's great, but it's rough and rocky. But so much of what happened to her is based on her decisions, and it happens onstage. I love that. I also really loved doing Isabella in *Measure for Measure*. That's oddly a favorite play because of the themes it speaks to of people trying to make the world black and white while the world is really gray. But I would say my ultimate favorite was Margaret in the *Henry VI* cycle into *Richard III*. I got to play her all the way through. We squashed *Henry VI* two and three together, so we lost a lot. But I loved the idea that I could play a character from teenage to ancient, go through her as an ingénue to a mother to a queen to a warrior to a vengeful whatever—spirit? soul? That journey was phenomenal; I got to live a whole life onstage. That's very rare. Yes, she's not the most likeable character, but that's okay; we don't get a lot of Iagos on stage.

I think all the characters you play are like you. They're all different aspects of you that are taken and exploited to become the predominant leading force, while the other aspects of yourself get pulled back. I do think if there isn't a piece of you in everything, then you're not doing the role justice. Shakespeare is so human and the characters aren't one-dimensional; they're multidimensional, including the female characters, of course, although if they were bigger parts they'd be even more so. It makes you just long for even more.

I teach a lot of Elderhostel and high school things, and if I ask, "What do you think the biggest role for a woman is in Shakespeare," people will say, "Lady Macbeth." And I say, "No, no, no." Her part is a really nice one-act, and there's almost a third of the play before and a third of the play after her. And then you have that nice little center section that's really interesting, but she's a supporting player. It's very rare in Shakespeare for a woman to be the protagonist. Rosalind of course is a big part. Cleopatra's up there, Imogen's up there, but it's usually so cut. Juliet is up there.

Shakespeare is the groundwork for all the other acting that I do. If someone can do Shakespeare, they can do anything. It all branches from that. I hadn't thought it would be that way. Most people put it up high and aspire to it, but I think if you get it as groundwork, as I was lucky enough to, it informs everything else you do. It informs musicals, it informs everything. The heart of Shakespeare is the language, and because of the language it keeps getting deeper. I've done seven *Twelfth Nights*, four Violas, two Olivias, and one Maria, and I can still do the play. I could do it again. I'd love to do it again because it's so rich and it can be interpreted in so many ways. And it's always going to be different with the chemistry of who's playing with you, who's directing it and what the situation is, what the audience is.

What is "Shakespearean"? I think the scope. Why is it still around after all these years? It speaks to so many people on so many levels. These are great stories, and they can be interpreted in different ways. Different aspects can be highlighted. It morphs and it continues to speak to everyone. And I think that kind of universality is so rare. And it speaks to the human condition and the journeys of humans through life. I mean, the Greeks do too, but for me Shakespeare has so much more of the humor, the life, the humanity.

He's also so good at putting the contradictions within the character, like with Margaret. On the one hand you're sympathetic to her journey and she's isolated, this French woman in court and all these things are going on around her. And yet she will kill people. And then you feel sorry for her when Suffolk's head is given to her, you think, "Ah, nobody should go through that." And then instead of becoming a victim, she decides to be a warrior and you think, "Good for you," and then again you don't like her. Things come out of her mouth that are a little bit abrasive. When she kills York, you think, "Couldn't you just kill him? Did you have to do that monologue?" It's especially amazing for a female character to have those kinds of contra-dictions because we want them to be virtuous. Virtue and victimization are acceptable for females, but Shakespeare makes females so multidimensional— even Desdemona, who I think is extremely virtuous and straightforward. I always hate it when actors say, "She's so boring," or something like that. No! She has that fabulous scene with Emilia at the end where one's in verse and one's in prose and they kind of switch and you wonder, "What are they talking about? Why does she sing that song?" She goes on this sort of journey of understanding, which is so deep. And that journey is what propels her into that final scene and the understanding of what Othello is thinking. And she knows, "I will never be able to change his mind. But I will try, I will die trying."

This upsets a lot of people, but I feel we don't know who wrote these plays, really, and the evidence we have for Shakespeare as a writer in his time is not enough to say, "Oh, yes, it was him." I think there's a strong possibil-ity it was somebody else. I don't know. And the beauty of Shakespeare is that we don't know, I think, because so many times we want to anchor plays to personal things: "Well, he wrote that because of what was going on in his life at that time," or "he did this because of this…." And if we don't know for sure, our imagination has to anchor it more closely to our own lives or to something else. We can stay in the story more than jump out and analyze it because we can't tie it to anything. Whereas if we did know a lot about him we'd be able to write off a lot of his language or categorize it as, "Well, he did that because he had a bad relationship with his mother." But we don't know and I am content to not know. I will say, however, that some of the stories of the other possible candidates are fascinating.

I'm very fond of a little quotation from *Twelfth Night*: "How will this fadge?" It's the only time "fadge" is used. Viola says it in the ring speech:

> How will this fadge? My master loves her dearly,
> And I, poor monster, fond as much on him,
> And she, mistaken, seems to dote on me.
> What will become of this? As I am man....

It's one of those speeches with a word that Shakespeare never used again. It's a question to the audience or to herself or both. I'm fond of that one. In life I get into situations where I think, "How will this fadge? What's going to happen? I need to pick up my income tax today—how will this fadge?"

I have also enjoyed "I am a feather for each wind that blows." Leontes says it in *A Winter's Tale*. And I love Hamlet's "there is nothing either good or bad, but thinking makes it so." I'll walk away from here and think of twenty more.

I was going to say *Two Noble Kinsmen* is a play I have a problem with, but I actually love that play. I think it's a connoisseur's piece. It is horribly hard to pick a least favorite play. I just did a workshop production of *Timon of Athens*, and it's a tough play. Even his bad plays—I shouldn't say bad plays—are better than everybody else's, so I'd still much rather do them. But, particularly from a woman's standpoint, *Timon* is very frustrating. It's a head piece.

Measure for Measure is definitely one of my favorites. Part of it is I had a really great experience with it. I've seen productions that I hated. In mine the director was very good at tying everything together with a concept. I loved the Isabel-Angelo scenes. Doing the back and forth of the love scenes was like playing a really good ping pong game: bam, bam, bam.

Measure for Measure is one of my favorite plays. But I love *Hamlet*. *Hamlet* is my favorite on a different level, on a level that is above the rest. Maybe your question should be, "What's your favorite play after *Hamlet*?"

BILL RAUCH

"*THOU ART THE THING ITSELF*"

*Since 2007, Bill Rauch has been the Oregon Shakespeare Festival artistic director, selecting the season's plays as well as their directors, design teams, and casts. He regularly directs two plays himself. From 1986 to 2006, he was artistic director of the Cornerstone Theater Company (which he cofounded). He was a drama professor at University of California, Irvine from 2005 to 2007. In 2012, Bill received the Zelda Fichandler Award (given by the State Directors and Choreographers Foundation to recognize past work, future promise, and community commitment); in 2010 he won the Theatre Communications Group's Visionary Leadership Award; in 2009 he won the Margo Jones Award (for "that citizen-of-the theatre who has demonstrated a significant impact, understanding, and affirmation of the craft of playwriting, with a lifetime commitment to the encouragement of the living theatre everywhere"). As well as directing many Shakespeare plays, Rauch has directed the world premieres of **All the Way**, **Equivocation**, and **By the Waters of Babylon** as well as opera and musicals. I talked with him in his office at the Oregon Shakespeare Festival, shortly before I saw his wonderful and one-of a-kind production of **King Lear**.*

The most formative early experience I had with Shakespeare was in 7th grade in Westport Connecticut. On a school field trip, I saw the Yale Rep production of *A Midsummer Night's Dream*, directed by Alvin Epstein. It was revelatory. I was completely transported. We were reading it in 7th grade, and I actually became impatient that my classmates weren't following the language enough as we were reading it in class. So I decided to translate it into contemporary American idiom so that it was more accessible to my classmates. I did this and I shared it with my teacher. Then my teacher decided that the next year when I was in 8th grade I should direct that year's 7th grade class in my version of the play. So that was a first directing experience. And of course I tried to copy all of the great staging from that Yale Rep production that had moved me so much. Doing that play was a huge, huge part of my life. So that's the first one. It was really something. I was very, very blessed.

I knew then that Shakespeare was going to be important in my life. I really did. And I put on a version of *Romeo and Juliet* with my sisters in my bedroom for my parents. I was very excited, very obsessed with Shakespeare.

My college mentor at Harvard, a woman named Joann Breuer, she was Joann Green at the time, was influential in everything I did, including Shakespeare. The first main stage show I directed in college was *Romeo and Juliet*. My husband Christopher was in that first show, so that's how we first got to know each other. That was a long time ago, and very significant.

And then in my Cornerstone years, in my former company we worked in communities, and Shakespeare was the playwright we went back to again and again. We did an adaptation of *Hamlet* in North Dakota in a small town, we did an adaptation of *Romeo and Juliet* in Mississippi, we did an adaptation of *The Winter's Tale* pulling people together from all the communities we'd worked in across the country. As a company, we on our own adapted *Twelfth Night* and *As You Like It*, so Shakespeare was a playwright that I went back to again and again—and he still is of course.

All of Shakespeare's plays are such deep mountains that you feel foolish even trying to climb them sometimes, but really I would direct anything written by Shakespeare anytime. I think I've worked on *Romeo and Juliet* four different times, *Midsummer* two or three times, the Scottish Play multiple times. Then there are ones that I've never done that I can't wait to do. This year will be my first time directing *King Lear* and *Cymbeline*.

As an artist, I sometimes struggle with what appears to be racism or sexism or homophobia or classism embedded in the plays, and I struggle with what was the playwright's point of view versus what are characters' points of view. I've got such faith in the artist William Shakespeare, knowing of course he was a man of his time as we all are, but I have debates with him and with myself about what is embedded in the work that is speaking from his heart and what he's critiquing. So that's always an interesting part of the journey when I work on the plays, with *The Merchant of Venice*, *The Taming of the Shrew*, with any number of plays. And embedded in the plays is the idea that class is born into you (as shown by who gets to speak verse and who has to speak prose). I struggle with those things because they're sometimes at odds with my own politics, but the deeper I dive into the work, the humanity of the artist and the humanity of the characters always comes out on top of those struggles.

The romances have a special place in my heart and that's why I'm so excited to be working on *Cymbeline*. I've directed *The Winter's Tale* and now *Cymbeline*. I look forward to directing *Pericles* and The *Tempest*.

I think the romances resonate with my world-view that life can be awful, tragic, but there is redemption that comes after; that there is tragedy and that there is hope. That appeals to me in terms of the way I look at the world and what feels true to me. A lot of people say that view is pure fantasy, but it resonates for me. To me, that is how the world works.

Look in *King Lear* that you'll see this afternoon at two minor characters: the servant that stands up and tries to stop Gloucester losing his other eye or the captain asked to kill Cordelia who says, "If it be man's work, I'll do it." Shakespeare packs unbelievable humanity into every character, whether it's one or two lines or a thousand plus lines. It's remarkable that achievement. So there's not any character written by Shakespeare that I don't love.

Twelfth Night does have a special place in my heart. We produced it at my former company, the Cornerstone Theater Company, and my husband Chris played both twins, Viola and Sebastian. And Allison Kerry, who's a very close colleague of mine, had adapted it. The intensity of that experience of the play and how successfully we realized it makes *Twelfth Night* special for me, but honestly every one that I've been able to dive into has a special place in my heart.

I think part of why I love the romances is the possibility of forgiveness, that there can be peace and reconciliation after great tragedy. But that's just one example. Shakespeare has shaped my life so profoundly in ways that I'm aware of and in ways that I know I'm not aware of, but the imprint on my life is huge. And the fact that my husband and I fell in love through working on Shakespeare together says so much. The fact that I have chosen and been lucky enough to be here at the Oregon Shakespeare Festival where every single project that we undertake, the yardstick by which we measure it is Shakespeare. Is the language rich? Is there great humanity? Does the work operate on a spiritual plane as well as a psychological plane as well as a political plane? All of the yardsticks by which we look at work are the Shakespeare yardsticks.

Shakespeare is the man of show business, not just Shakespeare the poet but the Shakespeare the populist. That Shakespeare's works originally entertained the groundlings and the nobles at the same time has been a huge driving force in my life. The democratization of art that Shakespeare represents has been a real through-line not only in the art I try to practice but in my life.

Yes, "What is Shakespearean?" is a really hard question. I'll try to not come up with the right answer but just some answers, because we could talk for hours about that. The shocking juxtaposition of tones and genres. The fact that you can have comedy in a piece like the Scottish Play. No matter what the genre is of the play, there's so many tones embedded in that work. Things that I've been talking about, the humanity, the absolute truth. The glory of the language, of course. The theatricality, absolutely. They're just good shows, right? When the play is well directed and well-acted, it's a great ride for the audience. And even sometimes if the play is not well directed and well-acted, it can be a great ride because they are so darn theatrical and entertaining, as well as moving. The thing I referenced earlier, the multiple planes, the fact that you can do a deep dive into the spiritual life of a Shakespeare play, the political life, the psychological life... well, I could go on but you get my point.

No doubt if I could get in a time capsule and bring somebody to this point in time or if I could go back in time I would want to meet William Shakespeare. I would give anything to meet that individual. There's such a generosity of spirit in his work. Whether he was able to practice that in his relationship with the people around him or not I can't say. But he sure was able to channel it as an artist. I feel quite adamant about the authorship debate. I mean, yes, of course, on one very deep level it doesn't matter. We have the plays, who cares who wrote them? But I can't accept the notion that it could not have been the man from Stratford because of class issues, education issues, rural versus court issues. To me it is really clear that the author was a person of the theater, a man who had spent his life in the theater and really, really knew the theater in his bones. This was not somebody writing isolated in a study. This was somebody who was writing for an audience and writing for a company. And there is the glorious human messiness of the plays; they are messy in all the great ways because they were written for a company and because they were written for an audience. You feel that in their bones. They were not the work of a poet holed up, not connected to company. So I feel very strongly that the man from Stratford wrote the plays. I also am struck by the interplay between the court and the country throughout the work. I feel the plays are the work of an artist who grew up in the country and then was privileged to spend time in the court. He was writing about his response to that dichotomy in his own life.

Lear's "Thou art the thing itself" has a very special meaning to me. That line is itself so naked in describing naked, raw humanity. The word 'thing' is as actively used now 400 years later. It's both nondescript and perfect! I don't know if I can articulate why it moves me, but it really does. But oh my goodness, Shakespeare's great lines go on and on and on. What I love about Shakespeare's language is how in every line great actors and great directors and great audiences can teach me truth that I hadn't heard before. So when I see a strong production or even just a spark of truth in a mediocre production, there are always line readings that take my breath away, and I think, "Oh, I never got that. Of course, of course, that connects to that." Or, "Of course you can see that as a cry of anger or see that as a plea"—whatever the new insight is. It's just bottomless, the ability to find truth through Shakespeare's language.

HUGH AND VELMA RICHMOND

"Pardon's the word to all."

*Hugh Macrae Richmond is Professor Emeritus of English at U.C. Berkeley, where he directs its Shakespeare Program and produces Shakespeare related videos. Among his books are **Shakespeare's Theater** and **Shakespeare's Sexual Comedy**. He has himself staged some forty Renaissance plays and edited two Shakespeare history plays. He helped rebuild Shakespeare's Globe Theatre in London, where he staged **Much Ado About Nothing**. He is Scholar in Residence for the California Shakespeare Festival. He also maintains an extremely useful website about Shakespeare in performance (http://shakespearestaging.berkeley.edu/).*

*Velma Bourgeois Richmond is Professor Emerita of English at Holy Names College in Oakland, where she chaired the Department of English, Speech and Drama, was Dean of Academic Affairs, and was a Director of the M.A. program in English. Among her books are **Shakespeare, Catholicism, and Romance**, and **Shakespeare as Children's Literature: Edwardian Retellings in Words and Pictures**.*

I talked with the Richmonds in their lovely home in the Berkeley Hills, where they served me a most delightful afternoon tea after our formal conversation was over.

Hugh: I grew up in a little town called Burton-on-Trent, which is about an hour's drive from Stratford-on-Avon. Immediately after World War II, when my father came back from Germany, he was very keen on finding amusing things to do. I must have been about 13 or 14 at the time. He started taking me to the Stratford Memorial Theatre — it wasn't called the Royal Shakespeare Company at that time. We did see a lot of theater in the 1940's. Obviously one rather laboriously tried to read the texts in school, but in early years they weren't terribly accessible from my point of view. It was the performances that fired me up.

The masters of the grammar school that I went to were very keen on theater, perhaps because it was near Stratford. We had an annual production, and one of the early ones I was in was *Julius Caesar*. I was lucky enough to be cast as Brutus. That gave me an immediate involvement in theater, not just reading Shakespeare in the classroom, which actually I didn't do very well at that time. In fact, despite some acting, even as an undergraduate or a graduate, I didn't have quite as much academic involvement as when I got here to Berkeley. The English department is very keen on Shakespeare and had eight or nine courses. They encouraged all faculty in the Renaissance to teach Shakespeare courses.

Velma: My own background is a little bit checkered. In school we did *Julius Caesar* in the eighth grade, which I think happens in the United States very often. Then in ninth grade I had a speech and drama teacher who was very keen about *Romeo and Juliet*, which we did. Then I suppose in my senior year, the English text was *Macbeth*. I remember my project was writing a diary of Lady Macbeth, which I suspect was incipient humanism or feminism, I suppose.

Hugh: …which turned into an article you wrote years later.

Velma: Many years later. In practice I had a rather bizarre situation because I didn't take an undergraduate class in Shakespeare at Louisiana State University in Baton Rouge. It was not required and I didn't take it as an M.A. student because, without naming names, I thought the person who taught it was very strange, so I just avoided it. I was obviously not going to get through a PhD program without studying Shakespeare, so I took a couple of courses in Shakespeare at that stage. It was a little bit unusual because I was reading, but not doing active things. It was all text-based, I suppose, because I was never a performer.

Hugh: Not never. At Berkeley, I had these big classes I had to teach—at one point I lectured to 400 students. This didn't seem to me to be a very effective way of communicating. We had English 117A/B, which is year-long Shakespeare course where you teach everything. If you do 117A, you have the three parts of *Henry VI*, and you have a week for each part with three lectures a week. So after eight lectures the class was stupified. I thought, what am I going to do with the ninth lecture? There was that terrific speech of Richard III—well, Richard Gloucester he is then (*3 HenryVI.3.2*). He plans out how he's going to become king and he develops this tremendous Machiavellian plot. I thought, we'll try this out theatrically. The result was astounding. People stood up and cheered. I suddenly realized that this is another way of dealing with big classes. If you've got two or three hundred people it's almost like a theater audience. You're teaching theater and I'd done a little bit of theater work, so it wasn't too hard. This worked so well that I recruited Velma—and that's why I was objecting to her saying she doesn't perform.

Velma: But I only read, I don't perform. I was never cast in a play, let's put it that way, and I didn't live close to Stratford-on-Avon, so for me it was film, rather than theater performances. When we were doing *Romeo and Juliet*, I remembered seeing that ancient film in which the balcony scene is separated by vast spaces. It did stay in my mind. And *Henry V*, the Olivier film, was very striking. It really did make a huge impression on me. On the other hand, I can remember going to see Orson Welles' *Macbeth* and the audience bursting out laughing. It was always a little bit varied. I was doing that kind of thing with film societies.

Hugh: I have to say that the English teachers who directed the productions did give me a real feel for theater. They weren't professional theater people. There was an ex-tank-commander called Norman Cleave, for example, who was very keen on theater. He directed me in about three plays and gave me a feel about how this kind of thing worked. What was so curious was when we got here, there was very little theater in the Bay Area. The Actor's Workshop had just started about a year or two earlier, in 1956 or 1955.

Velma: While I hadn't seen very many productions, I did have a wonderful introduction to Stratford when I was at Oxford because the first play I saw was *Macbeth* starring Laurence Olivier and Vivian Leigh.

Hugh: I think that's the same for me. It's interesting that I did *Much Ado* at the Globe because one of the first things I saw—it must have been in 1950—was John Gielgud and Peggy Ashcroft in *Much Ado About Nothing*. I still remember that. I was writing about it just last night, actually, because it had had such an impact. I guess it's very memorable because that's the play that I still enjoy most.

Velma: But there was a revival.

Hugh: There were several revivals. This is what I've just been writing up on the website. It started with Anthony Quayle and Diana Wynyard. Then Gielgud took over and then there was Peggy Ashcroft. It was so successful that it kept surfacing again. I think they took it on a world tour.

Velma: *Much Ado* is my favorite of that kind of play.

Hugh: The progression of the relationship between Beatrice and Benedict is archetypal. The tension and the resolution of it, by all kinds of accidents and so forth, seem to be the most memorable. I do think it came to be a kind of

model for *The Way of the World* and *The Importance of Being Earnest.* I wrote
an essay about Albee's *Who's Afraid of Virginia Woolf?* The older couple there,
George and Martha, are in the same pattern, recognizing the genuine richness
of their relationship. It's not the sentimental *Romeo and Juliet* relationship, like
Hero and Claudio; it's a genuinely complex and even inconsistent relationship. It's also been, after *Hamlet* and Falstaff and *King Lear* perhaps, one of
the great popular successes. But Velma should talk to you about her favorite,
which is quite different.

Velma: My favorite is *The Winter's Tale.* Although I'm very keen about Shakespeare and have done a certain amount of work and certainly been very much
enriched by all of Hugh's work, I suppose my heart is a little bit more in the
Middle Ages, particularly in the romance. So because of the way that Shakespeare handles the romance, *The Winter's Tale* is the one that I most value. It
is being performed a little bit more often now than it used to be.

I'm more interested in Hermione than I am in Perdita. I like the thematic
material, the false accusation of the queen and her own defense. I admire the
response she has as a woman when most fiercely accused of having betrayed
her husband, whose child she is carrying and whose other child is by his side.
And she can say in effect, "All I hope for is that someday you'll be sorry for
this." That is a real model in an extraordinary kind of way. Many feminists
feel that she is not being very assertive, and I will yield to say that Paulina is
necessary dramatically throughout. But the capacity for forgiveness and that
transcendence deeply appeals to me. I don't think any of the other plays quite
have it in the same way.

And the magic of the transformation in the statue scene is just breathtaking. Let me personalize for a moment. My favorite Shakespeare moment in
the theater was one in Stratford-on-Avon when we went to see *The Winter's
Tale.* Our then seven-year-old daughter was with us, as well as our ten-
year-old. Before the play all I did was to say to her, "Don't be too distressed
because you're going to hear that the little boy dies." But I didn't tell her anything else. She sat there and watched all of this and when the statue appeared,
she reached over to me and said, "Mommy, she's alive!" That's what the whole
play is about. If ever anyone wants to say this play is unconvincing, that's the
story to tell to make clear why it's so splendid.

Hugh: It's interesting that people prefer different parts of the play because I
think it goes in three phases. It's like a Greek tragedy at the start, then a kind
of pastoral comedy, and then a romantic, mystical ending—almost transcen-
dent. These three different parts are the play's crucial sequence.

Velma: At the last meeting of the Shakespeare Association of America in Seattle, I signed up for the seminar on *The Winter's Tale*. I thought, "Well, this is my favorite play. I'll see what people are doing." After 45 minutes of hearing people talk about their papers, I sat there thinking, "Who are these people? What play did they read?" We had torture, bizarre sexuality, and those kinds of things. That's just not the way I read the play.

Hugh: As for other characters, there is something about Falstaff that I find fascinating. For much of the time I think he's actually pretending to be somebody that he knows he isn't, which is a rather complicated mindset. I think he sets himself up for the teasing that he gets from those around him. I find the social awareness involved in this complicated interaction impressive. What's curious is that the same kind of quality appears in two other characters that are completely different in one way or another: Richard III and Cleopatra. All three of them have this multi-layered reaction. Richard III, though, is a pretty sinister case. But Cleopatra is coming back. The feminists started it, and the latest books on Cleopatra recognized that she was a major political figure and came within a hair's breadth of creating the future Eastern Mediterranean Empire.

Velma: I enjoy, to stay with the women characters, Beatrice and Rosalind. They are very engaging, and I like their playfulness. And one can't help but think about the fact that these parts were originally played by boys. Shakespeare's boy actor is a whole theme in children's literature, which is another one of my interests. There's a major industry of Shakespeare for the young adult reader: Cary Blackwood, Susan Cooper, and John Bennett, who wrote *Master Skylark*, an Edwardian novel that I very much like. It's the whole way of trying to introduce children to Shakespeare by telling the stories.

Hugh: In almost every threatening situation, I think "Shall I be King Lear? Or Richard III?" When the Registrar scheduled me in the wrong room with another person teaching a course at the wrong time and refused to make any adjustments, I decided I would try the King Lear thing. This was in a big room and this registrar was a particularly clownish figure. I noticed that people were drifting away from the room until in the end it was just the registrar and I. In the end he wearily said, "Yes, we will correct all that. You can have the room that you want."

I remember in the 60s or 70s seeing someone with a t-shirt that read, "We are so sincere; how can we be wrong?" I just said, "That's not the way to get things done. You need to realize that for every action there's a counterreaction, so if you just push too hard, you'll be pushed back, unless you stage-manage things." My book on Shakespeare's sexual comedy was written almost as an admonition to students about how to get things done by artifice not violence. This is a very unfashionable way of looking at Shakespeare and life. But students have usually reacted very positively.

I recently had a distressing experience, at a Shakespeare Association meeting, where I went to a session that was about secondary school teachers and how they taught, but it was being run by university academics. There was a complete split. The high school teachers wanted to teach students to enjoy Shakespeare, to understand Shakespeare and to learn from Shakespeare, and they spent all their time building up enthusiasm. The faculty people were all just horrified about this. They said, "You know he was a terrible conservative and a reactionary, and he was patriarchal and misogynist." There was almost a complete breakdown between the two attitudes. I do think that the high school teachers didn't really have a wholly defective view—I mean one like Horace's idea that you should enjoy literature and perhaps learn a little bit from it, and the enjoyment makes the learning better, so to speak. But a lot of the time recently, I read a scholarly book and think, "Well, this just makes one depressed." I'm afraid I'm a bit of a maverick about whole issue of negative thinking.

Velma: As you can tell from the conversation, we have spent a lot of our lives attending wonderful performances. It does sort of spoil one for other theater sometimes. But that has been a great enrichment. The other thing is, I think it would be honest to say, I started studying literature because I loved story-telling. There's no one who is a better storyteller than Shakespeare. One could say, "Well, he borrowed all of his stories." But he does extremely good things with them.

Hugh: He knows the good stories.

Velma: He's got a good eye. I go back to what I see as a trajectory in the development of Shakespeare's eye. We finish with the romances, where I find the most useful way of approaching human experience. It's a belief that, with God, everything is possible and that there is a happy ending. To go from the vision of the tragedies to the vision of the romances, to sound like a Victorian, is extraordinary. That moves me deeply and I don't know very many writers that do that in the same way. Although I so much admire Chaucer, he really doesn't have that struggle. I think the affinity between the modern age and Shakespeare is closer. That's probably what has moved me the most.

Hugh: There is a similar pattern, in fact, even in the middle comedies. You have these storylines about the seemingly dishonest woman, who then comes back—from the dead often.

Velma: And from the start, as with *A Comedy of Errors*, there is a recovery. There is a sense of human loss, but all is not lost. A good deal is recovered.

Hugh: What is Shakespearean? Velma's just talked to this a bit. I think it is the multitudinousness. He's never trapped. With Ben Jonson there is a real sense of a constraining aesthetic and a moralism even, so that you're trapped in a situation. And with Shakespeare, there's always a way out of the trap. There's a sense that there are so many options that you never really have to be caught. I literally think in terms of his way of approaching the situation. You look at the problem and think, "Do I have to look at it this way?" I've been thinking even about Shakespearean blocking because in Shakespeare, very often, you have a central problem, lovers quarrelling or a father or the daughter or whatever. But there are always other people around so that there are alternative perspectives. Even in *Lear*. So you're never trapped within your one view. Sometimes the blocking goes to extremes. In *Love's Labour's Lost*, Dumaine, Longaville, Berowne, and the King are all overlooking each other, so that you have about four different perspectives.

I've just been writing about Velazquez in exactly these terms. In his painting *Las Meninas* (*The Maids*), you have a whole set of different characters and they're all looking in different ways, and there's a strange figure at the back. Then you suddenly realize that in addition to all this, also at the rear, reflected in a mirror, there are images of the king and queen, who are supposed to be where you're standing. The situations are never constricted. There's this openness. That's partly why I think people say Shakespeare has no point of view. What he's got is infinite varieties of perspective. I think in the end that awareness is his preferred point of view, paradoxically.

The Sonnets have this. We have a bit of a debate because Velma especially likes 116.

Velma: "Let me not to the marriage of true minds. . ."

Hugh: Even there, you see, he's escaping. He's saying if there's something wrong we can get over it. And 138 ["When my love swears that she is made of truth/ I do believe her, though I know she lies"] is about, well, the fact that everything is relative and you can never be sure of what's going on. So there's always an alternative option.

Velma: Shakespeare is exactly the kind of person that I'd love to have tea with!

Hugh: The descriptions suggest, as with the battles-of-wit with Ben Jonson, that he was a charming and endearing person. The other thing was that he probably was a bit of a social climber, but he had the necessary talents. He comes from Stratford and finishes up performing in front of the queen and associates with Southampton and Essex and all those people. So he must have been a very attractive personality. This is where again I diverge a lot from the conventional view that we don't know very much about Shakespeare. I think he was absolutely an enthusiast, but aware of the dangers of enthusiasm, so that you get the best of both worlds. In the Sonnets, it seems to me that you get a vivid picture. It may not be historical truth, but he talks as if he's talking about himself. At the very least it's a way in which he wants to present himself. I find this very attractive. Again, it's the agility of his mind.

I had a weird experience because I worked with Marian Diamond, who is the person who dissected Einstein's brain. She's a physiologist. We had quite long discussions about the way the brain works and so forth. In the end, she finished up having a seminar for post-docs, which were recruited from various neurologists and brain surgeons in the Bay Area. There was a series of meetings about great minds like James Joyce and so forth. I was asked to talk about Shakespeare. We discussed the capacity of Shakespeare and the imagery, for example. Often the images work on half a dozen different levels. They work on the literal level, the moralistic, the allegorical, and so forth. We really got down to discussing what type of neurological set-up would allow somebody to work this way. I think Marian showed that Einstein's dendrites were very elaborate. And the neurologists got to the point of saying that certain types of mind don't think linearly. They think at different levels.

We didn't get deeply into the psychology of Shakespeare, but it was clear that he had a really rich response to things. He didn't just read things literally. Compared to Ben Jonson, who I actually quite admire, he's infinitely more agile. That's what's so funny about the description of the two. There's even a painting, I think it's from the Edwardian period, showing Shakespeare beating Ben Jonson at a game of chess. Poor old Jonson would be bewildered by Shakespeare's wit, as Fuller describes. It's not so difficult to visualize what his personality might have been like.

Our favorite quotation, which we got put on a tile at the Orinda Shakespeare Festival, is from *Cymbeline*. Now *Cymbeline* the play is written to produce an absolutely intolerable confusion. In the last act, everybody keeps discovering new things. And at the end the king sort of thinks, "Well, I don't know what to do. We'll just have to forgive everybody." So our favorite quotation is, "Pardon's the word to all." It's so brief, but it's the state of mind that a lot of the Shakespeare plays work towards. It's no use getting excited like Othello or Angelo. You need to be like the Duke at the end of *Measure for Measure*. He finally gives up and says, "Okay, even the ones who are murderers I'm going to let off." It's almost a religious kind of thing.

Velma: I was very happy with "Pardon's the word to all." It was a joint project—but I do like a similar phrase: "Banish plump Jack, and banish all the world," Falstaff's self-defense.

Hugh: People get so excited these days about being angry at other people. A college president, at one point, was fired because she was trying to defend one of the administrators. . .

Velma: . . .who said something about varying ethnic manners she shouldn't have.

Hugh: She was trying to protect the woman. One needed to say, "That's not very tactful," and just forgive it, instead of firing her. People get so angry. This is one of the reasons I'm relieved not to be teaching much, though I still do classes and lectures. If you are a teacher, if you don't watch out, you can say something ironic that could be misinterpreted, particularly when referring to some of Shakespeare's tricky characters, like Richard III, Othello, Shylock, or Petruccio.

The funny thing is that much censured film of *Shrew* I like most of all is the Burton /Taylor *Taming of the Shrew*, directed by Zefferelli. There's the scene on the way to Padua when she suddenly realizes how to outmaneuver him by saying something ironically. Sometimes the scene is played as if she's a zombie. But here it's as if Kate understands what Petruccio's playing at, and the two really come to some kind of mutual understanding that you don't need to be literal-minded and indignant all the time, which I think is how she starts out. It's like Beatrice and Benedict again. There are daggers drawn, and then they learn how to live with their mistakes.

Velma: I think in practice one of the things that's been a little bit sad, from my point of view, with some of the feminist writing is that I don't think anyone has given more illustration of nicely matched men and women than Shakespeare. "Nicely" in the old sense of the world, meaning "precisely."

Hugh: It's amusing looking at Shakespeare's reputation in the 17th century.

The Puritan ministers used to get very angry, saying, "If you go to the wedding chests of some of these young women, what do you find at the bottom? The Plays of Shakespeare!" Obviously they were regarding him as a very dangerous influence in encouraging young women to think for themselves. If you read the literary scholars on Beatrice and Benedick, they often think their marriage is doomed because they talk against each other on occasion, but every married couple does. I had a wonderful experience at a faculty seminar a few years ago. I got into a conversation with a very distinguished scientist who said, "When I was a graduate and my wife was an English graduate student, I used to sit in on your lectures about women and Shakespeare, and that's why our marriage has survived."

This is the whole thing about lively performance. It's very difficult, if one is just coldly reading it on the page, not to be over critical and negative. But every play has to be colored by the actors' positive physical presence and the rich resonances of the spoken quality. For me that's the only way to approach plays. I always start from performance.

PATSY RODENBERG

"Love is not love
which alters when it alteration finds"

Patsy Rodenberg is Head of Voice at The Guildhall School of Music and Drama in London and Director of Voice at Michael Howard Studios in New York. She has trained some of the finest and most successful actors in the world, has worked with the Royal Shakespeare Company and the Royal National Theatre (where she founded their voice department), and has had notable success as a director. She has also worked as a voice coach with politicians and business executives around the world. She has published **Speaking Shakespeare** *(invaluable for any teacher of Shakespeare) as well as* **The Actor Speaks**, **The Right to Speak**, **The Need for Words**, *and* **The Second Circle**. *She has recently released an 8-disk DVD set,* **Patsy Rodenberg Brings You: Shakespeare in the Present**. *In 2005 she was appointed Order of the British Empire in the Queen's Birthday Honours. I met her at the Guildhall School and we talked over lunch.*

The Shakespearean life guides you, doesn't it? It guides you because the ethics are so clearly there. And in all the chaos of it, Shakespeare comes back to what it's like to be a human being. I always think he comes back to liking human beings in a way that Jonson might not. He believes in us. He is compassionate. He even likes his villains.

If you go down, as I have done, and worked in Broadmoor [a high-security psychiatric hospital], where there are serial killers, they always say that Richard III and Iago are casebook studies of sociopaths. But even with sociopaths you can glimpse their humanity at some point; you're working with somebody who is a monster and yet you see a glimpse of something else—just as you see the glimpse of Iago realizing that his wife may be sleeping with everybody and the pain it engenders in him. That compassion is one of the great advantages of being with Shakespeare.

My mother was working class. She could have been very well-educated because she was bright, but her parents couldn't afford a very good school. So she wasn't really educated. My father was Dutch and never knew about Shakespeare. But I remember finding an old battered book of complete works and reading *Hamlet* when I was very young, nine-ish. I understood a lot of it, even if I didn't understand it. I thought it was wonderful. I remember going to my grandmother, who was really working class. She was smoking a cigarette—she would manage never to drop the ash. I was quoting her lines from *Hamlet* and said, "This is amazing, this work is amazing." She just went, "Mmm." Eventually she said, "I don't think that's so amazing because we've said those things all our lives." I said, "That's because he wrote them." She said immediately, "No, he wrote them because we said them." It does go both ways.

My mother was a bardic woman—she told stories. And, of course, story-telling is one of Shakespeare's gifts. Another of his gifts was to understand that the working classes are often the best-behaved people. It's the shepherd that picks up that baby in *The Winter's Tale*; it's the servant who tries to stop the blinding in *Lear*. Such people often provide the turning point in his plays. Dogberry is an idiot, but he's the one who saves the day.

I just enjoyed reading Shakespeare. It never seemed to me to be difficult. I can't bear people making Shakespeare so difficult. I read Shakespeare without a filter, without thinking, "Oh, my God, this is a remarkable piece of work and I have to bow at his feet." I remember reading some of the Sonnets when I was very young. I didn't understand them all, but I liked the feeling of the rhythms and the sensuality of the language. With Shakespeare you can't only think him, you've got to feel him.

Of course, I read him aloud. My students who come not having read Shakespeare aloud are bored by it. Shakespeare works on all the levels. He simultaneously works physically, intellectually, emotionally, and spiritually. I don't think any other writer's managed that one. There's both sound and sense. The glory of the English language is in its chaos because its physicality is fantastic. Sometimes when I've taught in so-called deprived areas I've deliberately not said, "This is Shakespeare." I just say, "Try this," and people say, "Oh, this is good." I do that all the time, and then I eventually say, "This is Shakespeare." "It's not." "It is." "Wow." There is this fear that you can't understand it.

I do a lot of work with world leaders. It occurred to me about three or four years ago that the scary thing in the West is that for the first time in our civilization we're being run by people who have never read the classics. We learn ethics and morality through stories, so now I teach Shakespeare to some of the people who are running the world. I have been asked to teach all sorts of people how to present, how to stay present, and how to impact. Then I started to realize that some of them were lacking; the bankers didn't understand that they'd done anything wrong because they never read these stories. Most of them are engineers who went on to get an MBA. So I introduce them to story.

I love teaching. When I was studying at Central School [The Royal Central School of Speech and Drama], I did the teaching course, which at the time was superb. Everyone was doing this teaching course because it was free (I really wanted to be an actor). I remember teaching in prison, in Holloway in Canterbury. Touch wood, I never really had a discipline problem. I was talking to them and I suddenly thought, "This is more interesting than acting." I remember thinking, "This is more important than acting." I started very early doing voice, and, of course, at some point you've got to put voice into text. And Shakespeare is the thing to do, so the two worlds collided very nicely.

I don't look at text as an academic. I look at text as something that has to be spoken and I try to facilitate that speech. I'm aware that I look at it differently than I would have done when I did my A levels. I've found another road, maybe because I was working with people who hadn't much education. I realized that this work really meant something to me. I get grown men crying. I use *Sonnet 94* in the business world, and the business people become those "that have power to hurt." Some of these people on 4 ½, 5, 6 million a year are wicked. I'll tell you the line that always gets them: "And husband nature's riches from expense." When I tell them what that means, really, many of them have said, "I've never looked after anybody. I have just wasted everyone." Shakespeare works. There's no doubt in my mind.

I talk about Beethoven to make students listen. I think that there are moments when artists are working at ideas; they work at an idea and then they bring it to perfection: like the symphonies of Beethoven, where he progresses from the first through to the ninth. And I think there are plays of Shakespeare when he's been working on ideas and then he comes to this sublime ability. *Winter's Tale* is a magnificent play, but he had to do *Cymbeline* in order to get to *The Winter's Tale*. There are plays where everything has come together at that moment.

I think you find the play you need to find in your life. There's always the play that you should be doing or the students should be doing or the actor should be doing. Or maybe certain plays are in the zeitgeist. When Clinton and Monica Lewinsky were the news in America, the first thing somebody should have done is put on *Measure for Measure*. Different plays surface depending on what we're going through.

In general I like to start with the Sonnets. But you have to be very clear; they're very distilled and they often open up all the essentials. There are only a few such things in Shakespeare; they happen to be among the most important things on the planet. In them there is often the misuse of power and on the other side of that the fact that if you have power you cannot not use it.

In both *The Tempest* and *Measure for Measure*, the Duke and Prospero should have used their power.

I think in every Shakespearean scene there is a tension between conditional and unconditional love. In that way you can understand that in *Sonnet 116* ["Let me not to the marriage of true minds"]. There's a tension between what I would call cosmic justice and man-made justice, as I talked about in that amazing scene I mentioned earlier, when the servant stands up to Cornwall: that amazing moment when someone actually says, "I know you've got the power, that you're the law, but this is wrong." That's why these plays are done everywhere, speak to everyone.

I've been lucky to teach Shakespeare all over the world. Sometimes it has to be in translation. Of course, then you lose a massive amount, but you don't lose his connection to what it's like to be human and to what matters. And I think he does say strongly again and again, "This should not be done. There are certain things that should not be done"—not in a puritanical or rigid way, but in a human way.

It's interesting how people say "Shakespeare's language," because he changes his language all the time. I'm very interested in how strong his women are, which I think is often overlooked. I think they are all strong. Does he write a wimp? Maybe Hero is in a way, but at the same time we see her spite, don't we? She's not a squeaky clean little girl. She has a wonderful opportunity to have a good old prod at Beatrice, doesn't she? So yes, she's not strong but she's not weak either. She gets somewhere.

I always say if you're going to say as a woman Lady Macbeth is evil, let's not rehearse the play. I was working recently on Lady Macbeth's speech "Have plucked my nipple from his boneless gums," about when the milk is still in her breast. They had a little boy, and he just gets a word about his boneless gums. But they had a son! So you can feel absolutely why she's doing this. Too often she's been directed as two-dimensional.

The evidence of the text is all there. It's very boring being married to Macbeth. He has a drink problem. You know the drunks who say, "Oh, yes, darling, I'll do that" and then the next day with a slight hangover, the wife will say, "Was the hope drunk?" He doesn't actually lie, but he doesn't fully tell the truth. She knows his flaws, so it's a marriage of flaws. One of the great themes is that if you get metaphorically into bed with somebody that you know is flawed, then you're in trouble. Cassius, in that scene with Brutus is completely brilliant, and so Brutus makes an allegiance with a man who is motivated by envy. It's like Blair and Bush. Blair probably thought he could control Bush, but he couldn't. It's going to end in tears. All Macbeth has to say is stop, no. But there is something in that relationship. Those scenes are used in Broadmoor a great deal because when murder is done by two people, it's more terrifying. Somebody says, "I don't want to do this," and then the other person says, "But if you love me, you'll do it." And that's what Shakespeare has written.

This is what happens in *Macbeth*: if you love me you will go along with this, if you love me you will clean up the blood. So when people say, "Oh, I don't get Shakespeare," I say, "Bring in the worst tabloid paper you can find, the one that everyone reads, that everyone just groans over, *The Sun* or whatever." And I can show you a Shakespeare story on every page. Flip it over, there it is. But what makes him even better is that he goes into this underworld through language.

Lady Macbeth only comes to consciousness through sleepwalking. She doesn't come to consciousness in her awake state, isn't awakened. I talk about "If it were done" as the center of the play: Macbeth does something knowingly, knowing that it's wrong in the way the Claudius doesn't seem to know. Claudius has to have the play to bring him to consciousness, and then he calls for light because light has come into his mind. He's been awakened by theater! That's how important theater is to Shakespeare.

Shakespeare reminds women not to be frightened of their power as women. I did a production here of *Richard III* where I kept all the women characters in. People were coming from Oxford and Cambridge to see it because they'd never seen these women played fully out. When Tony [Anthony Sher] did his *Richard III* in Australia, they cut out Queen Margaret. But the women are the survivors in the play. He wrote so sympathetically about powerful women. And he likes to struggle with those women, like Hotspur likes the struggle with his Kate. It's a relief to read those plays and see those women struggling with men—and being loved.

I think Shakespeare was married to an extraordinary woman, that Anne was a handful, just as all his female characters are handfuls—yes, except maybe for Hero. I did a production of *Hamlet* in a top security prison where they promised me not so bad boys, but I got the worst boys. Then we did it for the other prisoners in that wing, who were naughty boys as well. There could have been dodgy moments, even a riot, but they were absolutely attentive. And when the guy (who was a murderer) came forward as Claudius and said to the audience, "O, my offense is rank! It smells to heaven," there was a gasp. There was a gasp in the audience. They got it. It smells to heaven—I stink. I've got to bend my stubborn knees.

I go all over world and they get it. You can go into African villages or in India and it's going to be something that they understand. I worked with Aborigines in Australia on Shakespeare, and they got him. What a privilege to bring people this extraordinary spirit, who used to live just over the road there. There's a Pizza Express, and that's where his house was. And in that church there, St. Giles Cripplegate Church, that's where Milton is buried. Andrew Marvel used to worship there. My students do *Paradise Lost* in there. I think in a way Milton was one of the first people who really realized what a genius Shakespeare was. It took another genius to realize it.

I think that the contortion of language is important. We understand who Iachimo is because of his tortured language. Having worked with politicians, I understand Polonius's language. He's a deadly man, but he manages to mask it with his language. How clever that is! He's pretending he's a nice uncle, but he would set a spy on his own son. As you make the journey as a character in Shakespeare, your language simplifies. So Lear has to make that terrible journey so at the end of the play he can say please and thank you. He comes down to simplicity. There's a lovely game where you can look at a character's first speech and their last and see how they transformed. And then he has characters that don't transform, a warning to us that if we don't grow, our language doesn't grow. Yes, Polonius, and all the salads in *Merchant of Venice*— oh, you know, Salerino, Solanio, the salads— they're not people who grow.

The absence of characters in a scene is fantastically interesting. I like to ask why isn't Edgar in the first scene in *Lear*. He's probably the most powerful young man in the court, but he's not interested. He's interested in other things. He has to be pulled into politics. He doesn't want to be a leader. And if you look at the play objectively and concretely, he never seeks to be part of the action. They find him. And then his language is extraordinary because actually it's like the language of people who spend time on their own. I was once working in Oxford and a group of monks came to work with me. They came because they said that if you go into silence for maybe four or five weeks at a time, when you come out you speak a childlike language. It's like a silence burns off all the outer layers of your language. I think that's what Edgar does. His language is extraordinary.

And then why isn't Egeus at the wedding in the *Dream*? Because he hasn't changed! How the lovers change their language when they go to the woods is key. They become initiated into adulthood and out they come speaking blank verse. And the *Dream* is one of those superbly structured plays; it's sublime. It's like he'd come to some deep understanding of dramatic structure at that stage.

I imagine Shakespeare would have been very interesting to talk to, but he might also have been more of a listener. We know that he was gracious. That's obvious in the plays. Mind you, he must have had testosterone. This is going to sound odd, so you'll just have to bear with me, but I think he's in balance between female and male energy. I'm not in any way religious in the way a lot of people would take this, but I think that's what's the brilliance of Jesus Christ is too, that he had both. There are people who have both, and Shakespeare seemed able to balance both. Name me another male writer that can write about women as accurately. How did he know what women did in the Desdemona or Emilia scene? (That might be the influence of his daughters.) And, of course, he suffered the loss of a son, a twin. How many plays have twins in them and one twin is looking for another one? These are really potent things that he throws into the mix: all those boys of eleven who die in his plays.

There are so many great quotations. I think of the critical lines in *Sonnet 116*, "Let me not to the marriage of true minds/ Admit impediments. Love is not love/ Which alters when it alteration finds." I think that line is pivotal to his thinking. Almost every Shakespeare scene has to do with—though not entirely—not being able to take away love from someone if you've really loved them; if you can take it away, it's not love. It's Lear again: "Nothing will come of nothing." It is critical to Shakespeare, I think, that "Love is not love which alters when it alteration finds,/ Or bends with the remover to remove." Iago is the remover, one who removes love. Shakespeare is absolutely realistic here. Real love looks on tempests. It's not going to be easy. You're going to have the great waves crash over you. That whole sonnet is so relevant: "Love alters not with his brief hours and weeks." That's an amazing concept.

I was thinking about *Macbeth* the other day, just that idea that sometimes you have to stop a student and say, "Can you really understand 'that if we but teach/ Bloody instructions, which, being taught, return/ To plague th' inventor.'" A child can understand that if he bullies, it's going to come back on him; every politician on the planet should understand this idea. And that's when you can blow a young person's mind because they just go dramatic about it. I talk similarly about the "the plague of custom" and "the curiosity of nations" that Edmund describes in his "Thou, nature, art my goddess" speech. The students understand that young Edmund is an outsider. And I always tell them about a moment I had with my father years ago when I asked, "Why did my brother get a better education than I did?" It can be a "curiosity of nations" that women get inferior educations.

So I think sometimes Shakespeare's poetry is wonderful, but sometimes the ideas are so extraordinary they blow your mind. And the ideas come out of the story. We have to see the idea in operation. We have to see the unbearable, bear the unbearable thing that Edmund manages to bear by feeling how unfairly he has been treated. And that's when the story becomes educational. Almost the last thing Edmund says is "Yet Edmund was beloved," remembering that two of the most powerful women in the land fell in love with him. That is so human. And that's where we started, I suppose, that humanity is Shakespeare's great gift.

Shakespeare is so much fun. We are lucky, aren't we? It is amazing that we get up in the morning and look at this. But I always say it seems to me that when you think you've got to the top of the Shakespeare mountain, he's seven mountains away waving, "Over here. Come over this way." The other great thing is that whatever you're going through in life, the play will throw light on it. You will find all the resonances that you need in whatever play you happen to be working on.

He was a balanced human being, not afraid of life—not frightened of getting involved in money-making, getting his hands dirty. Good for him. And he's not frightened of mess, either. So many young actors want to make the text tidy. They've got to understand how messy the scenes can be—because life is messy.

Mark Twain was very naughty to suggest that Shakespeare wasn't Shakespeare. I'm so bored with Americans coming up and saying, "But Shakespeare didn't write Shakespeare." I'm interested in ornithology; I know a lot about birds. And the Royal Society for the Protection of Birds some years ago published an article about how Shakespeare was the first person to notice certain bird behaviors. His attention is to actual nature, and I argue that a courtier wouldn't have such attention to nature. Shakespeare knows how to milk a cow, he knows about gardening. There isn't a play without mention of particular behaviors of birds, the way they feed or fly. In *Sonnet 29* ["When in disgrace with fortune and men's eyes"] a skylark arises, just as you can see skylarks do. He saw those things.

Allen Bennett and Maggie Smith have a wonderful story (I haven't got it exactly but it's in one of his memoirs) about "Fear no more the heat o' the sun... As chimney-sweepers come to dust." In Warwickshire, only in Warwickshire, there's a children's game where they get a dandelion, blow it, and chant, "Chimney-sweepers come to dust. Chimney-sweepers...." And it's only in that area. But it gets even better: they also call old people dandelion heads because of their white hair. So he fuses together two rural references of the old head of a dandelion and that song. And that's only in Warwickshire.

JAMES SHAPIRO

"There is a world elsewhere."

James S. Shapiro is Professor of English and Comparative Literature at Columbia University. Among his books are **Rival Playwrights: Marlowe, Jonson, Shakespeare***;* **Shakespeare and the Jews** *(winner of the Bainton Prize for best book on sixteenth-century literature);* **1599: A Year in the Life of William Shakespeare** *(winner of the Theatre Book Prize as well as the BBC Samuel Johnson Prize, awarded to the best nonfiction book published in the UK); and* **Contested Will: Who Wrote Shakespeare?** *(winner of the 2011 George Freedley Memorial Award by the Theatre Library Association). I talked with him in his office at Columbia University, where, memorably, he seemed to have programs for all the many Shakespeare plays he had ever seen.*

I have distinctive memories of when I first encountered Shakespeare. It was in ninth grade, in a New York City public school. We were assigned *Romeo and Juliet*, and I hated it. I did not get the dirty bits and I did not understand why everybody thought this was the greatest writer in the world. We just read it and analyzed it, and it turned me off to Shakespeare in a huge way. I have to say the teacher was not a bad teacher. He was great on plot, villains, and the like, but he was not somebody who made me find Shakespeare accessible. And as a result, when as an undergraduate I went to Columbia, where I now teach, I did not take a Shakespeare course at all. But I did study a Shakespeare play in the great books curriculum. I liked plays. I studied drama, classical drama, some medieval drama, but I never took a Shakespeare course. I studied some other Elizabethan playwrights, but Shakespeare for some reason had been tarnished.

When I was 18 or 19, just finishing college, or even a year earlier than that, I started going with my brother to Europe, bumming around. In those days you could do that for a couple of hundred bucks, sleeping in church basements and youth hostels. When we found ourselves in London, I started going to plays, Shakespeare plays. And they were electric and extraordinary. Then I then started going back myself. I'd take a summer job for a couple of months, then spend August in London, Stratford, and up to the Edinburgh Festival.

This was from 1977 to 1981. And if you look to your left there on the bottom shelf, you'll see all the playbills going back to those years. For the next eight or ten years, I went over almost every year and probably ended up seeing a couple hundred productions of Shakespeare. So, in my training, even in graduate school, I never took a formal course on Shakespeare. I took a lot of Renaissance literature. But my experience with Shakespeare is through seeing productions, and now that I teach Shakespeare, which I've done for a quarter century at Columbia, I make students get on their feet, act out scenes, and see live productions—so that I try to do something that will free them from the kind of problems I faced at first. Shakespeare on paper can be not just formidable but alienating.

So how do you get to a position where you spend fifteen hours a day on Shakespeare, which is what I've done for the last couple of decades or so? My story is probably a version of that Malcolm Gladwell argument, that if you do something 10,000 times or for 10,000 hours, you get good at it, and then you get better at it. I understand how a lot of these plays work in an intuitive way. And some of that comes from studying the period and seeing the plays and talking to actors and other scholars, but some of that comes from a kind of gift. I don't have a gift for languages; I've studied a half-dozen foreign languages that I've forgotten. But I do have a gift for understanding the deep currents within not all of the plays, but within many or most of them. And it's a gift that I have built on because I got smarter by spending more and more time thinking about these things.

You should ask everyone you interview, their A-list and B-list plays. I got to interview Peter Brook, the most wonderful and influential director of Shakespeare in the 20th Century, and I asked if there were plays that he didn't really understand (Michael Boyd was part of that conversation as well)—this was a few months ago when the Royal Shakespeare Company was in town. And they both didn't really want to engage that question, so I didn't press the issue. But there are plays that I know and like but don't really grasp: *Twelfth Night* is a play I could see many times, and just saw again and loved it on stage, but I don't really get it. And I don't teach it. And *Love's Labour's Lost*—I have friends that think it's the greatest of the plays. It is a foreign language to me, that play. I can translate it into my own terms, but plays like *Hamlet* or *Julius Caesar* I really have a deep, deep feel for, which I don't have for plays like *Twelfth Night*. I don't think one chooses which plays one understands. I don't really get *Much Ado*, but I have friends who edited the Arden edition of it. I just understand *Julius Caesar*, for example, very well, compared to my understanding of other plays. I don't want to be vainglorious about it, but I have a deep comfort level with the play and understand a little bit about why and how it works.

There are very few academics that work with theater companies. We're cats and dogs in the way that we both lay claim to Shakespeare. But I've been working for the past few years with the Royal Shakespeare Company, and it has been one of the most exciting things for me. I go over when they are opening a season and tell them what I know and kind of pick their brains and work with the actors and directors. I'll be going over in November and doing that for the next season. They are going to be doing *Twelfth Night*, *The Tempest*, and *Comedy of Errors*. David Farr, a brilliant director, is doing *Twelfth Night*. To go out on a rope, I'd say I'm really good at *Comedy of Errors* because I really understand it and think it is undervalued. I'm pretty good on *The Tempest*. Most people are. It's one of those things where some people are brilliant on it. I'm pretty good on it. But I said, "You know, I'm really not going to be as good as you think I am, or would like me to be, on *Twelfth Night*. Maybe we could arrange a different session than that." And they haven't written back yet. I could talk about it, but they'll walk away scratching their heads thinking they didn't have enough caffeine that day, or I that wasn't punching my weight. I just don't get the play at all. I can sit through it, but I do not know what Shakespeare was doing in that play. I can make up an answer, but in all honesty it eludes me.

I never have been one of those people who over-identifies with any character. I actually think Shakespeare, however many hundreds and hundreds of characters he created, identified with all of them. And I think it's quite dangerous to get into the identification game because that's at the heart of the movement to deny that Shakespeare was Shakespeare. In other words, you begin with identification and then you say, "Well, Shakespeare himself was… Romeo in love was… Hamlet in depressive moods was…." Then you say, "Well, the Earl of Oxford corresponds more closely with this persona." So I think Shakespeare loved the servant in *Lear* who tries to intervene in Gloucester's blinding as much as he loved and identified or didn't identify with Lear. So I never saw myself in those terms. I don't bring that, although I recognize that lots and lots of people see themselves through these characters. I like all the characters and see complexity in all of them. Even when I was younger, I really never left a play feeling a powerful identification.

You're talking to one of the luckiest people in the world, somebody who gets to teach really smart and talented students, gets to work with some of the best actors and directors in the world and gets to spend his time out on sabbatical this year. I'm working on a documentary on Shakespeare. I'm working on a Shakespeare in America volume. I'm working on a book on Shakespeare in 1606. These are quite thrilling things so to the extent that has Shakespeare has shaped me, it has probably forestalled a midlife crisis. Every day I wake up thinking about one of these problems or another.

I have a kid who is now as old as I was when I first started studying Shakespeare. When you are the kid of a Shakespeare professor and your mom teaches literature as well, you are going to spend a lot of time going to plays. So since he was three he has seen, on both sides of the Atlantic, some of the most spectacular productions. The RSC comes over here and he hangs out with them. He spent last summer at a brilliant NYU program putting on a production of *A Winter's Tale*, and he is in a production of *As You Like It* right now at his current school. I was the most shocked person when he came home and said, "I want to be in a play." I have never been in a play— I can't act. I have a Brooklyn accent, which will not be picked up in your transcript, but on tape clearly shows why Shakespeare did not write a lot of roles for a Brooklyn accent. But I can see the confidence and excitement in a 15-year-old who is supremely confident navigating through these plays. And that's made my life more pleasurable.

He has a bit role in this *As You Like It*. I think they created a role as Duke Ferdinand's servant. They usually pad out these casts to accommodate a large group of students. And I said, "Does it bother you that you have a bit role?" And he said, "Nah, I really understand this play." He has seen *As You Like It* several times, has had the play committed to memory from having seen it. And he is able to help the other kids who are in the leading roles who are lost in the play.

I wrote my dissertation on Marlowe, on his verse style—quite far away from Shakespeare issues—and I spend a lot of time thinking about Dekker, Jonson, Middleton, and others. I really think about dramatists who worked around Shakespeare, and I would say a couple of things make Shakespeare distinctive. He seems, to my mind at least, to be less judgmental of his characters. He is able to put out very powerful plays that are not morality plays. Jonson can't hide his likes and dislikes in the way that Shakespeare does. I'd say "Shakespearean" also has to do with a kind of brilliance of construction that the more you study and read and teach and see his plays the more you grasp—and also a real love of language, which sometimes goes too far, or even in the later plays a level of difficulty in language, which also sometimes goes too far. There are probably many, many other hallmarks of the "Shakespearean." His contemporary playwrights might have said what is "Shakespearean" was his ability to walk right up to the line of what is politically dangerous without overstepping that line and, unlike every other major playwright, without ending up in trouble.

The question of Shakespeare's personality is a much more loaded one than most people acknowledge. Having written a Shakespeare biography, having reflected hard on what it means to write Shakespeare's life, I think one of the great faults of most of the biographies that have been written is that people have been given too free reign to believe based on their reading of Shakespeare and what evidence is out there that they are in touch with the man and not the author. And I'm interested in the author. Oh, I'm interested in the man as well, but what we know about his feelings, his belief systems, his attitudes about his family or anything else, we could put on the back of a napkin. So I made a decision a long time ago to keep those two parts separate, although some of the best minds in the business have let them cross-fertilize. I think that 50 or 100 years from now scholars will look back and shake their heads at the speculation about his sexuality, his personal crises, his religious beliefs, his politics. He had all of those, but we just do not have a clue about them. So people write things like, "Shakespeare didn't like dogs."

That exemplifies for me the real danger of reading the life out of the works. I try not to do that. I understand that we've all trespassed, but I try to be really careful about that sort of thing. I don't think is possible to write about Shakespeare, either as a critic or a biographer, without slipping into some kind of autobiographical moment. It is just not possible. Harold Bloom is the great example of that. He has a brilliant, brilliant mind, but he thinks Falstaff was like Shakespeare—to talk about the over-identification with a particular character. And he also thinks that he is like Falstaff, and you know, it is not all that hard to make the third angle of that triangle.

There are so many great quotations from Shakespeare. In *Coriolanus*, when Coriolanus, in a huff, leaves Rome, he says, "There is a world elsewhere." That's a great line. One of the very few things that I've learned in my professional life, watching people go from university job to university job, or for that matter from marriage to marriage, or anything else, there is no world elsewhere. And, that fact is one of the cruel, tragic ironies of that play. It's a lovely line to say. With David Kastan, who used to be my colleague and now teaches at Yale, I would end many conversations with that tag line: "There is a world elsewhere." And we would just laugh. We know, for example, that Yale is not that different from Columbia. We don't have any fantasies as Coriolanus did that the world is different someplace else.

TIFFANY STERN

"THE RAIN, IT RAINETH EVERY DAY."

Tiffany Stern is at Oxford University as Professor of Early Modern Drama (English Faculty), and as Beaverbrook and Bouverie Fellow and Tutor in English (University College). She specializes in Shakespeare, theatre and book history, and editing. Her first book, **Rehearsal from Shakespeare to Sheridan**, *was followed by* **Making Shakespeare**, *which focused on Shakespeare's London, actors, theatres, props and music. Theatre companies attempting 'original methods' of Shakespearean production use both books. She subsequently co-wrote (with Simon Palfrey)* **Shakespeare in Parts**, *focusing on Shakespeare as playwright and actor performing from, and writing for, 'parts' (the texts actors received, consisting of cues and speeches, nothing else). This book was followed by* **Documents of Performance in Shakespearean England**, *which examines other performance papers: plot-scenarios, playbills, arguments, prologues, songs, scrolls and backstage-plots. Stern has also edited the anonymous* **King Leir**, *Richard Sheridan's* **The Rivals**, *George Farquhar's* **The Recruiting Officer**, *and* **The Merry Wives of Windsor** *(forthcoming). She is one of three general editors responsible for the New Mermaids play series, an Arden Advisory Editor, and on the boards of the RSC, the* **Greenwood Shakespeare Encyclopedia**, *the Queen's Men internet editions, and the journals* **Shakespeare Bulletin**, **SEDERI**, **The Hare**, *and* **Shakespeare Quarterly**. *I talked with her in her rooms at University College in Oxford, which were a wonderful mix of the old (antiques and old books) and the new (a Macintosh laptop). This blend seemed to me much like Stern herself, comfortably at home both in the early modern era and in our own time.*

My uncle, Patrick Tucker, was a Shakespeare director. He had a little company called The Original Shakespeare Company. He was a great influence on me. I used to be taken to the theatre from when I was five or six. That was really helpful. My mother would tell me the story in advance, so I never thought Shakespeare was difficult to understand. Experiencing it first in the theatre gave me a love of Shakespeare performance and theatricality, which has carried through.

Shakespeare was a treat and an exciting outing: you put on a pretty frock and you go to the theatre! And as I say, because I'd been told the plot in advance, it never struck me that one had to struggle to understand the language or anything. I just always assumed I understood it.

So as a child I loved the theatre and I loved and admired my Uncle Patrick. I used to follow him around, and he'd allow me backstage and I'd see props and fall in love with his actors. I grew up with that as a very important part of my life. Then as I grew older and started specializing in English at university, my uncle would ring me and ask me to look things up in the library. And one time he said he wanted his company to rehearse in the original way and he couldn't find out what an original rehearsal was like. I told him I'd go to the English faculty library, look it up, and tell him later. And, of course, there was no book on rehearsal. I thought, "This is a strange gap. There are lots and lots of books about performance but no books about rehearsal, and yet performance comes out of rehearsal." People were making assumptions about how these plays were rehearsed, which when you looked at them didn't make sense. So that ended up being my doctorate and then my first book. I never had to think about what my doctorate might be. It had been presented to me. I was very lucky. That gap then sort of became my possession in the profession. I owe all of this to my uncle.

I think that the only Shakespeare play I really don't like is *Titus Andronicus*. I can't work out whether it's very bleak humor or just a bloodthirsty sort of Hammer House of Horror play. I find rampant mutilation difficult. I don't think the lyricism is good enough to make up for the horror of the play. I am slightly appalled by it. And students always love it. They always want to do it, are a bit enthralled by the bloodthirsty nature of it. I try to steer them away from it, trying to suggest, "What about Shakespeare when he's more philosophical and kind of better?" I really can't stand that play. All the others I love in one way or another. They all have problems, but the problems are some of the things that are exciting about the plays.

My favorite play has often changed. I think everyone has a *Hamlet* phase. And some people stay in it. When you're adolescent, *Hamlet* issues are especially real to you, relationships with parents, relationships with the person you love. So certainly I had a *Hamlet* phase when I was young and passionate. Now I know *Hamlet* almost too well. It's hard to be reinvigorated quite as much as I'd like. I need to see a really fresh, exciting, fantastic production to be re-Hamleted. And I think for that reason I now find more intriguing the slightly less well-known plays. At present I'm very, very fond of and interested in *Pericles*.

There are tons of things I find very moving about it. The father-daughter recognition scene at the end, with the celestial music, is one of the most moving scenes in Shakespeare. I love that. And there are great lyrical moments when Pericles thinks he has to bury Thaisa at sea: "A terrible childbed hast thou had, my dear." I think that's one of the loveliest, most beautiful bits of Shakespeare. And *Pericles* is also such a funny play. Of course, it's cranky and difficult in some places, was probably co-written, and comes in a not very good quarto. I love that the whole play is narrated by Gower. Shakespeare in his late phase got so interested in narrative, and he slightly de-dramatized all dramas, playing around with what drama is. I keep being drawn to *Pericles*. One thing that makes me sad this moment is that the RSC have a season that they're calling their shipwreck season. And they haven't put *Pericles* in there. I thought *Pericles* was a main shipwreck play. In *Comedy of Errors*, the shipwreck is just a device that happened. But in *Pericles* you have wet mariners, as you do in *The Tempest*.

It is fascinating to imagine spending time with Shakespeare characters. I guess it would depend on what sort of evening I wanted. You said you would like to drink with Falstaff, so I'll drink with Toby Belch and his group. I'd love that, to be a kind of Maria to them. I'd like to have a conversation with Feste. I'm interested in *Twelfth Night*. I like those astute, melancholy clowns who understand things but sort of Cassandra-like can't actually change things by their knowledge, who sing songs that cryptically reflect on what's happening and tell jokes that are telling but that no one really hears. So I would love to talk to Feste. And, yes, in my ambitions, I'd maybe like to be Cleopatra. You've got to dream. She really lived, she really died, and she was passionate and wayward and troublesome and fascinating. I've outgrown some of the younger heroines but Cleopatra remains a good one anyway to have in my sight. But against Shakespeare's many feisty women there are those weak, accepting women that things happen to, the Heros of this world. I don't dislike her, but I wouldn't really want to hang out with Hero.

So many of his evil characters are fascinating as well. I would love to talk to Iago or Richard III. And who would not like to meet Edmond the Bastard?

I read Shakespeare, I teach Shakespeare, I go to the theatre, I listen to music of the era. I work a lot on contexts. My way is trying to understand Shakespeare's context. And I suppose there's a bit of my heart and soul that's kind of early modern. They say the past is another country, and I suppose I've lived mentally in that other country a little bit. I have a lot of Shakespeare phrases in my head. I do think Shakespeare must have fashioned the way I think, but I can't say exactly how.

I often reflect starting from a Shakespeare phrase because that's so much in my head. I don't have moments like Laurie Maguire has. She wrote a sort of self-help book using Shakespeare. I think she can isolate moments in her life that were invigorated, revivified, or given a new direction because of a Shakespeare play. And I don't have anything as clear as that, perhaps because he's infused everything a little bit.

I think Shakespeare is some weird combination of many things, which is why he's so good. Obviously, there's a high quality of poetry and great lyricism. Also a range of different thoughts—which dramatists can do because they think through different people—but Shakespeare thinks in especially different ways through different people. He has a philosophical way of thinking combined with an extreme use of language. He has a profound sense of theatre. So reading Shakespeare is different from reading an epic poem or anything else, because it's got in it almost living figures. I think the Shakespearean is some mixture of theatre, poetry, thought, and emotion. It is an emotional business reading or seeing or hearing Shakespeare. Ben Jonson's characters each have of an emotion; you see a consistency of emotion in his characters. But with Shakespeare people are emotionally changing, developing, or falling apart. The Shakespearean happens in the minute. You can get instantly gripped because you're seeing some extraordinary focused mental development happening. And you're also being struck by the tortured power of the words at the same time you are struck by the thought and the emotion of a person.

If you research in that period, you will find jests and various things about Ben Jonson and even about George Peele. They were people who gripped the imagination of the people around them and were big characters. It's clear to me that Shakespeare was not one of those. I don't think he was charismatic. I don't think his charm was of that kind. I think he was the person in the corner of the room, absorbing, not actually the center of attention, not the focus of everyone's gaze, not exuding brilliance. I think he was the man with the beard in the corner of the room taking it in. He was introverted.

He clearly knew unhappiness around the subject of love, and he knew the tension around the subject of parents and children. I take it he was not a totally happy and fulfilled man. You don't write like that if you are. I think he had an angry or frustrated phase in middle life. Yes, I take it he was a quiet, troubled person.

As to a favorite quotation—as I said I have *Pericles* in my head at present, and I have that reconciliation scene very much in my mind now—I could pick the dialogue: "Wherefore called Marina?/ Called Marina for I was born at sea." And then the whole plot unfolds from that, which I love. Days like this one cannot help but think, "The rain, it raineth every day." That has been much in my mind of late, throughout the summer, in fact. I like it. It's a profoundly English thing to say, and it is locally the case and will have been specifically the case many times when the Globe was in operation, but it's also to do with maybe a big sorrow as well.

DAVID SUCHET

*"Life's but a walking shadow, a poor player
that struts and frets his hour upon the stage,
and then is heard no more."*

David Suchet was born in London. He attended Wellington School
in Somerset, where he became interested in acting. He joined the
National Youth Theatre at age 18, and subsequently trained at the
London Academy of Music and Dramatic Art. He joined the Royal
Shakespeare Company in 1973 and was there, off and on, for
thirteen years, playing Iago, Bolingbroke, Mercutio, Hotspur,
Orlando, Caliban, and other such roles. He is doubtless best known
for his television portrayals of Hercule Poirot. He was awarded the
OBE, the CBE, and the London Critics Circle Award, and nominated for the Laurence Olivier and Tony Awards. As well as many
stage performances, he has often been featured in movies and on
television. He is one of the principal actors in John Barton's **Playing
Shakespeare** video series. I interviewed him in 2011, backstage
at the Apollo Theatre in London, where he was acting in **A Long
Day's Journey Into Night**. Since this interview took place in a
theatre, in accordance with theatrical superstition we could not say
name of the play **Macbeth** out loud.

My first memory of Shakespeare is. . . . I can't say the name in this
theater. It begins with an "M." It was the first and the most important
meeting that I've ever had with any playwright in my whole life—because I
played that part when I was sixteen at Wellington School in Somerset. It was
as a result of the success of that role that my English master and director, Joe
Storr, said, "Why don't you try to join the National Youth Theatre?" I used
that performance as an audition. I got into the National Youth Theatre, and
when I was 18 or 19 while still there, I decided to try to be a professional actor. Without my first meeting with Shakespeare and that part, it would never
have occurred to me. I never did that part again, and now I'm a little old for
it. That role is a young person's ambition, isn't it? But there you are. So that's a
momentous meeting that grew later on into my career.

I started becoming a professional actor in 1969. When my wife and I first
met in 1972, we shared a conversation about our ambitions as actors. Now,
don't forget in 1972 there was theater, there was a certain amount of radio

drama, and there were three channels on television. Big TV shows and series and all that were around, but they weren't huge. So over our very first meal, my wife and I discussed our ambitions as actors, and both of us had the same ambition: to be a regular member of one of our two national theaters, either the Royal Shakespeare Company or the National.

And it so happened that during that year, 1972, I was seen by the late Morris Daniels, who wrote to me and asked if I ever considered joining the Royal Shakespeare Company. I said, "No, but I'd love to try," only because I wanted to be part of the company. I didn't really know much about Shakespeare. I went for an audition that summer, and I went back for a recall. Just before New Year's Eve 1973, I heard that they had accepted me. And I started rehearsing with Sebastian Shaw as the boot boy in *Richard II*, the wonderful production where Ian Richardson and Richard Pasco alternated Richard II and Bolingbroke. That is when I joined the Royal Shakespeare Company.

But before that I did have two other Shakespeare experiences, that really started, if you like, an infatuation, which turned into a love affair when I was in the Royal Shakespeare Company. The infatuation started in 1970 when I was invited at the age of 23 to do Shylock in *The Merchant of Venice* at the Gateway Theatre in Chester, where I was doing a year's apprenticeship, from 1969 to 1970. I played it for three weeks, and I go down in history as the youngest professional actor to ever play Shylock. It was a difficult role for me at the time, but it got very well reviewed. My next Shakespeare play was in 1971 when the late Anton Rodgers was directing *The Taming of the Shrew* at the Exeter Northcott Theatre. I had been in a play that he'd directed already, and he said, "I think you'd make a wonderful Petruccio." I said, "Oh, I don't know, it's Shakespeare." So he said, "Well, we could manage that. Would you play him?" So I said yes. The director of the Northcott Theatre Exeter at that time, Tony Church, was as an actor a member of the Royal Shakespeare Company. (He's no longer with us either.) And when Tony was back at the company, and he heard that Morris Daniels had called me for an audition, he pushed me in my auditions and said good things about me. So you see life is like a spider. You spin your web and you don't know what you've spun until you turn round and say, "Look how that led to that led to that." A spider spins from behind. He can't see his web when he's going forward. He has to look back to see it.

I was in the web of the RSC. I was there from '73 to '75 and then from '78 to '86. So really on and off I was there for 13 years. I was one of their boys. I started off cast in two roles, Oliver in *As You Like It* and the boot boy. I was the understudy, so because dear Bernard Lloyd hurt himself I ended up in my first season playing Orlando, Mercutio, and Hotspur I think. And that shot me into the ranks.

When I went to join the Royal Shakespeare Theatre Company, John Barton was very clear. He said, "I think you get the worst verse speaking prize." When I left in '86, I got the best verse speaking prize. He taught me. He gave the company the Sonnets classes to teach us how to speak properly. He taught us all the clues to the verse. I did all the Sonnets with him in class-work, and then he used to take me privately and teach me. And he directed me a number of times in the company. And, of course, I made the video series with him, *Playing Shakespeare*. I learned how to speak Shakespeare from him. A lovely man.

Shylock, of course, I've now played twice. But for myself the transforming character for my development as an actor was Caliban. I chose to play him—though I couldn't do it now—as the universal native, the put upon. And I played him black with a sheen, so that I seemed to be from another world. My body changed color almost. Sometimes it was black, sometimes it was gold and sometimes.... I didn't play him deformed at all because close examination of the text shows— and John Barton helped me here— that Caliban is human and not deformed. And I knew that I had to release my own rather inhibited emotions. I knew I had to release especially when he started singing, "Freedom, high-day, high-day, freedom." And it took me weeks before I had the courage to just let go. And that transformed me as an actor. It didn't end up as my favorite part, but it was a big milestone in my development of re-leasing emotions. Shylock remains a favorite along with Bolingbroke and Iago. I played Iago in 1986 with Ben Kingsley as Othello.

I know what I tend to do as an actor in plays. When I'm in plays, I always enjoy playing the underdog. Iago is an underdog. And Bolingbroke's the underdog. Shylock's the underdog. Poirot is an underdog—in this country. And I always like playing characters that fight for what they believe is right. Even Iago, he wants to be better than he is. And he suffers from jealousy. He's the one that has the disease and he gives it to everybody else. That was an amazing role. But there are also characters that I admire in Shakespeare that I wouldn't necessarily play. I mean, look at the language Shakespeare puts into John of Gaunt's mouth. He is a person who has such integrity and such love for his country, such devotion to our England. I think his "This sceptered isle" speech is extraordinary.

Shakespeare, I don't believe, was in the business of drawing characters to make people admire them. I think Shakespeare was in the business of put-ting on plays to show raw emotions of the human being and encompassing the whole gamut of those emotions, especially with love, hate, jealousy, greed. This is what he centered on: universal emotion. The characters that he shows us are pretty much all flawed, except perhaps Henry V, although his behavior in Harfleur is not very nice, either. I think I'll probably stay with what I'm saying, that they're all flawed. He understands human beings and he gives them those cracks. I'm not surprised that there's no other writer really to touch him.

My problem is what do I do now. This is a very difficult choice for me. Every year now I'm asked to do either Claudius, Prospero, or Titus Andronicus. I've not been asked to do Lear, and I don't want to yet. I'm not ready. Yes, I know I could play it now, but I know that if I did it now, I'm not going to repeat it later. And that's just about it. I don't really want to play Polonius. So I don't know if there is any other Shakespeare role for me now.

The problem with Prospero is that the best scenes in the play are the ones with Caliban, Trinculo and Stephano. I find the lords not very interesting. Prospero is all right with Miranda and Ferdinand, but he's best when he's with Caliban and that lot. *The Tempest* is not a play that really means much to me. It's wonderful to read, and Caliban was great to play. Caliban is the best part in the play, actually, and although Prospero is a great role, I don't believe it is the best role. I've done *Timon of Athens*, which I loved to play. Oh, I loved playing him. Such a lonely man. I loved that. And I loved playing Iago. So I don't know what there is now, which is a bit of a shame.

Shakespeare has affected me in a number of ways. First of all, as an actor, you can't do major roles in Shakespeare if you're not fully equipped technically to do it. So playing Shakespeare for so many years nonstop gave me the chance to develop my vocal abilities, my breathing, my sustainability of language on a single line, my diction, and, most of all, my appreciation of language. And I start from the text now in every play that I get. It's all text, text, text, text, and the word, the word, the word. That is what he says with *Hamlet*: that the play is the thing. It's the written word. He gave me an enormous respect for text, an enormous respect for playwrights, created in me subconsciously the reason why I ever wanted to act: to be a servant of the playwright, to be the playwright's voice for that character. And that's why, looking back, I now know that in my first performing Shylock as a professional (not my first performance as a student, but when I started doing it professionally) I found the reason that I wanted to act. And my reason to this day is to be a servant of my playwright, because without my playwright, there are no roles for me. And without an actor in a role, there's no voice for the playwright.

I couldn't have done this without Shakespeare. Couldn't have done *All My Sons* without Shakespeare, without the knowledge of how that playwright [Arthur Miller] may have wanted me to speak and why I'm in the play and all that. So Shakespeare gave me the reason for being an actor. Shakespeare also taught me that human beings are illogical. Having done a lot of Shakespeare's plays, I spent my time studying Shakespeare, thinking, "Why does he make him behave like that? That's not logical." I tried to make it logical until in the end, Shakespeare won. So you just play what's there. By the end of the play you realize that logic with illogic, illogic with logic, all comes together to make a human being. So much of our lives and our personalities are so illogical! How often do we find ourselves saying, "Gosh, I never expected that of him." Well, actually, you're wrong, you should because people are illogical. And that is Shakespeare. Shakespeare also taught me poetically—through language— the pain of love. Nobody does it better. He taught me about humanity, he taught me why I want to act, he taught me about language, and he equipped me technically for the rest of my life.

The heart of the Shakespearean has got to be language. What other great playwright do I know who writes in iambic pentameter? There's no other playwright in the world that has so captured in iambic pentameter the rhythm of our English language. And therefore, for his day, he was the most modern playwright. He was avant-garde because he put the rhythm of our language into this poetic da-dum, da-dum, da-dum da-dum, da-dum. And in his day because the language was so appreciated, you would have heard when the iambic pentameter turned to prose. Now you don't as much, because people spoke differently then.

The main thing is, if you want to be truly Shakespearean, don't make the verse too naturalistic because it becomes almost like prose. And don't forget the English accent at that time was more like American. You only have to look at rhyming couplets to see that. You'll get words like s-l-a-n-t rhyming with p-a-n-t and you realize it's slant and pant, it's not slahnt. It's slant and pant, so it's more like American. But obviously today we wouldn't speak Shakespeare like that. So now we honor Shakespeare's verse, of course we do, and we honor antithesis and we honor rhyming couplets and we honor the stresses. But I believe it's less stressed now than it would have been in Shakespeare's day. It's more naturalistic now.

I'm not sure that's a loss. I've been brought up to do it in the modern way. Now it would be more theatrically false if it was overstressed. But then that was the style of the acting. You know that from Hamlet's speech to the players. That's what Shakespeare was fighting against too, I think. He wanted it to be more realistic and naturalistic, so perhaps it was. So for uniqueness, I would say Shakespeare's language. There's lots of playwrights who have written similar themes in different plays, but nobody with such language.

I played the part of Shakespeare in Edward Bond's *Bingo*. And it's a portrait of a very, very difficult, irascible man, and I kind of agree. I think for anybody to write with such an understanding of human beings and emotion, he must have been so aware of all those things in himself. And I think that he would have been an extraordinarily difficult, moody poet. How many years did he write? It poured out of him, poured out like with Keats or Tennyson or Donne and all of those other complex people as well. And Shakespeare's even more complex, I think. He had to get it down on paper.

There must have been enormous pain involved. He understood jealousy, the most painful of all emotions. Jealousy, as he says, is like a snake; it's the green-eyed monster. And he must have understood that or he would never have written Iago; he must have felt that too or he'd never have understood Othello. So he had to understand all of them, so he couldn't have been easy.

I have a quotation in mind. It sounds a bit depressing, but then it's something that I think that all human beings should be aware of. I often think about it. It's not just a depressing thought; it's actually quite a positive thought. We live our lives in a sense of thinking, "Oh, I'm young, I've got all the time in the world." We don't have a sense of death. If we had a sense about death, we'd have a sense of what the Biblical writers, especially David in the Psalms was saying, that man is like a plant. It grows and it withers and it's gone so quickly. And since I'm allowed to quote that play in a theatre, it starts with, "Life's but a walking shadow, a poor player/ That struts and frets his hour upon the stage, / And then is heard no more." And then he goes on to say, "It is a tale/ Told by an idiot, full of sound and fury, / Signifying nothing." Well, who's the idiot in that sentence? He is so depressed, he gives up on God. Without awareness that's where it can take us all. But I think Shakespeare is saying, "You've got to come back. You've got to come back and do your best." So that's the moral for me in that speech. It's not total despair, it's Shakespeare saying, "Yes, that's what it is. You've got to live life." If you live as though it could be tomorrow when you snuff it, then you make the best of today. Yes, "Life's but a walking shadow, a poor player/ That struts and frets his hour upon the stage, / And then is heard no more." Full stop. That's true. It's absolutely true. So take that for what it is and give your love to people, make them happy, enjoy the moment that you have. I've always said you are who you are now as the result of the past, which you can never regain. You have a hope for the future, but you are living in the present. And what is a present? It's the greatest gift. So make the most of now before it's gone.

ANN THOMPSON

"WHAT'S PAST AND WHAT'S TO COME IS STREW'D WITH HUSKS
AND FORMLESS RUIN OF OBLIVION."

Ann Thompson is Emeritus Professor of English at King's College
London. She is a General Editor of the Arden Shakespeare (third
series) and has (with Neil Taylor) edited all three texts of **Hamlet**
for Arden (2006). An updated edition of **Hamlet** *appeared in*
2016, along with a volume of essays on the play. Other publications
include an edition of **The Taming of the Shrew** *(1984, updated*
2003), an edition of **Cymbeline** *for the Norton Shakespeare*
(2016), **Shakespeare's Chaucer** *(1978),* **Shakespeare, Meaning**
and Metaphor *(with John O. Thompson, 1987),* **T**eaching
Women: Feminism and English Studies *(edited with Helen*
Wilcox, 1989), **Women Reading Shakespeare**, *1660-1900*
(edited with Sasha Roberts, 1996), **In Arden: Editing Shake-**
speare *(with Gordon McMullan, 2003) and* **Macbeth:**
The State of Play *(edited, 2014). Current projects include a*
book on Shakespeare and metonymy.

I must have studied Shakespeare in school, as one does in this country. I was at school in a small town in South Devon called Totnes.

We were lucky because just up the road we had Dartington Hall College of Art and Drama—which put on plays. I remember going to plays at Dartington when I was 14 or 15. In 1964 I saw their *Richard II* in the Great Hall for the centenary. I also remember hitchhiking when I was 16 or 17 over 100 miles to the south end of Cornwall to see *King Lear* at the Minack Theater, a theater built into the side of a cliff.

I was supposed to do classics at university. I did Latin and Greek in my final years at school, suddenly changed my mind and decided I wanted to do English. I didn't particularly want to do Shakespeare at that stage. Right at the end of my undergraduate career, here at King's, I was all set to do a PhD in Contemporary American Poetry and was accepted at various places. We had a very charismatic teacher here, Eric Mottram, but I knew that I wouldn't be able to work with him because you either had to agree with him all the time or you had to really fight to disagree, and I didn't feel sufficiently confident to disagree. So I was going to do American Literature at the University of Essex, which was the place you did it in those days. But then

I got a much better degree than I expected, so I was offered various scholarships, and in order to take the scholarships I had to stay in London. I decided at the last minute that the person I would most like to work with and who would be challenging in interesting ways was Richard Proudfoot, a Shakespeare scholar. He had taught me Shakespeare in my final year, had got me interested in editing, in variant texts, and things like that. I thought he would be good for me, that I needed somebody who would teach me to do things that I didn't already know how to do.

He wanted me to edit a text for my PhD, but I didn't want to do that immediately, so I did a PhD on Shakespeare and Chaucer. At the undergraduate stage, here at King's, I was taught also by Geoffrey Bullough, who co-edited the big *Narrative and Dramatic Sources of Shakespeare*. I suppose the sources thing came about partly because of him, but it seemed to me back then in 1969 that it was rather strange that people were still saying there was no clear evidence that Shakespeare read Chaucer. I thought, "Who else was there for him to read?" But Bullough retired after my first year as an undergraduate. And then I got my first job at the University of Liverpool, where my head of department was Kenneth Muir. Kenneth was the kind of person who would say to a 24-year-old coming in with no teaching experience, "Well, we've got this Shakespeare course. We do half the lectures each. Which do you want to do?" And he also appointed me as his assistant editor on the journal *Shakespeare Survey*, which he was editing from Liverpool at the time.

The first play I edited was *The Taming of the Shrew*, which obviously is a problematic play. I took on that job at the same time I was becoming a feminist critic and setting up the first courses at Liverpool in women's writing and feminist criticism. Kate's long final speech is very difficult. Obviously people still struggle with it. People want to distance Shakespeare from it, but you can't. It is the longest speech in the play, and she dominates the stage while she's saying that she is submitting, so there is a lot of irony built into it. But I don't like the play; I don't like most productions of it. The only production of it I ever enjoyed was an all-female production at Shakespeare's Globe. This was in 2003, with Janet McTeer as Petruccio and Katherine Hunter as Kate. That worked because the women playing the men's roles were kind of parodying them. They were being laddish and having a lot of fun with it. But usually it's a pretty painful experience. Back in the '70s, I saw the Michael Godunov one with Jonathan Pryce, which was semi-tragic and was interesting from my point of view as someone who was then painfully editing the play.

Troilus and Cressida and *Cymbeline* are two of my favorite Shakespeare plays. My fondness for *Cymbeline* probably has to do with the language. One thing that interests me about Shakespeare is the density and the brilliance of the language. I like editing because for a series like The Arden Shakespeare you're doing extensive commentary notes, so you really do have to attend to the language. As an editor, you have to punctuate the stuff and all that, so you have to work out what each sentence means word-by-word and why you think it means this. Both *Troilus* and *Cymbeline* are in quite different ways linguistically difficult plays. They're both very self-conscious plays.

Obviously, *Troilus* was part of my study for the Shakespeare and Chaucer project. In *Troilus and Cressida* one can see Shakespeare taking on Homer on the one hand for the war stuff and Chaucer on the other hand for the love story, and satirizing them both. And there's so much in *Troilus* about re-membering and being remembered: Ulysses threatens Achilles that he will be forgotten, and Troilus and Cressida both have these speeches about how they will be remembered in the future. There's a self-consciousness about Shake-speare saying, "Well, these people are only remembered because of writers: the Trojan War wasn't a very big deal, but it became a big deal because of the dramatists and the poets who wrote about it." Shakespeare as a writer is inter-vening. And Shakespeare's Achilles perhaps would prefer to be forgotten than to be remembered as Shakespeare depicts him. And the same is true of, say, Cressida. I sense that Shakespeare was really measuring himself up against both Chaucer and Homer.

Cymbeline is very different. It's a self-conscious play that recapitulates every other play Shakespeare had written; there's a sense that this is a rewrite of *Othello, Romeo and Juliet*, and *As You Like It*. There's a sort of kaleidoscope going on there; so many things from Shakespeare's past are coming back, and we recognize things that we have encountered before in Shakespeare. The lan-guage, the syntax is very strange. The Folio text literally is full of parentheses. That's probably partly due to the scribe Ralph Crane, who was very fond of parentheses. But as an editor you find yourself using parentheses a lot, un-less you're editing for the *Oxford Shakespeare* where you're not allowed to use parentheses. There's not a single round bracket in the entire Oxford Complete Works because Stanley Wells thinks they're not as appropriate for oral texts as they are for written texts. But in *Cymbeline* a character will start a sentence, interrupt himself or herself, and then interrupt himself or herself again. And sometimes characters never finish a sentence; another character will come and interrupt. Actors complain about *Cymbeline*: it's hard to learn because the sentence never completes, never gets to where you think it should be going. I think parentheses are useful. At least in modern usage they come in pairs, so you know that you can set aside a bit of a sentence while you're trying to puzzle out the rest, whereas what you get in the Oxford Shakespeare is endless dashes. Dashes do so many other things and they don't always come in pairs, so it's very difficult to follow. I think there's a kind of experiment going on with syntax in that play, that Shakespeare is pushing the medium in a way that he hadn't done before. John Porter Houston has written a book called *Shakespearean Sentences* in which he works through the canon. He says that in *Cymbeline* the idea of a coherent syntax has clearly been abandoned. We all speculate about why Shakespeare might have stopped writing plays, but perhaps the actors were beginning to say to him, "Look, we can't learn this stuff," or the audiences were unable to follow.

There are speeches in the other late plays like that, and it's interesting to see what editors do about them. We still haven't gotten the third series of *Cymbeline*, but in the second Arden series the editor in his notes on the very first scene says how this speaker is excited, which leads him to be breathless and incoherent. You think, well, if that's the case then everybody in this play is excited and breathless and incoherent, because they all speak like this.

In *The Tempest*, Ariel has quite a complicated speech around the banquet he delivers and then makes disappear. The syntax there is more like *Cymbeline*, a really dense, convoluted style. I think Steven Orgel in his edition says something like, "Clearly Prospero wrote this speech for Ariel because it is more like Prospero's style." He brings in Prospero as the author to explain the density of the syntax. And there are similar speeches in the other late plays, but *Cymbeline* is really full of this stuff.

I've never really subscribed to the notion that what you do when you read books or see plays is identify with the characters. I think half the pleasure of it is to learn about people who are unlike yourself, who you might not want to be or even meet. I think it's also more difficult for women in the case of Shakespeare than for men because one would not want to identify with most of the female characters in Shakespeare. The women don't get to do a lot apart from their choice of a husband. That's about as far as they're allowed to go. One has to search hard for female characters one sort of likes.

I spent a lot of time working on *Hamlet*, and the character in that play that I found more and more interesting was Horatio, who is very puzzling. One of the things that we ask all our Arden editors to do is a casting chart of their play, to show what is the minimum number of performers you could do the play with, with doubling and so on. Theoretically the actor who plays Hamlet or the actor who plays the Queen could in the opening scene double Francisco, who has a very tiny contribution then vanishes. But the only person who can't double at all is Horatio. And you have to wonder why? Is it somehow that Horatio has to go on being Horatio because he in some ways means so much to Hamlet that he can't be anybody else? There are many prequels and sequels where Horatio figures very largely—perhaps not surprisingly because he's about the only person who isn't dead at the end—but he often turns out to be the villain. He often turns out to be in league with the king or with Fortinbras. He's a very puzzling character. I've talked to actors who've played Horatio. Scott Handy played Horatio in the Peter Brook production with Adrian Lester as Hamlet. (Actors either hate working with Peter Brook or love working with Peter Brook. Scott did not enjoy working with Peter Brook, even though he was allowed to both open the play and close it as Horatio.) Scott didn't understand what Horatio was doing much of the time, but quite late on when they brought the production to London (it had started in Paris), he broke or sprained his ankle and had to do the part on crutches. This mischance gave him insight into the character. He thought that Horatio is somebody who really wants to help Hamlet, but is impotent. Horatio can't help Hamlet. We ended the introduction to the Arden *Hamlet* with the puzzle of Horatio.

I think it was Judi Dench who said, "Shakespeare is the man who pays the rent." And he has given me a good living. I'm grateful for that. With the possible exception of Jesus Christ, who perhaps was cheating, Shakespeare must be the human who has provided a living for more people in the history of the planet. Think of all the teachers, all the actors who have all done very well!

I didn't realize when I chose to do a PhD on Shakespeare that it would be the way to travel a lot. I've been lucky to go to conferences in North America, Japan, all over Europe, and so on; Shakespeare has global interest. There are some notable areas where there isn't much of a Shakespeare industry, like most of Africa and South America, but there are a lot of countries where people do study Shakespeare. I've supervised quite a few international PhD students. A lot of my friends are Shakespeare scholars. Having the job here, I've had a happy relationship with Shakespeare's Globe Theater in that we have an MA program that we teach jointly with them, which started off just after I came here, so it's been running about sixteen years now. And I'm often involved in Globe events. I give lectures there, and go to conferences.

There is a longevity about Shakespeare. He keeps going in a way that others don't so much. Perhaps that isn't fair because we don't get the opportunity to see many productions of plays by Jonson or Marlowe, or certainly not Lyly. But you sort of feel, okay, I've seen a production of *The Roman Actor* or I've seen a production of *The New Inn* and probably that will do, whereas one keeps wanting to see more productions of plays like *Hamlet* or *King Lear* or *Othello*. I've taught Shakespeare every year for the last 40 years and I don't get tired of it. I don't find that you can go on autopilot. I still find it difficult. I could not claim to be able to answer all of the questions my students ask about Shakespeare. I often say, "I know where you might be able to find that out," and give them some suggestions. Shakespeare keeps giving you a lot more.

And he's more a man of the theater than some of the others. Jonson was rather a reluctant man of the theater and would rather have been writing for a private commission or some such. There's something that's engagingly democratic about what Shakespeare did through his career. He didn't write for the court. His plays were performed at the court, but they weren't specifically directed to the court in the way that, say, Jonson's masques are. He didn't do some of the things that almost everybody did. Around the time of *Cymbeline* you get the double royal events of the death of King James's eldest son and the marriage of his daughter. And just about everybody else who has any pretentions to be a poet at that point writes both a marriage poem and a funeral poem. Not Shakespeare. He just doesn't seem to want to do that sort of stuff. You wonder if he is alluding to these events in *The Two Noble Kinsmen* or *The Winter's Tale* or elsewhere when you get funerals and marriages juxtaposed, but he doesn't seem to think it would be a good idea to write complimentary poems about the royal family. He doesn't need to be bothered.

He obviously could have been a poet rather than a dramatist in terms of the early success of his narrative poems. But he must have decided that wasn't what he wanted. He must have enjoyed working with other people in the way that drama is collaborative. He manages to combine that with having been apparently a very private man, in the sense that he doesn't write about himself personally. It's been very frustrating for biographers that you can't pin him down in some ways. We do not know what effect the death of his son had on him and so forth. It would be more interesting to meet Shakespeare than to meet any of his characters. There has been a more negative view recently because of Katherine Duncan-Jones's book *Ungentle Shakespeare*. It's not perhaps fair to anybody of that period to reconstruct their life from minimal legal records and so on. There was obviously so much more going on. It seems from the efforts people took to publish his plays and the prefatory poems in the First Folio that he genuinely was well liked. Ben Jonson, who had been a great rival, writes very movingly about Shakespeare at that point. I don't think he would have done that if he hadn't really liked the man.

Shakespeare's treatment of women is problematic. We don't know what his marriage was like, though people speculate on it. I find it regrettable that it seems neither of his daughters could read or write, but he was a man of his time. I dedicated my edition of *Taming of the Shrew* to Susanna and Judith. People want to say, "Oh, well, there are people in the period who made their mark who could nevertheless read and write," but we have absolutely no evidence that either of them could read or write. And yet in the plays you get a romantic notion of the daughter taking over the role of the father, like Helena in *All's Well that Ends Well* or Portia— an image of the educated and elegant daughter.

There are many passages I could pick as favorites. One of my favorite moments, if I have a favorite moment in *Taming of the Shrew,* is when after the wedding Petruccio and Katherine have traveled back to his house and are preceded by Grumeo, who was sent ahead to make a fire. Curtis keeps interrupting him telling his story, so eventually Grumeo says "Tell thou the tale. But hadst thou not crossed me thou shouldst have heard how her horse fell and she under her horse, thou shouldst have heard in how miry a place," and so on, a whole paragraph, ending "with many things of worthy memory, which now shall die in oblivion and thou return unexperienced to thy grave." I always liked that passage.

Another one I like is from *Troilus*, Agamemnon welcoming Hector to the Greek camp when Hector and Ajax are about to fight:

> Worthy of arms! as welcome as to one
> That would be rid of such an enemy.
> But that's no welcome. Understand more clear:
> What's past and what's to come is strew'd with husks
> And formless ruin of oblivion,
> But in this extant moment, faith and troth,
> Strain'd purely from all hollow bias-drawing,
> Bids thee with most divine integrity,
> From heart to very heart, great Hector, welcome.

I find "What's past and what's to come is strew'd with husks/ And formless ruin of oblivion" such a striking metaphor. It's easy enough to see what's past as some kind of landscape strew'd with husks and ruins, but why would one envisage the future as a landscape strew'd with husks and ruins? There's something odd about the way the past and future are symmetrical in what Agamemnon says. And one can make some sort of sense of that by saying from the point of view of Shakespeare and his audience around 1600 and for us today, this is all the past, that the whole Trojan War is in the past, but for the characters it's partly in the future. One of the things I find interesting about *Troilus* and also *Antony and Cleopatra* and *Julius Caesar* is the way that Shakespeare is telling a story where everybody knows the outcome and the extent to which the characters are allowed to know the outcome or not. I think that makes a big difference in productions. I think it wrecks *Antony and Cleopatra* if you play it in such a way that they know the outcome.

But with Troilus and Cressida, much of the time they do know the outcome; they are already kind of ironizing themselves, their own fame and their own roles in the plot. I find that metaphor striking.

ZOË WANAMAKER

"*But then there was a star danced*"

*Zoë Wanamaker was the first person I interviewed for this book, and her interview is a "one-off," to use the English term, different from the others in this book. It was only after talking to her that I felt able to do the interviews that became this book, that I came up with a formal set of questions. Zoë Wanamaker is an American-born British actress who has worked with the Royal Shakespeare Company, the National Theatre, on Broadway, and in movies and television. She is a multiple Olivier Award and Tony Award nominee. She has won two Olivier Awards and was awarded a CBE for services to drama in 2001. While she is a renowned actress, Shakespeare is not her specialty. I talked to her in large part because she is the daughter of Sam Wanamaker (who is responsible for the creation of the new Globe Theatre in London and who is the dedicatee of this book). In 1997, in recognition of her father's role in creating the new Globe, she was the first person to speak on its stage. She subsequently became Honorary President of the Globe. I interviewed her in the summer of 2010 in her dressing room at the Apollo Theatre in London, where she was starring with David Suchet in Arthur Miller's **All My Sons**. Her graciousness and encouragement made me want to continue the project.*

My father gave 27 years of his life to the new Globe Theatre. He must have started the project in the late 60s. I started work as an actress in 1970. I think the project was in his head from 1968. I was at drama school at the time. While I was at drama school I was living at home, until the last year, 1969, when I moved out. That's when my parents left Highgate, where they lived, and moved to Southwark—to a house where my mother cooked on what was called a Baby Belling, which was something that you have in student flats. It was a tiny little thing. So she was suddenly living in an area that was uncomfortable, where nobody wanted to live. In those days, nobody wanted to live in Southwark. But he went to Southwark because that's where the Globe was. He figured at the time that you can't build something in an area where you yourself don't live. He wanted the people of Southwark to be involved, so he couldn't live in Highgate when all this was happening in Southwark. He wanted to be in the community.

I guess he must have always been interested in Shakespeare. There's a famous photograph of Daddy when he 17 or 18, when he was doing summer stock, standing in front of posters for *Midsummer Night's Dream* and another play (they had two shows a day). So he was into Shakespeare from very early. The reason why the Globe happened was that his brother came to visit London, they walked around Southwark, and they couldn't understand why there wasn't any indication that Shakespeare's Globe had been there. He first came in '48 when he was doing the movie *Christ in Concrete*, or as it was called in Britain *Give Us This Day*. They couldn't make this movie in the States, which was about an illegal immigrant worker, so they came to England. And he went to look for the Globe and found nothing. He was even told it was in Stratford, which of course has nothing to do with the Globe.

My father certainly battled for the Globe. Speaking of living the Shakespearean life, he said once that he felt like a beggar, going around with his model of the Globe and asking for help. He said, "I feel like a beggar." And for sure being an actor means at least being a gypsy, living a gypsy's life. It's a tough life; rogues and vagabonds, that's what we are.

I really haven't done much Shakespeare. When I left drama school, that was the last thing I wanted to do. In the late 60's and 70's new work was the most important thing. That was when new writing was at its absolute peak. And Stratford had opened the studio theatre called The Other Place, in what used to be a costume warehouse. And when it went to London, they took over what is now the Donmar. That's where the RSC brought their Other Place shows. And that's where I wanted to work. I wanted to work on new writing. So when I first went to Stratford in '78, where I met David Suchet and many others of my generation, we all wanted to do new work. We weren't interested in Shakespeare. But I did one Shakespeare then, *The Taming of the Shrew*.

And I have done three productions of *Twelfth Night*, playing Viola; I've done a production of *Twelfth Night*, playing Olivia; I've also done *Midsummer Night's Dream*, playing Hermia, and I also played Titania at drama school. Those are the only ones I did in repertory theatre, with good directors I must say. We had a repertory system here that was similar to America in the sense that it was high quality, so when kids came out of drama school, they could go to the provinces, to Leeds, to Nottingham, to Edinburgh, to Glasgow. Although when I went to the RSC the first time it was like going to Mecca; I thought that this was where I wanted to do new stuff. Then later I was asked back, and I did *The Comedy of Errors, Twelfth Night*.

I was never tempted to go to the Globe. It would be too much for me— and too much for everybody else. I don't want that, but if I did it would have to be a really fine director—and that's the only way I work anyway. A director for me is very important.

I lived a Shakespearean life for all the time that my father was totally obsessed by the Globe. And I couldn't understand his obsession. It was his baby, his passion, his dream. He said he wasn't going to do it himself, but he couldn't understand why nobody else had done it. Daddy told me that another American had made some moves earlier to try to get the Globe going. I remember talking to Jonathan Miller about it, and he said, "Why do we need another Globe? It's inherent in the English language." Dad's vision was that the whole of the South Bank would be given over to the arts, and that's what happened. He was a visionary. Daddy had that whole vision for the South Bank.

I don't remember a play when I finish it. It goes straight out of my head. I wish I did remember. So it's hard to pick a favorite line from Shakespeare. I just did *Much Ado*, and there's a lovely line there: "But then there was a star danced"—and I think that could be a favorite line for Daddy too.

I just did *Much Ado* with Simon Russell Beale at the National. Nick Hytner directed and brilliantly cut something like 150 to 600 lines, and he even changed some words. He cut to the quick, so the audience didn't sit listening to old jokes that nobody understands. For some people Shakespeare is hard enough without making it totally inaccessible. He started cutting with Beatrice in the first scene of the first act, where Beatrice has this whole thing about Cupid and his arrow's point where you have to go to a glossary and even then you don't understand it. So we cut that and gave the rhythm of the play that much more energy, made the play more beautiful. Cutting is not a sacrilege.

Let's face it, most of Shakespeare's plots are pretty terrible. And that's what you have to get over. And none of the plots are original—nothing wrong with that, stealing from the best. *Antony and Cleopatra* has a terrible plot, terrible! And Antony and Cleopatra only meet twice! They don't have very much time on stage together, but the play is supposed to be about Antony and Cleopatra. We want to see them, and the rest of it is all this other *mishigas*.

I love Shakespeare when I get involved in it, but when I'm not involved I don't live it. I don't read the Sonnets. It was only when I was at Stratford, during that time in 78-79, that I began to appreciate what Shakespeare was about. We were with people like John Barton, who was fantastic. In Stratford at that time there were even Sonnet classes on Saturday mornings, which hardly anyone went to, because people were so tired and had Saturday matinees.

I've been asked to do Cleopatra. Mark Rylance asked me to do it at the Globe, but I didn't want to do the Globe. Then he did Cleopatra himself, and he did it beautifully. But for me the play always has this problem with all the generals and the war. At the Globe recently I saw the best *As You Like It* I've seen in years, beautifully cast, beautifully performed, beautifully costumed, beautifully staged—it was perfect. The Touchstone was so brilliant, funny, funny. And I only saw the last twenty minutes of it. It is one of the easiest plays to do well.

Hamlet is easy. *Hamlet* is one of the easiest because it's so emotional; it has so much emotional truth. And the language is actually easy to understand. There's nothing really difficult in it, just the odd word: "Who would fardels bear?" But you immediately know what fardels are. It's like Yiddish. You understand it even if you don't know the word. It's onomatopoetic. You don't worry about it. When you worry about the words, it stops the brain. It's wonderful to hear somebody just speak it, like it's a normal language, because it just comes to life and you understand it. And if you don't understand the odd word, it doesn't really matter. And it can be like listening to French, so lovely to listen to: if you don't understand the odd world, it really doesn't matter. But the beauty of Shakespeare is that once you get involved in it, like my year at Stratford, you understand it like music; there is a secret in Shakespeare's language, like music has a secret, like all those dots where somebody who knows the secret can play them and make music. Once you understand the dots, once you understand the rhythm, you can let it go and then just do it. And it's just beautiful. And the imagery is just wonderful if you can just wait and listen to it. And once I do it, I become immersed in it, but not until then. I love the research into Shakespeare's language, all the details, but eventually you just have to absorb it and throw the rest away. That's the way with everything, even with Arthur Miller, with every good bit of writing.

People come to England in part because of Shakespeare. And we do have to carry that tradition on, the love and understanding of Shakespeare, what makes him such a genius, why on Desert Island Discs the person's choice of a book is usually between the Bible and Shakespeare. Part of what makes a country is the debt it owes to great writers, like Shakespeare, for the country's language. And, of course, Shakespeare is about the human heart.

JIM WARREN

"*It is required*
you do awake to your faith."

*Jim Warren is the Artistic Director and Co-Founder of the
American Shakespeare Center (ASC) at the Blackfriars Playhouse
in Staunton, Virginia, the world's first re-creation of Shakespeare's
indoor theater. The ASC evolved from the Shenandoah Shakespeare
Express, a traveling troupe Jim Warren and Ralph Alan Cohen
founded in 1988. Warren directed ASC's first production in1988,
and, by the end of 2012, he will have directed more than 89 ASC
productions and more than half the Shakespeare canon. In 2008,
Governor Tim Kaine awarded Jim Warren and Ralph Alan Cohen
the Virginia Governor's Award for the Arts for their work with the
American Shakespeare Center. (The Virginia Governor's Awards
for the Arts have been presented only three times.) The American
Shakespeare Center's motto is "We do it with the lights on" because
all performances are staged with the lights on. To understand how
dramatically this changes audience-actor interactions, it is neces-
sary to see a play there. I can attest to the wonderfulness of the
Shakespeare plays directed by Jim Warren at the ASC, which, for
one thing, bring more and louder laughter than I am used to at
Shakespeare plays. I talked to Jim Warren in October 2011 in the
basement of the Blackfriars Playhouse, during the sixth annual
Blackfriars Conference (where Warren directed **The Tempest,
Hamlet, Tamburlaine the Great**, and **The Importance of
Being Earnest**).*

The first time that I remember encountering Shakespeare was in a high
school, a public high school in Northern Virginia, Fairfax County,
supposedly one of the better counties in the country. I got through the first
few years of high school with *Romeo and Juliet* and *Julius Caesar* (those are
the two I remember the most) not particularly caring, just another assign-
ment. I don't remember those teachers as being particularly bad, but I don't
remember them being inspiring. I got lucky my senior year when the AP
English teacher (who had won all these awards) stuck around for one more
year. She had taught my brother the three years prior to that and she probably
lied to me when saying, "I stuck around just so I could have another Warren

in my class." She was the first one who cracked the door open where we read in class in a way that I thought was interesting. So a seed was planted. There was one play in high school, the senior class play where I had some actor friends who convinced me to try out for a show. But I didn't love Shakespeare until I was in college and started to act.

I got bit by the bug and started looking at acting in my undergraduate college days. Getting cast into Shakespeare plays really opened things up. I got to play a small part in *Hamlet* in my second year. But even before that went on, I got cast in *Antony and Cleopatra* playing Enobarbus. I had no idea how great a role it was. And it was the first play that Ralph Cohen, the professor I started this company with, directed by himself. That kicked everything open. Crawling inside the lines as an actor made me love Shakespeare, then made me want to direct him, then made me want to play every part and direct every show.

Different people at different times added different layers. After I had played Enobarbus, I went to England to study for a semester in a program that my now business partner Ralph had started. And I happened to be there when George Williams, the person Ralph did his dissertation with at Duke, was there. I got to do an independent study with him. So seeing a billion shows, working with Dr. George Williams, and then coming back from that experience and choosing to direct *Romeo and Juliet* in my junior year as my honors thesis began a whole other layer of wanting to explore the plays. In my senior year Ralph taught a seminar on Shakespeare's staging conditions, and we put on *Henry V* using those staging conditions. I played Henry, and at the end of that experience I said, "You know, we should keep doing this. We should start a professional company." And so it was really the educational process that got me to the place where I not only loved Shakespeare but I wanted to start this company that snowballed into what we are now.

I was a double major, Theater and English. And Ralph was an English professor who had started directing for the theater. So we were starting in some of the same places, and that seminar was not something that he had done a bunch of times before. His premise was, "You know, the plays that I like the most tend to be the smaller ones and they tend to use more of these principles. Let's study how Shakespeare put on his plays, and then let's put on a play trying to do that." So a student and a professor hooked up at the right time with the right partnership, and so built this company.

The *As You Like It* you saw in the spring with our touring group was, I agree, great. I think one of the big things about our theatre is—as silly as this sounds—that when you leave the lights on and you surround the stage with that visible audience and you include them in the world of the play and you talk to them, the plays are funnier. And you find the lighter stuff even in the darker plays because all the darker plays have funny stuff too. And without sending them up, without trying to goose it, there is more entertainment value when you turn the lights on. So it's just the set and the costumes that are separated from the audience. It's a different experience, putting everything in a different perspective. After you experience it that way, you want to keep doing that.

We're going to be finishing the canon for the first time when we celebrate our 25th anniversary. This is our 23rd year, so within two years we will have done all Shakespeare's plays. And I myself want to direct them all eventually. I was scared of *King Lear* when we first decided to put it in the schedule, around 2003, so I had a guest director do it. I was intimidated, thinking in theory that I was too young to understand the play—I just had one kid, a baby. Then I directed it a few years ago. By that time I was older and had two kids. I think it was being around that guest director's production that made me realize I shouldn't be intimidated. I'm sure that when I direct it again, I'll have different life experience to bring to the table, just like an actor playing the part would. I think to be in this business you have to be arrogant as all get out, and it's a matter of tempering that arrogance with some reality and not being stupid about it and not overthinking your abilities. As this company grew, I think I let the pendulum swing a little far in the "don't overvalue yourself" "make sure you let other people in" direction. And though I still do let others in, I'm a little less likely to say, "Oh, I don't think I can handle that." I can handle anything now.

I did *Titus Andronicus* a couple of years after *King Lear,* and it posed even more staging issues than *Lear.* But boy that was fun! The way Genius Boy— oh, I like to call Shakespeare "Genius Boy"—crafted his plays, they just feel like they open up more and more as the years go by and as we do them more.

It used to be that I would answer the question about my favorite play by saying, "It's the one that I'm working on right now." But now I'm directing so many of them at one time—with the economy tanking, we had to figure out economical ways of doing things, shortening the rehearsal processes and getting rid of guest directors—that my old answer can't be literally true. You hear musicians say things like their songs are their children so it's hard to pick favorites. I don't quite feel that strongly, but I tend not to go into superlatives because they all offer different things.

I'm excited about directing the *Henry VI* plays when they come up again and I'm excited about doing *Timon of Athens* when that comes up. It's really hard, but I've seen some decently horrible productions that made me think, "Oh, no, this can work." And you don't have to mess with the script so much. I'm going to be directing *King John* in the upcoming year, and that's a great play.

I don't think of it in terms of any character being particularly challenging. Part of the trick is to see yourself in as many of them as possible. For me, David Lynch as a film director does some interesting visual things, but I almost never care about the characters in his films. But Genius Boy wrote even tiny characters that you have to identify with. So I tend to identify with them all or find something in them that feels like, "Oh, I understand what he or she is going through." I'm fascinated at how incredibly he was able to write for women when he was writing those roles for young boys to play those parts. And I assume those young boys kicked butt in those characters, that they must have been trained to be good enough for Shakespeare to be able to write those characters for them to play. When you see all male productions today and you see adult men playing the women, that to me is no more like what Shakespeare did than having women play the parts. But having really a good young boy before his voice changes play Lady Macbeth, wow. I'm excited about someday getting to the point where we could scour the country to find the best boys and train them in our way of doing things, just to see what that way of doing the plays is really like. We'll get there.

I apologize to the board members that have been around long enough that they've heard it a billion times, but I try to say at every board meeting that experiencing great art, in particular Shakespeare, makes us better human beings. He was able to tap into humanity so that we see ourselves, we see our friends, we see our parents, we see our kids, we see our neighbors, we see the good sides and the rotten sides of being human. And if we pay any attention at all we get to be better human beings because we are exposed to that. And us being better human beings one by one I think makes the planet a better place to be. So night after night seeing Shakespeare or doing Shakespeare, we are contributing to making a better world. Shakespeare allows us to see what's heroic about us, to see what's tragic and horrible about us. Shakespeare puts on display how deeply people love, how they love deep and dream big, all kinds of lessons that would make most people say, "Yes, that is the human experience." So I'm affected on a daily basis.

I love that we also do a lot of Shakespeare's contemporaries. There are a lot of really good plays written by other people; they churned out plays in the English Renaissance. Not to be too cynical, but I think Shakespeare got romanticized by the Romantics. Shakespeare got put into the English public schools and then the American public schools in part because the Romantic poets were so influential. They put him in that mold so we would be taught the beauties of Shakespeare and his great poetry. We back-doored our way of putting him into our modern American psyche because we put him in public schools. I think that's one of the big reasons we're doing his plays rather than somebody else's. Gary Taylor would tell you Middleton is the other Shakespeare and is as good as Shakespeare. But having worked with these other playwrights, I think Shakespeare is just better. And not that there aren't great plays by other people, but he is consistently at a different level. Even in his own career he got better at what he did; you can look at middle plays and later plays and see how they're better than his early plays.

Harold Bloom said it in different ways, but there's something about the way he dramatized the human condition that's deeper and more true than the way the other guys did. The most popular television movies, dramas, and comedies won't necessarily stand the test of time as being great art several generations along the way; they are popular because they hit something in the moment. Something is popular for years and years and years and decades and generations and centuries because it connects to something in our human hearts that is the same four hundred years later. The great artist just does it better than a medium artist or a hack artist. And how much Shakespeare wrote by himself is rare. There was so much tag teaming, just as the way that Hollywood and television scripts are done today.

I think there's something more eternal and enduring about a Shakespeare moment than a Jonson moment. Jonson speaks to your head; Shakespeare speaks to your head and your heart. Heywood speaks to the adventuresome side of you and he creates some rollicking fun action plays. Shakespeare didn't play in the city comedy realm the way a lot of the other people did, but his comedies have a depth, a heart, and a warmth that's rare, that helps him rise above the other ones. In the end a Shakespearean moment is something that touches your head, your heart, and your soul, makes you think and makes you feel. Those other playwrights were only able to accomplish that in fits and starts rather than as consistently as Shakespeare.

I'm fascinated that when he wrote something it became the property of the company, so he didn't own it in some way. I want to know how much he directed, how much he told people, "Why don't you try this?" or "Don't do it like that." I wonder about the relationship between Richard Burbage and Shakespeare.

I think Shakespeare was a pragmatist who we often put on a pedestal because he was so great. He was probably an everyman too, the kind of guy you'd want to hang out with and have a beer with. He wouldn't be stuffy and over-intellectual, like all of that crap about the Earl of Oxford. That Shakespeare couldn't have written his plays because he was not a member of the nobility is just classism. I find it interesting about him as a human being that he didn't have an upbringing inside the court, that he was a "regular guy" who was just frickin' smart and full of soul and able to create stuff beyond just his personal experience. All the great artists are like that and the great scientists too. If you started saying you could only be great if you have a pedigree, we wouldn't have a country. We often categorize him as this great poet, and though he was—he is—a poet, he's a stage craftsman as well. That often gets lost. He knew how to write a play so that his actors could put it on without an auteur director. He was a theater craftsman as well as great poet.

Paulina in *The Winter's Tale* says, "It is required you do awake your faith," and that phrase is something that I have in my head all the time, that the way life is, you'd better have faith in something to help you get through the difficult times. Most of us have faith in something, and it's required that we shake it up and wake it up. So that's the quotation that comes to mind.

Part of what Paulina is doing in that moment is saying to the audience, "Your imagination, your sense of make-believe, is also connected to your faith in our ability to put on a make-believe show that you're going to buy." So it is your faith that will awake this statue, make this statue come alive. Performing the plays under the conditions that Genius Boy was writing for forces there to be a kind of theater of the imagination that is different than what we normally do in the 21st century, which is create a theater of illusion that is much more like a movie. So the chorus of *Henry V* at the beginning is trying to get the audience to go on that ride, saying, "Here's this great story that we're going to tell, but you know, we're really not able to do it. We can't do all this stuff, so piece out our imperfections with your thoughts." That's as literal as he ever got to saying, "Pretend along with us." A lot of times in theater today we're not asking the audience to pretend. We're trying to show them; we think our job is to show them a slice of life and then we try to do something that doesn't require imagination. But Shakespeare wasn't writing for a set. He can go from Rome to Egypt in *Antony and Cleopatra* and back and forth just by saying, "Welcome to Rome." "Now we are in Egypt," and you don't have to change the lights or move the set. And we modern theater practitioners too often think we're supposed to create Rome and Egypt into something big and beautiful so that you're not using your imagination, but you are delighted by the illusion that we create on stage. Here at the Blackfriars we try to awake the audience's faith, awake the audience's imagination.

STANLEY WELLS

"*WHY SHOULD A DOG, A HORSE, A RAT, HAVE LIFE, AND THOU NO BREATH AT ALL?*"

Stanley Wells is a Life Trustee and Former Chairman of The Shakespeare Birthplace Trust, Emeritus Professor of Shakespeare Studies of the University of Birmingham, and Honorary Emeritus Governor of the Royal Shakespeare Theatre, where he was for many years Vice-Chairman. He is a PhD from the University of Birmingham, has been awarded numerous honorary doctorates, as well as been made Honorary Fellow of Balliol College, Oxford, and of University College, London. He was awarded the C.B.E. in 2007. In 2010, Shakespeare's Globe awarded him the Sam Wanamaker Award. And in 2011 The Shakespeare Birthplace Trust elected him its first Honorary President.

Room doesn't allow for all (or even most) of his publications, but his books include **Literature and Drama**; **Royal Shakespeare: Studies of Four Major Productions at the Royal Shakespeare Theatre**; **Modernizing Shakespeare's Spelling**; **Re-editing Shakespeare for the Modern Reader**; **Shakespeare: the Poet and his Plays**; **Shakespeare in the Theatre: An Anthology of Criticism**; **The Oxford Dictionary of Shakespeare**; **Shakespeare For All Time**; **Looking for Sex in Shakespeare**; **Shakespeare's Sonnets** *and* **Coffee with Shakespeare**, *both co-authored with Paul Edmondson;* **Shakespeare & Co.**; **Is It True What they Say About Shakespeare?**; **Shakespeare, Sex, and Love**; **Great Shakespeare Actors**, *and* **William Shakespeare: A Very Short Introduction**. *His editions include* **The Oxford Companion to Shakespeare**, **The Cambridge Companion to Shakespeare**, **The Oxford Shakespeare Series** *and the* **Penguin Shakespeare** *(General Editor), numerous individual Shakespeare plays, and the annual Shakespeare Survey. In 2009 Wells revealed the existence of the Cobbe portrait, arguing from his extensive research that it is indeed a life portrait of William Shakespeare. I interviewed him at a restaurant in London.*

244

When I first went to grammar school and high school we had some Shakespeare, but I wouldn't say I got enthused about Shakespeare until I went into what we call the sixth form, at about 17. I had a fine teacher there, who in fact taught a number of distinguished actors, including Tom Courtenay. He was a very good speaker of Shakespeare and would act the parts in the classroom. And in the provinces just after the war, I was able to see some real Shakespeare on stage. I deliberately chose to go to London to do my degree, partly for the theater and the music. I was able, for example, to see Olivier on the stage as Richard III, and that was thrilling. I saw Olivier with Vivien Leigh. I saw Alec Guinness and Michael Redgrave play Hamlet. I also had some fine teachers for my degree, including one very distinguished literary critic: Harold Jenkins. So I had quite a bit of inspiration from the academic side as well as from the theater.

And there was Winifred Nowottny, a very introverted lady who was my personal tutor. I just briefly mention her, but she was a very fine critic, and she gave very intense lectures, quite difficult in some ways for the young student, on *Troilus and Cressida*, for example, the most difficult of all the plays, and on *King Lear*, which for me remains the greatest role to play.

My PhD was an edition, not of Shakespeare but of two pamphlets by Robert Green. And soon afterwards I edited a big selection of the works of Thomas Nashe and a short masque by Ben Jonson for *A Book of Masques*. So I had edited other writers before I edited Shakespeare. Then I began to write for Terence Spencer, who became general editor of the Penguin Shakespeare. I was a dogsbody for him, which was extremely good experience because I had to deal with a lot of scholars who were editing for him. I checked their typescripts and corrected a lot of them.

I'd had good training in scholarly techniques. At college as an under-graduate, one of my teachers was C. J. Sisson, who himself edited a complete works of Shakespeare. But he, like most people, edited it from a previous edition. I was insistent when we edited the complete works that we should not edit from a previous edition. So we're the only people since Edward Capell in the 18th century to edit a complete edition from original texts.

I was a poorly paid schoolteacher for six years, so I was outside the schol-arly world, though I did keep up scholarly reading during that time. Every year I read the annual publication Shakespeare Survey, which later I edited for 19 years. I knew that C.J. Sisson after retiring went to the Shakespeare Institute at Stratford as a senior researcher, so finding myself more ambitious than to be teaching in a not very good school, I offered to do voluntary work at the Institute for a couple of weeks, having a sort of holiday. While I was there I did some transcribing of Elizabethan manuscripts because at college

I'd learned paleography, learned to read Elizabethan handwriting. And during that short time there, I transcribed a 17th century poem. I published an article about that in *Shakespeare Quarterly*, one of my earliest publications. At the end of my time there, the director, Allardyce Nicoll, a great historian of the theater, asked if I would like to apply for a scholarship to do a PhD, so I did and was accepted. I started when I was 28, a little older than the average graduate student. I also had some teaching experience, so I was asked to do some teaching for the British Council for Visiting Groups. That, quite apart from my own natural instincts, took me to the theater a great deal. The pattern was I gave them a talk about the play, then they went to see the play, then we had a discussion afterwards—something I've been doing all my life! In that time I saw some great productions, some very frequently.

I saw the *Twelfth Night* that Peter Hall directed at least a dozen times, usually standing at the back of the stalls. The really great season was 1959, with Olivier's *Coriolanus*, which is the greatest thing I've ever seen. It knocked me back. I talked about this in lectures I gave at Furman University when they gave me an honorary degree. And they published the four lectures as a book called *Royal Shakespeare*: one is on Olivier's *Coriolanus*; one is on John Barton's *Twelfth Night* with Judi Dench as Viola; another is on John Barton's *Richard II* with Ian Richardson and Richard Pasco; and the other was on Peter Hall's *Hamlet* with David Warner. But that was 20 years or so after I had seen some of these productions. If you were to read that you would see how strongly I felt about Olivier's *Coriolanus*. I did have help because I was able to consult the prompt books. I was able, with great difficulty, to find a recording, an informal recording that had been made on stage. It took me months to dig that out and it wasn't complete, but it was a very important document. As I sometimes say I'm one of the very few people who can actually tell you how Olivier spoke the very last line of *Coriolanus*. And the same season Paul Robeson was doing Othello, though not very well. He'd lost it by then. He had a wonderful voice, but there was no passion. Charles Laughton was doing Bottom, which was very good, and Lear, which was not very good. And I was working part time in the theater gallery. So all my life I've combined scholarly work with the theatrical. And even now I'm starting a book that is going to be called *Great Shakespeare Actors*.

I think *Troilus and Cressida* is the most difficult play, linguistically, and also theatrically in some ways, partly because of the long speeches and the two long debate scenes. For modern audiences, too, the classical background is not easy. But again I have seen a great production of it. I was lucky to see the great Peter Hall-John Barton production, which had Dorothy Tutin as Cressida. I wish I'd actually been able to write about that. I could have, but I didn't.

John Barton is my favorite director in some ways. I loved the productions that he did in the '70s of the comedies with Judi Dench, who is my favorite actress.

There are some obviously difficult plays like *Timon of Athens* because of the unfinished state of the text. *Love's Labour's Lost* is a favorite play of mine, but as I sometimes say to students, it's the last play to read first. The language is so intelligent, so clever, so self-conscious. *Lear* is not a play that one goes to lightly. *Lear* is more like a religious experience, like "Missa Solemnis" or the Verdi "Requiem." It's a great play because it's the most fundamentally concerned with the human condition. One of the greatest lines in all Shakespeare is, "Why should a dog, a horse, a rat, have life, / And thou no breath at all?" That should speak to anybody.

I don't think all that much in terms of individual characters. I'd love to be able to talk to Shakespeare, of course, but I don't think of the characters quite as individuals, I think of them as part of the play in which they occur. But Berowne *would* be fun to talk with.

One of the things I would like to ask Shakespeare is whether the Sonnets (or any of them) are autobiographical. My own view, for what it's worth, is that some are and some aren't. But I would love to know whether the most intense of the Sonnets come, as I suspect they do, from his own interior experience, including sexual experience. Some of the Sonnets are very sexual, like 151, and I'd like to know whether they are about his own experience. I can't believe that they're not, but I'd like to have his assurance. I published a book about the Sonnets, originally with my friend Paul Edmondson, and in that we tried to destroy the idea that the Sonnets are a sequence and that they have a singular addressee.

The Sonnets are sometimes said to be more like one end of a telephone conversation. Many of them need to be delivered with spontaneity as if they were just being coined. Some of them are more formal than others. "Shall I compare thee to a summer's day" is more formal. But others where he's joking, where he's punning on his own name, "Will," are deeply personal, and they need to be spoken as if they were coming spontaneously, which always means dramatically.

One of the questions I've put to people recently is, "Is Shakespeare good for you?" I mean, does Shakespeare have any moral effect on people? It's a very difficult answer because some very objectionable people are very interested in Shakespeare. Shakespeare has certainly given me a very great deal of intellectual stimulation, pleasure of many different kinds. I suppose there's an interaction between one's relationship to Shakespeare and one's relationship with people. And certainly some of my friendships have had as a major basis a shared interest and pleasure in Shakespeare.

The "Shakespearean" is difficult to encapsulate, but one part is romanticism. Shakespeare, to me, is a romantic. He's a romantic partly in the sense that his plays are almost all set in the past and almost all set outside England. This is one of the reasons why he goes on being of interest and importance; his plays are not tied down to the society of his time like Ben Jonson's and Middleton's are. On the other hand, Marlowe is also a romantic dramatist. Shakespeare became an old-fashioned writer in the last ten years of his life in some ways, and I suspect he started collaborating with Fletcher because he was a bit out of date. My book *Shakespeare & Co.* tries to place Shakespeare within his own time but also tries to suggest not that he is greater than all the others (which I think he is) but more to say he was one of a crew, that he was working within a sympathetic intellectual theatrical environment, that he was learning from others as well as teaching others, that he was not an isolated figure.

If I had to compose a list of the fifty greatest plays, there would be quite a few that were not by Shakespeare. In other words, some Shakespeare plays are important to me mostly because they add to my picture of the overall man Shakespeare, and this is one of the reasons why I've been fighting hard recently against the anti-Stratfordian school. Sometimes people ask if it matters who wrote the plays. And I respond that partly it does just because I like to know what the truth is. But also it's important to me to know what man had the range of imagination and skill to encompass plays as different as the *Comedy of Errors* and *The Tempest* or *Two Gentlemen of Verona* and *King Lear*. This tells us something about the power of the human imagination. Of course, one of the most important movements in Shakespeare scholarship over the last 30 years has been the realization that Shakespeare collaborated with other writers more than we used to think, but that doesn't affect, to my mind, the overall picture.

I think Shakespeare was a listener. I think he was sympathetic. And I think he was not a person who gave himself away easily. I have another little book (only 20,000 words) called *Coffee with Shakespeare*, which is literature d'esprit, really. It's recently been republished as *Q&A Shakespeare*. It's an imaginary conversation with Shakespeare. I was trying to get at what sort of a chap we might think he was. I think he was a modest man but knew his own worth. He was a businessman. One of the questions we don't know the answer to is how he made all his money. He was able to buy the great house New Place in Stratford. He owned a house with 20 to 30 rooms! I don't know how big your house is, but he owned that when he was 33, only three years into the partnership with the Lord Chamberlain's Men. I've recently examined a PhD thesis [by David Fallow], as yet unpublished, whose author believes that both Shakespeare and his father were better off than is often thought and that both Shakespeares may have had considerable business interests that we don't know about. We know that John Shakespeare was a wool dealer, and this chap thinks that the reason he withdrew from public affairs in Stratford was not because he was broke but because he wanted to make more money by pursuing business interests rather than giving public service.

My faith that the Cobbe portrait is indeed of Shakespeare is only 90%. My instinct is strongly that it is, but I admit that there are scholarly reasons not to commit oneself totally to it. On the other hand, I think there are good presumptive reasons for it to remain as the major candidate along with the Chandos portrait. I think those are the only two that have any claim. I think the Chandos is not a very attractive portrait, which is irrelevant in a way. But the Cobbe does conform to some of my ideas of Shakespeare as a listener. It is a portrait of a listener I think. It's a man of high intelligence, I would say a man with considerable human sympathy, which certainly Shakespeare had. And one of the grounds that people have argued against the Cobbe is that it looks like too wealthy a man. But that's nonsense because you've only got to look at the portraits of Fletcher and Beaumont (both of whom made a living out of the theatre) to see that they are even more elaborately dressed. Shakespeare also was to a degree a wealthy man. He was a member of the court, a courtier. The other objection to the portrait that people sometimes say is that he looks too young to be the age which we believe him to be at the date of the portrait. I admit that, but I also have found a line in *The Spanish Tragedy* where somebody says, "Paint me five years younger than I am."

I think you could use the *Lear* passage as a favorite of mine. But I'll tell you another one from *The Winter's Tale*, one of my favorite plays: "It is required/ You do awake your faith." I gave a lecture in Prague last year at the World Shakespeare Congress. The lecture hasn't been published yet, but it's called "Shakespeare, Man of the European Renaissance," and I think it's one of my better pieces. I explore the idea that essentially Hamlet and Lear are two humans in similar works of art, and that they're both concerned with the deepest things about human life. But Hamlet does so through an exploration of the Christian idea, and Lear does so through an exploration that is totally destitute of the Christian. Famously, Lear is stripped of all Christian reference. There's only one possible reference to a single God ("God's spies"), whereas Hamlet is full of Christian references. And this lecture comes partly from my feeling that there is a totality which does work from one play to another. I would link, for example, *Comedy of Errors* with *Twelfth Night*. That's why I get cross when people say *Comedy of Errors* is just a farce. It's a romantic comedy. In fact, it's the only play in which he uses the word comedy in the title. It's a lovely play, a great play, a mature play. It used to be thought to be his first play, but its craftsmanship is so sophisticated that I can't believe it to be a really early play.

JOHN BOE

"Speak what we feel,
not what we ought to say."

John Boe received his PhD from the University of California at
Berkeley. He is a Lecturer Emeritus at UC Davis, where he taught
for thirty years and edited the journal Writing on the Edge
(WOE). He recently co-edited Teachers on the Edge: The WOE
Interviews, 1989-2017. He has published various articles on
Shakespeare, including two included in his collection Life Itself:
Messiness is Next to Goddessness and Other Essays: "To Kill
Mercutio: Thoughts on Shakespeare's Psychological Development"
and "The Introvert in Shakespeare." He also wrote about
Cymbeline for the Facts on File Companion to Shakespeare.
He won First Prize in the 1991 H.R. Roberts Literary Awards,
Informal Essay category, and has won teaching prizes from UC
Davis and Phi Beta Kappa. He wrote his answers to his own
questions at his home in Berkeley.

In eighth grade in Ridgewood, New Jersey, Mrs. Church made us write a
biography of a famous person's parent. In a random selection, I was given
Shakespeare's father, John. My father worked for Collier's Encyclopedia, so
he had their research department write up the story of John Shakespeare's life.
Though morally questionable, the resulting paper that I wrote (or rewrote) was
indeed very good. I'm sure at that time I knew more about John Shakespeare
than I did about William, since I doubt my parents ever read or saw a Shakespeare play.

When I was at Amherst College, English majors were required to take
a year-long Shakespeare course from Theodore Baird. For the first semester
final exam, we were given one essay question. In writing my response I felt I
was brilliant, was doing the best writing of my young life. And sure enough,
in that course I ended up getting the highest grade of my college career. I was
gratified to have confirmation that at least some of the time I could tell when
I was doing well as a writer. Listening to Professor Baird for a year made me
realize how much a lively mind could find to say about Shakespeare, and
writing that exam made me feel that I could have something to say about
Shakespeare too.

The biggest influence on my Shakespearean life was Sam Wanamaker, a man I met briefly in the 1990s when he was trying to raise money to build the new Globe Theatre, a project I thought was unlikely to succeed. It was, of course, totally successful. From 2000 to 2015 I taught Shakespeare in London to American college students for UC Davis Summer Abroad. Each summer, I would see all the plays at the Globe, go to other Globe events and to other Shakespeare plays. For sixteen summers, I lived a fully Shakespearean life, centered around the Globe.

My problems with *King Lear* began in high school. We were studying *King Lear* in Mr. Reid's advanced placement English class, and after school one Monday, I told my girlfriend (now my wife) that I could write an amazing paper on *Lear* if only I had a few days to do some research. Later that afternoon, a kid (not me) set fire to the chemistry lab, and school was closed for the rest of the week for repairs. My research was on astrological references in the plays (Ursa Major, together with bear images and, I assume, Draco). I was wildly proud of the work. But Mr Reid gave me the lowest grade I had ever gotten, something like a C+. I went to see him to complain and soon realized he thought I had plagiarized the paper. Disgusted, I threw away my essay. I can't now imagine what was actually in it.

Studying for a PhD qualifying oral exam in graduate school at UC Berkeley, I took to staying up all night reading, playing with my small children when they awoke, then going to sleep. The night I read *King Lear,* it went to my heart but I felt unable to discuss the experience. So I went to the man who was to question me about Shakespeare (Stephen Booth, who is in this book), and told him I that for personal reasons I was unable to discuss the *King Lear.* He kindly agreed not to bring up the subject and graciously acted as if I weren't bonkers.

To earn money during and after graduate school, I sometimes taught Shakespeare classes to adults at UC Extension and the San Francisco Jung Institute. One November night in 1977, after teaching *King Lear,* I came home to learn that my father had died. Then a few years later I was teaching *King Lear* again, and I came home to find an old friend who told me his girlfriend had just committed suicide with a gun at their home. I was getting a little superstitious about teaching the play, but I taught it again in February 1987. When I came home from teaching that class, I discovered my wife's father had just died. So two old fathers and one young woman had died while I was teaching *Lear* (a play featuring the death of two fathers, Lear and Gloucester, and of the young Cordelia). I vowed never to teach *Lear* again, which is hard for someone who regularly teaches Shakespeare. But a Jungian analyst, Neil Russack, convinced me that I was being irrationally superstitious; surely the deaths occurring when I was teaching *King Lear* were a meaningful coincidence, but they were an example of synchronicity, which is not causal. And so I have taught *Lear* a number of times since then without anyone dying, and recently I have been able to actually enjoy productions of the play. Still, I sympathize with Samuel Johnson who was "so shocked by Cordelia's death" that he never read again the last scenes of the play until he had to revise them as an editor.

As I grew older, *Othello* became much the same for me, too powerful for my heart. In 2004 I watched Greg Doran's *Othello* in London and was the last person to leave the theatre because I was still in my seat crying. But recently I have finally found myself able to enjoy productions of *Othello*. *Othello* and *Lear* are two of Shakespeare's greatest plays, surely, but they have caused me emotional problems.

My favorite play is *Cymbeline*. I can understand why Tennyson was buried with a copy of the play and why, supposedly, he read it on his death-bed. It contains beautiful and serene poetry. Like most fairy tales, it is a tragicomedy (though as Polonius might say, it is actually tragical-comical-historical-pastoral). For me it heals the pain of the tragedies. The villain Iago becomes little Iago, Iachimo, a villain who repents in Act V. Wife-murdering Othello becomes Posthumus, who repents what he thinks was his murder of his wife even while still thinking her guilty of adultery. Desdemona becomes Imogen, who escapes death, then puts on pants and become the boy Fidele. And King Cymbeline, who has a Lear-like lack of feeling, miraculously regains all three of his lost children. As in *The Winter's Tale*, what is lost is found again. I think it wonderful that Shakespeare ended his career with so many tragicomedies, my favorite genre.

My favorite male character is Hamlet. He is a genius, smarter than any reader or audience member. It is a pleasure to be in the presence of a mind like Hamlet's (which is, of course, a mind like Shakespeare's). I especially like it when actors really bring out the madness of Hamlet's behavior. In the out-of-joint sick world he is living in, Hamlet's madness (whether feigned or not) can seem an appropriate response to his world. Eventually he shows, as a mythologist once wrote of Dionysus, that madness can be a companion to life at its healthiest. One great thing about Hamlet is that he gets somewhere with his madness (though of course he ends up dead, as we all do). In the first half of the play, he seems a young depressed and confused semi-lunatic, but in Act V he has become a mature thirty-year-old man. He can answer his earlier "to be or not to be" query with the accepting attitude of "Let be."

My favorite female character is Cleopatra. I love her on the page and I can really love her on the stage. She is beautiful, sexy, funny, maddening, moody, poetic, brilliant, vibrant, full of the "infinite variety" that women can have, at least in the eyes of certain men. Like me, Antony is fascinated by Cleopatra but isn't at all sure he understands her. I would like to be alone in a room with Cleopatra, but I am sure she would not want to be alone with me.

The characters I especially dislike are the criminally minded politicians. Polonius is a low-rent version, Octavius a high-rent version.

What have I learned from Shakespeare? First there are the lines that live in my mind and mouth. Whenever my wife talks about how I am "seeming," I cannot help but say, Hamlet-like, "Seems Madame?...I know not seems." Just as *Cymbeline*'s "Fear no more the heat of the sun/ Nor the furious winter's rages" haunts both Septimus and Mrs Dalloway throughout Virginia Woolf's novel, so lines from Shakespeare come into my mind every day. I assume this situation applies to most Shakespeareans. There is the profound ("We are such stuff as dreams are made on"), the obvious but still profound ("And therefore take the present time"), the wrong-headed ("How sharper than a serpent's tooth to have a thankless child"), the resigned ("Signifying nothing"), and so many more. These lines play for me the part proverbs used to play for many people. And, of course, some of the lines that I have learned from Shakespeare were originally proverbs. The other day I found myself quoting to a grandchild the proverb Lady Macbeth made famous: "What's done, is done." When I dream of my parents, I wake up thinking "Sleep, thou hast been a grandsire to me" (*Cymbeline*). When I am being lazy (as happens more and more the older I get), I think of Hamlet's "What is a man/ If his chief good and market of his time/ Be but to sleep and feed?" And when I meet people who seem to have no inner life, I think of Lear's daughter Regan's "Yet he hath always but slenderly known himself." There is a famous poster, "Quoting Shakespeare," that shows many of the phrases in everyone's everyday language that come from Shakespeare. For those of us with Shakespearean lives, the contribution by Shakespeare for our "words, words, words" is even greater.

I also know the stories from Shakespeare plays better than any other stories (second would be fairy tales and myths). Even for non-Shakespeareans the stories are lodged in the "collective consciousness," are our archetypal stories. Almost everyone knows the ghost story that is *Hamlet*, the witch story that is *Macbeth*, the family tragedy that is *Lear*. I used to take the power of Shakespeare's stories for granted. I was first drawn to Shakespeare by the language and thought the stories by themselves were best suitable for a children's book (like the famous *Tales from Shakespeare* by Charles and Mary Lamb). After all Shakespeare probably made up only one plot on his own (*The Tempest*), so his genius seems not to have been in making up stories.

But he certainly seems to have had an amazing talent for choosing and for retelling other people's stories. The recent Hogarth press series of novels based on Shakespeare plays has brought home for me the power of the stories. Edward St. Aubyn, Jeanette Winterson, Jo Nesbo, and Anne Tyler, Margaret Atwood (the five I have read so far) bring to life and make new *Lear, Winter's Tale, Macbeth, Taming of the Shrew,* and *The Tempest.* These novelizations have made me realize how deeply I (and the writers) have internalized Shakespeare's stories, characters, and dramatic scenes. No wonder that whenever I suffer an unsuccessful dinner party, I think, "Well, that wasn't as bad as Macbeth's dinner party when Banquo's ghost showed up."

I have lived closely with Shakespeare's characters for a long time. When I talked with Stephen Greenblatt, he suggested that many Shakespeare characters (and not just the major ones) have the "weird effect" of seeming in one's imagination to live outside of the plays they are in. Surely many of us have in a private moment thought, "I am much like Hamlet." Emily Dickinson wrote a note to accompany of gift of flowers she had just picked: "I send you a flower from my garden—Though it die in reaching you, you will know it lived, when it left my hand — Hamlet wavered for all of us." I too learned about the space between life and death from Hamlet; he wavered for me. In a similar vein, Goethe wrote, "Ein alter Mann ist stets ein König Lear" (An old man is always a King Lear). The Hogarth Press series makes clear that Shakespeare's characters can exist in other settings and other times. Who hasn't met a Beatrice and Benedick, the musical comedy couple whose fighting suggests attraction, or a Bottom who wants to play every part, a sociopathic Iago, or even an introverted, scholarly Prospero (I identify here) who wants mainly his book.

I have been changed by Shakespeare because his characters, his stories, and his lines live within me.

I once had a dream in which Shakespeare told me that his favorite emotion was tears mixed with laughter. I find that combination very Shakespearean, the way he can get laughter in the tragedies and tears in the comedies and in some plays (especially the late ones) tears and laughter at the same time. Also Shakespearean is the fact that his plays play so well, were written by someone who as an actor himself uniquely understood how theatre works.

I've written about Shakespeare's personality, so I have fantasies of what he was like. I think the best description of him came from Keats, who talked about Shakespeare's negative capability for "being in uncertainties, mysteries, doubts, without any irritable reaching after fact and reason." Reason is not Shakespeare's strong suit; he is most definitely not a thinking type, to use Jung's term. I think Shakespeare's dream life was important to him.

Dreams are more important in his work than in any other writer I have read. Consider Romeo's two dreams, one Mercutio won't let him tell, the other Romeo doesn't take seriously enough; Clarence's and Richard III's dreams; Calpurnia's dream the night before the Ides of March, which her husband Caesar ignores; Antigonus's dream where Hermione advises him to leave baby Perdita in Bohemia; Posthumus's big dream, which leaves a tablet behind in the morning (a sure sign that dreams are real). I could go on. I think Shakespeare was deeply introverted, needing to live alone for much of his life. I have always thought appropriate the epithet 'gentle' that was so often attached to him by those who knew him. He clearly had deep feelings, a great wit, and was a genius (like Hamlet). Like me, he was a father, a husband, and a gardener. And he was a professional man of the theatre who clearly loved some of his company's fellow actors (he left money in his will to buy rings for three of them). In her 1935 book *Shakespeare's Imagery*, Caroline Spurgeon talked about Shakespeare's love of movement in space, how more than any other dramatist his imagery is drawn from bodily movement, from quick and nimble action: jumping, dancing, climbing, running.

My favorite quotation has always been the third to last line in *King Lear*, Edgar's, "Speak what we feel, not what we ought to say." The challenge in this advice is twofold. First you have to know what you feel, to be in touch with your feelings. And, more important, you have to have the skill to put feelings into words, which is what Shakespeare was so good at. I think of this quotation as advice, and often misremember it as in the second person, Edgar giving me advice: "Speak what you feel." And often for me speaking what I actually feel is a source of humor, as what I feel often turns out to be humorously discordant with what I ought to say. In any case, I do better psychologically the more I speak what I feel and not what I ought to say. Shakespeare reminds me to do that.

CPSIA information can be obtained
at www.ICGtesting.com
Printed in the USA
BVHW071941190519
548592BV00005B/97/P

9 781587 905000